BY RODNEY BARKER

Dancing with the Devil

The Broken Circle

The Hiroshima Maidens

DANCING WITH THE DEVIL

Sex, Espionage, and the U.S. Marines:

The Clayton Lonetree Story

Rodney Barker

Simon & Schuster

New York   London   Toronto

Sydney   Tokyo   Singapore

SIMON & SCHUSTER
Rockefeller Center
1230 Avenue of the Americas
New York, NY 10020

Photo credits appear on page 336.

Designed by Jeanette Olender
Manufactured in the United States of America

10   9   8   7   6   5   4   3   2   1

Library of Congress Cataloging-in-Publication Data
Barker, Rodney, date.
Dancing with the devil : sex, espionage, and the U.S. Marines :
the Clayton Lonetree story / Rodney Barker.
p.   cm.
1. Lonetree, Clayton. 1961–   .
2. Spies—Soviet Union.
3. Lonetree, Clayton. 1961–   —Trials, litigation, etc.
4. Trials (Espionage)—Virginia—Quantico.
5. Courts-martial and courts of inquiry—United States.
I. Title.
E839.8.L66B37   1996
327.1247'073'092—dc20
[B]   95-42856   CIP

ISBN 0-684-81099-9

This one goes out to

Tom Barker and Jean Fortner,

my father and mother,

who extended our family to include

other people from other cultures

around the world.

CONTENTS

FOREWORD

The call came early one morning in the fall of 1993. I was told authorization had been given for me to view the previously classified videotape of the intelligence debriefing that Sgt. Clayton Lonetree submitted to after he was convicted of committing espionage, and for a private screening I should show up at the headquarters of the Naval Investigative Service at 10:30 A.M.

The news had been shocking when it was announced in January 1987. A United States Marine security guard at the American Embassy in Moscow, a twenty-five-year-old American Indian by the name of Clayton Lonetree, had confessed to being seduced by a beautiful Russian woman named Violetta and initiated into the espionage business by a high-ranking KGB officer who posed as her "Uncle Sasha." And when the subsequent investigation indicated that even more Marines had been compromised by KGB beauties, forming a spy ring that had allowed Soviet agents to enter the code room at the embassy with disastrous consequences to national security, coming in the wake of a series of major spy cases, this one seemed bigger than any of the others. Government spokesmen touted it as the most serious espionage case of the century.

Then something very strange happened. After a series of Chicken Little pronouncements, officials began to scale back their damage estimates. Press reports suggested the investigation had been mishandled. The focus shifted from Marine olive drab to State Department pinstripes, with allegations that the Corps was being asked to pay for the sins of negligence on the part of American diplomats. Soon it was conceded that the sanctity of the code room may not have been violated after all.

When espionage charges were dropped against everyone except Sergeant Lonetree, who was convicted of spying at a military court-martial, the dramatic reversal was complete.

Spy stories were not supposed to end this way. The satisfaction that came at the conclusion of any good espionage thriller, in which the guilty were exposed and put behind bars for life and the world was again safe for democracy, was missing. The Sex-for-Secrets Marine Spy Scandal, as the media billed the case, stood out as an ambiguous variant to the usual stories that came in from the cold.

It was obvious to any discerning observer of national affairs that there were levels of mystery to this story that had yet to be revealed. The untidiness of the Lonetree affair left nagging questions: What moved Sergeant Lonetree to the deeds that brought his convictions? What went wrong with the government response that kicked in when it appeared that espionage had been committed? What precisely was the impact of the Lonetree affair on national security?

Then there were the lingering questions known only to the Soviets: What kind of planning had gone into the recruitment of Lonetree? In the minds of the KGB, how valuable a spy was he? How did they rate the overall outcome of the operation? Was he the only Marine recruited?

Perhaps most tantalizing were the questions swirling around the beautiful Russian woman who seduced Lonetree. Her name was Violetta Seina, and she was described as tall and lithe, gray-eyed and Garboesque in demeanor. Spymasters were convinced that Violetta was a "swallow"—a lovely female who used sexual favors to lure foreigners into the "honey trap." But the way Lonetree described their relationship, they were two young people, each educated to fear and distrust the other, who simply found love in the wrong place.

Clearly, this was a story that cried out for independent scrutiny. It was unfinished. Its intrigues had only been superficially scratched. And having followed the story in the press, I wanted to be the one who took it on, the one who dismantled and inspected its parts and determined whether an injustice had taken place.

But the timing wasn't right. I knew that for me to get at the underlying truths of a story like this, time would have to pass. Key people in the military and intelligence community would have to retire before they could talk freely, and classified material would have to go through review processes. Most important, there would have to be the kind of change in superpower relations that would allow for research opportunities in the Soviet Union.

With the meltdown of the Soviet empire, the last of those conditions was met. In the way other investigative writers have gone back to celebrated cases in criminal annals, turning up new information, tracking down surprise witnesses, and presenting them to the court of public opinion, I decided to reopen the Marine Spy Scandal. I moved from my home in Santa Fe to Washington, D.C., and initiated a two-year inquiry that included a two-month stint at the scene of the crime: Moscow.

Now I felt that I knew certainly not everything, but more than any other individual on earth about what really happened. One of the few pieces of the puzzle I had yet to examine, however, was Lonetree's post-trial intelligence debriefing. A specially trained NIS agent "went eyeball to eyeball with Lonetree," I'd been informed, "and cleaned him out." It was a provocative characterization, which explained why I felt the chance to view the videotape of the debriefing was as important to my research as the original interrogation had been essential to the intelligence community's assessment of the damage he'd done.

After a uniformed sentry at the gate to the Washington Navy Yard checked my driver's license, I navigated a maze of brick buildings that had stood since this was a shipbuilding facility, parking in a lot along the Anacostia River that was a short walk to the administrative headquarters of the Naval Investigative Service. At a counter on the second floor I identified myself, and several minutes later a door opened and I was shaking the hand of John Skinner (not his real name), a special agent of the Naval

Investigative Service whose expertise was counterintelligence. Skinner had played a prominent investigative role in the Marine Spy Scandal. He was Lonetree's interrogator.

With a visitor's badge clipped to my shirt pocket, I followed Skinner up a stairwell and down a corridor to his office, where a VCR had been set up on one side of his desk. After I'd taken a seat, Skinner set the scene for me. What I was about to witness had been taped through a one-way mirror by a stationary video camera and broadcast live to the representatives of an alphabet soup of intelligence agencies, who had been sitting in an adjoining room with notepads in hand—NSA (National Security Agency, CIA (Central Intelligence Agency), DOS (Department of State), DOJ (Department of Justice), FBI (Federal Bureau of Investigation), DOD (Department of Defense), NIS (Naval Investigative Service). Hundreds of hours were recorded, and the highlights were edited into a counterintelligence training tape that began, as I would soon see, with Sergeant Lonetree's admission of contemplated suicide just days before he voluntarily surrendered to American authorities.

A moment later the black-and-white image of a young Marine appeared on the TV monitor. He wore camouflage utilities and was leaning back in a chair with his hands locked behind his head. His wide, flat cheeks and ethnic features identified him as an American Indian, the high-and-tight military haircut adding a Mohawk touch. At the moment he seemed calm and relaxed, like someone who had kicked back and was spinning a good yarn.

"I was on the midnight shift, at the desk, and I bent over and my cover fell off. I picked it up and brushed it off. Then I looked at it. I looked at the emblem. I looked at the eagle. It took me back to boot camp. They told us the eagle is a representation of our nation. The globe is our additional duties. I didn't care about the anchor. I kept looking at the eagle and thinking about the things it represented. . . ."

As I listened to Lonetree talk, my eyes picked at the details. The date and time pulsating in the lower right-hand corner. The low-grade quality of the programming you would expect from a surveillance camera. Lonetree's peculiar mannerisms: Asked a question, he would lapse into a long pause during which he stared straight ahead, eyes wide, mouth slack, as if he were watching memories . . . and when at last he spoke, his rambling, stream-of-consciousness response would frequently appear to miss the point.

As if reading my mind, the NIS agent recalled that Lonetree's delivery bothered him at the beginning. "With a normal criminal suspect, if he's not making eye contact, he's probably lying. Of course some can look you in the eye and lie, but in the initial stages of the interrogation, when he was doing this, I thought he was making up stories. Later I realized it was just his way."

After several discursive digressions and another interminable pause, Lonetree seemed to recover the thread.

"To get back to where I was, I didn't do anything on that post. But then I figured what am I gonna do, carry on till the day I die? Be an old man? . . . I was going against my principles. What I believed in . . . I cried once."

If any of this made sense, it was only to him. But he glanced at his interrogator for a reaction. My guess was he didn't receive one, and after taking a deep breath, he continued.

"I pulled the thirty-eight out of my holster. It was loaded. I was wishing I was dead. . . . I thought, If you kill yourself, there's gonna be an investigation. They'll want to know why you did this. They'll probably search your room. You're going to puzzle the hell out of them. They're not going to rule out espionage. But that's probably as far as they'll get."

His concentration was absolute now.

"It was the easy way out. I toyed with it. I put it up to my head. My forehead."

He squinted, as though once again feeling the pressure of oblivion against his skull.

"Then I brought it down. Put my mouth around the barrel. Put it under my chin. They would find me that night. It would be a mess, of course. People trying to get in contact with the post. When they found me, I'd probably still be sitting in the chair. . . ."

A sudden case of the sniffles overcame him.

"But I valued my life more than that."

There was a quaver in his voice when he delivered a line that I was told had, to the note takers, the kick of the shot he never fired: "I remember thinking, It's only espionage."

Passion, and passion in its profoundest, is not a thing demanding a palatial stage whereon to play its part. Down among the groundlings, among the beggars and rakers of the garbage, profound passion is enacted. And the circumstances that provoke it, however trivial or mean, are no measure of its power.

HERMAN MELVILLE, *Billy Budd*

A TROPHY
OF SOVIET
ESPIONAGE

1

Several days after Sgt. Clayton Lonetree unholstered his .38 Smith & Wesson, cocked the hammer, and put the muzzle under his chin, but was unable to apply the pound-and-a-half pull to the trigger that would have ended his life, he decided to turn himself in.

The date was December 14, 1986. The place, Vienna, where Lonetree had been transferred after an eighteen-month tour in Moscow. The occasion he chose was the annual Christmas party at the residence of Ambassador Ronald Lauder.

The ambassador lived on the opposite side of the city from the embassy, in a mansion that claimed historic interest. It was here that President John Kennedy met with Premier Nikita Khrushchev before the Cuban missile crisis and, legend had it, Khrushchev decided that if one of them blinked, it wouldn't be him. By the time Sergeant Lonetree arrived in a van loaded with barracks buddies, the reception was in full swing. In a ballroom graced by a Christmas tree whose top touched the ceiling, embassy personnel, from the clerks and telephone operators to the ambassador and deputy chief of mission, stood in chatting groups, and a piano player was summoning the holiday spirit with a medley of Christmas carols.

Helping himself to a drink, Sergeant Lonetree pointed his attention toward a tweedy professorial type about whose posture there was a distinct slouch in the shoulders typical of Austrians, who liked to say they carried the weight of the world on their backs. Officially the man's position at the American Embassy was "political officer," but Lonetree knew better. He knew the man was the CIA station chief.

It was an open secret in the diplomatic world that foreign embassies housed covert branches of the "silent services." In all of the American embassies abroad there existed a station staffed by Central Intelligence Agency personnel who were dedicated to conducting intelligence-gathering operations and undercover missions deemed important to U.S. foreign policy and national security, and who went through elaborate charades to disguise their identities, posing as everything from State Department clerks to commercial attachés, while engaging in clandestine activities. Everyone knew it, everyone did it, and the United States was no exception.

As Clayton Lonetree would later describe his movements: "So I walked up to him and introduced myself. I could tell he recognized me, because he said, 'Oh, yes, I've seen you around. What can I do for you?' I told him I had some serious problems and wanted his advice. He asked what sort of problems. I said, 'It concerns my tour of duty at our Moscow embassy. Can we talk privately?' "

Taking a last swallow from his drink before setting it down on a small table, Big John (as he would be referred to throughout the proceedings that followed in order in protect his real identity) guided the young Marine by the arm into a corridor outside the reception area. And there, in a shaky, emotional voice, Sergeant Lonetree blurted out the admission that while he was stationed in Moscow he had become involved with Soviet intelligence agents.

Big John took the announcement casually, seemingly bent upon pretending that nothing unusual was happening in case anyone was watching. "Have you reported these contacts to anyone else?"

Lonetree shook his head. "No, sir. You're the first."

Big John then asked about the classic vulnerabilities. "Sergeant, do you have a problem with liquor or drugs?"

Lonetree came to attention. "No, sir. I take pride in the fact that I have kept my body clean of drugs."

"Was a woman involved?"

Not so quickly and with less assertion, Lonetree said, "No, sir."

"Was any money exchanged?"

Lonetree admitted he had accepted ten thousand Austrian schillings, about seven hundred dollars.

Flicking a glance to see if there were any guests within earshot, Big John asked the important question. "Did you give them any classified information?"

"No, sir," Lonetree answered.

The CIA station chief studied the Marine at this point, and under his scrutiny Lonetree all but wailed, "Sir, I really fucked up my life."

Lowering his voice, Big John said, "Well, Sergeant, we're at a party now. This is not the place to discuss this matter. Call me in the morning at my office."

Lonetree took a deep breath. "All right."

"Use the code name Sam."

Lonetree nodded.

"And Sergeant, if the Soviets should contact you unexpectedly before we talk again, do not let them know you discussed this situation with me. Understand?"

Lonetree had recovered his composure by now. "Yes, sir," he replied smartly.

The conversation had lasted no more than ten minutes, and when it was over, the depths of Sergeant Lonetree's turmoil were stirred by a mixture of relief and disappointment. A tremendous amount of agonizing had preceded his decision to come forward with his story. He'd spent numerous sleepless nights. He'd had a headache for a week. He'd reached the point where he wished he were dead. But lacking the courage to take his own life, he had fantasized about going AWOL and joining the French Foreign Legion. About being gunned down in a terrorist attack on the embassy, which would allow him to go out in a blaze of glory, not humiliation. It had been a major decision for him to come forward—which accounted for why he was so dissatisfied with the way the station chief had acted. The CIA official's response had been perfunctory. What you would expect from the typical bureaucratic head of a department tipped to malfeasance, who saw whistle blowing as more work. Lonetree felt he'd been treated as if he were a mere functionary. Big John had seemed more interested in returning to hobnob at the party than hearing the details of an espionage confession.

Nevertheless, the process had been set in motion. At nine o'clock the next morning, "Sam" called the station chief's office. He was asked if he knew where the McDonald's was in the center of Vienna. Lonetree said he did. They arranged to meet there at two that afternoon, after the lunch crowd had cleared out.

But Lonetree was fifteen minutes late, because paranoia was gnawing at him as much as guilt, and he employed a series of counterintelligence moves to lose a tail he suspected either the CIA or the KGB might have on him. Drawing on spy books he'd been reading for years, he took a trolley downtown, pretending to read a newspaper while peering over the top. When the trolley stopped, he waited until it was about to start up again before jumping off. He hurried into a department store, exited through another door, and hailed a taxi that took him to a spot where he caught another trolley that dropped him off in the vicinity of McDonald's. He walked the rest of the way.

Big John was waiting for him at an outside table, wearing a trademark trenchcoat. The Marines were never let in on who the intelligence personnel were operating out of the embassy, so one of the guessing games they played was Who's the Spook? The guy with the red eyes who's been up all night analyzing data? The fellow who never says hello, just comes and goes? No one knew for sure, but according to the stereotype, they all wore trenchcoats.

When Big John stood and shook his hand, Lonetree immediately thought, He's using some kind of signal. As he sat down, he scanned rooftops and parked cars for surveillance. He noticed a university student on the opposite side of the restaurant reading a newspaper who was also wearing a trenchcoat, but ruled him out because he looked too young for the spy game.

"Don't be nervous, Sergeant," Big John said. "Coffee?"

Lonetree shook his head. "Hot chocolate."

After returning with the order, Big John asked Lonetree how he had known that he was the CIA station chief.

Lonetree took a sip before answering. "The Soviets told me who you were."

Big John smiled grimly before admitting that yes, he was the station chief, but he did not personally handle counterintelligence matters. He left that up to his operatives. And with that he cast a sideways glance toward the student. "If you don't mind, I'm going to let my best CI man handle this matter."

Only in retrospect would Lonetree realize that this was a critical juncture for him, and if he'd thought ahead of time, he would have realized his tremendous bargaining position at this point. Any number of deals could have been struck that would have been to his advantage, including immunity in exchange for his story. But overwhelmed by the momentous decision he had made, consumed by regret, and not just a little caught up in this real-life spy drama, he missed the opportunity.

After a cordial introduction to Little John (as he would be referred to in all future dealings), Big John left the two of them alone. But it was apparent that Little John was not comfortable with the location, and after a brief exchange of small talk he asked, "Do you know the location of the Intercontinental Hotel?" Lonetree said he did, and Little John suggested they meet there in the lobby bar at four o'clock. `now was L-the Jranged?`

Lonetree arrived at the Intercontinental early, standing across the street and watching those who entered and exited the front door. At four precisely he went inside and found Little John sitting at a corner table. The agent put on a little act, as if this were an unexpected encounter with an old friend, inviting Lonetree to join him for a drink. Lonetree passed on the alcohol, but his mouth was dry, so he accepted a ginger ale. After some light conversation Little John whispered he had rented a room and when he finished they could go up there and talk. Downing the soda swiftly, Lonetree said, "Let's go."

It was an ordinary hotel room—two double beds, a dresser, a

TV—that lent itself to the Agency's preferred debriefing environment: anything to put the subject at ease. A decision had been made to bring Lonetree here because the Agency did not want to take a chance on alerting anyone else to this meeting by having him enter their secured spaces within the embassy, and they did not want to blow the location of a safe house by taking him there.

For almost five hours Lonetree talked about his involvement with Soviet intelligence. It had begun in Moscow, and had continued in Vienna. Indeed, he said, he had yet to break off relations. He was scheduled to meet with his Soviet handler on December 27 to finalize plans for a surreptitious return to the Soviet Union.

Little John asked him a lot of questions, focusing primarily on the potential damage done the CIA station in Moscow. Gathering intelligence data from inside the Soviet Union had always been difficult, encumbered by the relentless surveillance of Soviet internal security forces. Nonetheless an important network of informants had been developed—communist diplomats, military officers, intelligence agents, scientists. Over the years they'd fed classified information and documents to the West about everything from Russian military plans and weapons models to subversive diplomatic thrusts and internal shake-ups. Little John was trying to determine to what extent these assets might have been compromised by Lonetree's actions.

Of course, in order to gain this information it was essential that Lonetree continue to talk, and toward that end Little John made a number of assertions. He assured Lonetree his disclosures would be kept "confidential." Told him it would be in his best interest to continue with his debriefings uninterrupted by independent advice. Even discussed the possibility of double-agentry.

Lonetree was encouraged. Fully acknowledging wrongdoing, he was anxious to make up for what he'd done. All along, he said, he'd thought about exposing the KGB operation.

Over the next nine days Lonetree would be debriefed in the same hotel suite on five different occasions. Then, on December

24, Christmas Eve, Little John laid out a collection of photographs and asked him to identify the man in Moscow who had been his handler, and his Soviet contact in Vienna. After picking two faces out of a pictorial lineup, Lonetree was informed that another set of counterintelligence people wanted to talk with him and were waiting downstairs.

"Are you willing to meet with them?" Little John asked.

"Sure," Lonetree replied, unaware that the people he was about to be introduced to were special agents from the Naval Investigative Service, whose interest in him was less damage assessment than criminal prosecution.

2

At this time the NIS headquarters filled the top floor of a gray, three-story building of World War II vintage in a government complex that did nothing to improve the low-income neighborhood of Suitland, Maryland. Long, dim, poorly ventilated corridors that smelled of asbestos led to depressingly small offices divided into cluttered cubicles, and the atmosphere reflected the morale at NIS, which was at an all-time low.

Throughout the eighties the United States had been rocked by one major spy scandal after another. After plundering Navy secrets for eighteen years, the Walker family spy ring was exposed. Jonathan Jay Pollard was caught turning boxloads of top-secret material over to Israel. Ronald Pelton was identified as an inside source of information to the KGB on the National Security Agency's multibillion-dollar electronic eavesdropping program. Edward Lee Howard, trained by the CIA to be a spy in the Soviet Union, defected to the Soviet Union. And these were just a few of the high-profile cases that explain why, in the intelligence community, the eighties would be referred to as "The Decade of the Spy."

Because key elements of America's national security strategy involved maritime power, it stood to reason that U.S. Navy personnel would be prime targets of hostile intelligence services, and that conclusion had brought increased pressure on the Naval Investigative Service (NIS), the senior criminal/counterintelligence investigative agency for the Department of the Navy, to initiate programs that would ferret out other spies among Navy and Marine Corps personnel. The pressure to aggressively pursue traitors in their midst, added to the usual business of conducting criminal investigations into murder, robbery, arson, and fraud, had magnified the workload such that it was wearily joked about among agents that there was no life after NIS. One agent, driving home after a sixteen-hour workday, had been stopped for driving while intoxicated when he was simply exhausted.

The strain was also taking its toll on Lanny McCullah, director of the Counterintelligence Directorate, the most prestigious position in NIS. A dapper-dressing pipe smoker in his late forties, McCullah was a first-class foreign counterintelligence (FCI) man, a crisp thinker and quick decision maker who was known for developing concepts that were marketable to the Soviets and successfully running double agents against Soviet military intelligence trying to spy on Navy operations. After twenty-five years with the Naval Investigative Service, he was the man responsible for all investigations, operations, and the collection of counterintelligence information for the NIS.

The sequence of events that would alert McCullah to the Lonetree situation began with a phone call on the open line from someone on the counterintelligence staff at the Department of State's Bureau of Diplomatic Security at eleven o'clock in the morning on December 22. Responsibility for security of U.S. diplomatic missions throughout the world rested with the Diplomatic Security Service. When serious espionage cases came up, they were referred to the FBI if the subject of the investigation was a civilian American citizen, but if a member of the armed forces was suspected, the appropriate military investigative agency was contacted. McCullah was asked if he would mind dropping by. Jim Lannon, head of the Counterintelligence Bureau, wanted to have a few words with him.

McCullah glanced at his watch. The annual NIS Christmas luncheon at the Officers Club was scheduled to start in about an hour. "Can it wait until tomorrow?" he asked.

"Let me check," the man at State replied. "I'll call back on your secure line."

As he hung up, McCullah had a feeling that the purpose of the call was other than had been stated. Within minutes he received a call back on the secure line with an explanation.

"What's the deal?" he asked.

That's when he first heard the news that a Marine security guard might have passed secrets to the Soviets. He was told a more detailed briefing awaited him at the headquarters of the Central Intelligence Agency. Jim Lannon had just left and would meet him there.

After instructing his key people to lay off the liquor at lunch and stand by the secure phones in case he needed to talk to them, McCullah drove to Langley, Virginia. There, a deputy director in counterintelligence at the Agency briefed both him and Lannon on what had happened.

McCullah wasn't all that surprised by what he heard. Putting himself on the Soviet side, he'd have gone after Marine guards. Not only were they young, frequently immature, and susceptible to a variety of temptations, they had strategic importance. As he likened it in his mind, if you want to rob a bank and you recruit a teller, all you get is what's in the cash drawer. If you want access to the vault, you compromise the night watchman.

Next they were shown the message traffic between Langley and Vienna that had started with Lonetree's approach to the CIA station chief eight days earlier. McCullah was a speed reader, and he digested the contents of the cables quickly. Most of what he read dealt with the debate over whether or not to turn Lonetree around and run him back at the Soviets. Having considered using Marine security guards himself as double agents, McCullah thought it was a bad idea. Given an MSG's access, if the Soviets started tasking him to do things and he did what they asked, in a relatively short time he could do a lot of damage. And if he didn't, it would get back to them quickly that he wasn't doing what they asked. Either way, it would be hard to keep up an operation like that.

But basing its judgment on what was contained in the message traffic, the CIA had rejected Lonetree as a possible DA for other reasons. The advantages they thought would be gained by sending him back with disinformation to discredit everything he had given up to this point, or to introduce a flow of information whose path they could follow, were offset by their assessment of his reliability. Included in the cables were character and personality analyses based on their agents' contact with Lonetree, which had led them to conclude he was unstable and untrustworthy.

So why had they held on to him for eight days? McCullah wondered with annoyance. It shouldn't have taken them that long to make that determination.

He knew what their answer would be without bothering to ask. They would say it took them that long to do an internal damage assessment based on his debriefing. Had Lonetree identified any of their people? What did that mean? Who had to be transferred?

While some of this was valid, McCullah's irritation had to do with the Agency's history of complicating investigations with its obsession for keeping its business to itself. In the case of Edward Lee Howard, the notorious CIA turncoat, this practice had contributed to the loss of a suspect because the Agency had not shared information with the proper investigative and enforcement agencies in a timely fashion. Here they had been dealing with an espionage suspect for over a week before letting the organization with investigatory responsibilities know about it.

His voice rising, McCullah said, "Damn it, I thought you guys were going to try to do a better job of cooperating. This sounds like the same old crap."

McCullah's concern was that in its single-minded interest in damage assessment and by stringing Lonetree along, the Agency might have taken the case down a path that would make his own job more difficult. If the CIA had had Lonetree in custody for over a week and had not properly informed him of his rights, for example, that could have serious legal implications. It might mean that whatever information he disclosed would not be admissible in a court of law, which certainly complicated an investigation aimed toward criminal prosecution.

The CIA man's reaction was calculated to let the air out of McCullah's wrath. He apologized while trying to put a positive spin on things. "Technically he was not in custody. He was allowed to go about his rounds. He was even late to a couple of meetings, missed one, and returned to his barracks each night."

It was an arguable point, sure to be raised by a sharp defense attorney.

"What about physical evidence? Have any of your agents checked out his quarters?" McCullah asked.

The CIA man shook his head. To his knowledge Lonetree's quarters had not been searched.

"And his handlers. Have they been ID'd?"

The look on the Agency man's face was enough to let McCullah know the answer to that one.

"Jesus Christ," he muttered. Even though the CIA wasn't a law-enforcement agency, he'd have thought they would at least have covered the basics.

"I'll see to it," he was assured.

His mind racing as he scanned the cables, McCullah came up with another idea. "It says here Lonetree is supposed to meet with his Soviet handler next on the twenty-seventh. That's five days off. How about having one of your guys cover the meet? If Lonetree says he's supposed to meet Ivan Yakovich on Saturday at ten in front of the church, and Ivan shows up Saturday in front of the church, I want that established."

McCullah was promised it would be done, and that he would be kept informed of all developments from here on out.

I doubt that, McCullah thought. The Agency had a reputation for releasing information on a need-to-know basis—and even then only when it was to its own advantage. He just had to hope that nothing was being withheld that would be critical to the investigation.

In the meantime, now that the case belonged to him, the most important thing was to get on the line to the regional director in London and order him to send his best counterintelligence agents to Vienna and discreetly withdraw the suspect.

Waiting for Sergeant Lonetree and Little John in the coffee shop of the International Hotel were three NIS agents who had flown in from London the previous afternoon. Special Agent David Moyer combined the comfortable corpulence and easygoing manner you would expect of a desk sergeant with the smarts of a street cop. He was accompanied by two junior members of his counterintelligence squad, Gary Hardgrove and Andrew Sperber, whose clean-cut, conservative appearances were almost interchangeable. This was going to be their first encounter with Sergeant Lonetree, but earlier that morning they had been updated by Big John and Little John and presented with three stapled packages of cables and a summary of what Lonetree had revealed. There were blank spaces on a number of the documents, indicating the Agency was supplying them with a redacted version of the communications, but this didn't concern the agents because they didn't expect their interrogation to proceed along the lines of tell-us-what-you-told-them.

"Clayton, these gentlemen are government agents," Little John said. After a round of handshakes, Little John excused himself, saying, "Sergeant, I'm going to leave you with these guys. Try to help them with what they want."

Lonetree said, "Okay," and when Moyer suggested they take a cab back to his hotel, where they could order some sandwiches and continue to talk, he agreed to that, too.

It was snowing heavily outside, blizzard conditions and no taxis waiting. Trying to be helpful, Lonetree dashed out into the street to flag a passing cab. His quick movements startled the agents, who mistook them for an escape attempt, and they lunged toward him. When they realized Lonetree's real intention, they tried to laugh it off and casually called him back to the curb. But an exchange of looks sent a signal to the Marine: This was different from what had gone on before.

Once they arrived at the Strudelhof Hotel, Agent Moyer took Lonetree up to his third-floor room while the other two agents stopped at the desk to order some food. Upstairs, they took their coats off and made themselves comfortable. It didn't even faze Lonetree when Moyer pulled out his NIS credentials and explained, "Clayton, we are going into a criminal phase of the investigation now. Any statements you made to Little John are completely inadmissible and can't be used against you. It is your right not to talk to us unless you want to. You are also entitled to have a lawyer present."

Sitting on a couch, Lonetree said he understood. Not only did he initial the boxes that waived all his rights, he put his signature on a form giving the NIS permission to search his room for evidence.

Special Agent Moyer was not surprised at Lonetree's complete cooperation at this point. Eighty percent of the people he warned didn't ask for a lawyer. Most tried to lie their way out. In Lonetree's case, he thought the sergeant was forthcoming because he felt bad and wanted to make amends. Moyer was touched when, just before Agent Hardgrove was about to leave to search Lonetree's room at the Marine barracks, the sergeant expressed concern about what his buddies would be told. So they devised a cover story. If asked, the NIS agent would say it was a drug investigation.

After Agent Hardgrove left, Moyer and Sperber sat around and basically let Lonetree talk. They obtained biographical data, asked him if there had been any problems in his relationship with Big John, and inquired about his contacts with Soviet intelligence. But they listened for the most part because they did not want to do or say anything that would lead Lonetree to terminate at this time.

After almost three hours of conversation, much of it taped, Moyer asked Lonetree if he would mind staying at the Strudelhof with them overnight. If Lonetree had declined and insisted on returning to the barracks, he would not have been free to go. He would have been officially apprehended, and there were handcuffs and restraining devices in Moyer's briefcase in the event he resisted. This was a point that Lonetree's lawyers would later harp on—their client was under arrest but didn't know it, and if he had been informed, he would have stopped talking and requested an attorney. But Lonetree wasn't thinking along these lines, and said that would be fine with him.

Long after Lonetree had retired to an adjoining room, Special Agent Moyer remained sitting in a chair in the company of troubled thoughts. His instructions were to withdraw Lonetree as rapidly and quietly as possible, and he had made reservations on an early-morning Air Austria flight to London. Between now and then he had nothing better to do than worry. About whether the KGB had them under surveillance, and if they would be daring enough to try to intercept them. About whether Lonetree was a defection risk and would make a scene when he was told they were going to London to continue the conversation.

Moyer did not sleep at all that night. He turned on the TV and found an English-language channel that was running the movie *Silverado* on a continuous loop. It was entertaining the first time around, but by the third and fourth time the images on the screen might as well have been wallpaper.

3

They arrived back in London on the twenty-fifth, Christmas Day, flying into Heathrow Airport. Lonetree was continuing his cooperation. Not only had he agreed to the proposal they move their meeting to London, after they had checked into a suite of rooms at the Holiday Inn, when Moyer asked him if he wanted to hold off answering more questions until after Christmas, the sergeant said, "No, I want to go ahead with it right now."

For the next three days Sgt. Clayton Lonetree was interrogated by NIS agents on a rotating basis. After that, a statement was presented to him that represented his "confession." It wasn't a verbatim transcript; it was drafted off notes scribbled by the agents and typed by a secretary sitting at a computer in an adjacent room. But Lonetree was given the chance to proofread it for accuracy, crossing out mistakes and misunderstandings and writing changes in the margins that were authenticated by his initials.

It ran fifteen pages in length, and in it Lonetree admitted to violating the regulation against fraternization with Soviet nationals and becoming intimately involved with Violetta Seina, who was employed at the embassy as a translator. He characterized their relationship as a friendship that turned sexual in late December of 1985 and became something even more clandestine in early January of 1986, when she introduced him to a man she identified as her Uncle Sasha.

Lonetree indicated that he did not report this contact either, because initially it was uneventful and there was no harm done. He admitted that gradually, however, he had been drawn into a web of conspiracy with Uncle Sasha, and that he had disclosed confidential information about the Central Intelligence Agency's presence within the embassy—the location of CIA spaces, the identity of CIA agents—as well as data about the embassy's seventh floor. This was where all the top-secret offices were located, including the Communications Programs Unit. Known as the CPU, it was the secure workplace where code clerks from the CIA, National Security Agency, and State Department went about their business. Within its chambers crypto machines transmitted and received encoded messages by satellite to and from Washington, D.C., and Langley on matters that ranged from the results of NSA's electronic eavesdropping successes on Kremlin communications and instructions from the President and Secretary of State to the ambassador, to information about CIA informants in the Soviet Union.

Lonetree told the investigators that many times he seriously considered reporting his encounters with Uncle Sasha to the security officer in the embassy, but did not because he knew if he did, he would be relieved of duty and transferred back to the States, where he would face disciplinary action. He said he decided to take Sasha's word that no one in the embassy would find out if he just cooperated.

While acknowledging he was disregarding his obligation as a security guard to protect classified material, Lonetree defended his actions with various rationalizations. It was apparent to him that Sasha already had a pretty good idea who was CIA. What he'd done was wrong, but to his way of thinking none of it was critically important.

Lonetree said that this went on for about three months, until he was transferred to Vienna in March 1986. At that time Uncle Sasha said that he planned to visit Vienna in the summer and suggested they should get together then. When Lonetree agreed to continue their relationship, Sasha gave him a slip of paper that had already been prepared, indicating a set of dates on which to meet, along with an enameled wooden jewelry box, which he said was a gift for being a friend.

In Vienna, Lonetree said, he purposely did not make the prearranged meeting with Sasha, and secretly he hoped this whole business would end there. He missed Violetta but felt guilty about what he was doing with Sasha. Then one night while he was on guard duty, the phone rang and it was Sasha. In a disguised voice he rescheduled the meeting.

They met in front of an opera house and Sasha gave him a big hug, expressed concern that he looked worried and thin, said Violetta sent her best regards, and took him out to dinner. Things were very friendly between them, and Sasha did not ask him anything about the embassy. Nor did he for the next few meetings, during which they took walks in the countryside and strolled in the Vienna parks.

Nonetheless, to his interviewers Lonetree would say, "I thought for sure he was playing a dangling game to draw me in deeper," which prompted him to try to break it off with Sasha through a harebrained scheme. Since Sasha had something on him, he would try to get something incriminating on Sasha.

"I knew this girl called Alexandre who was a waitress who worked at a bar called Slambos in Vienna. I went to her and told her that a Soviet I'd known in Moscow had followed me to Vienna and was bothering me. I told her I wanted something on him so he'd leave me alone. I said he was married and offered her one hundred dollars to meet him in the park and entice him into a compromising position I could photograph and use for blackmail, but I didn't tell her any other details."

He told her where he was to meet Sasha in the park; then he went and hid in the bushes near the rendezvous point with his camera. Sasha arrived and waited but she never showed. Lonetree found out later she got the directions mixed up and went to the wrong part of the park.

After that, Lonetree said, he accepted the inevitability of his situation, and Sasha made it easy. He would deliver letters from and pictures of Violetta. He would put his arm around Lonetree's shoulders and refer to him as "one of the family." And he would overwhelm Lonetree's resistance with grand gestures. After they had gone to an inn for lunch one day, he laid out a thousand dollars in Austrian currency on the table. He said it was a present. Lonetree said he couldn't accept it. Sasha became indignant and said, "If you don't accept it, you'll be insulting me."

By this time Lonetree was convinced he and Sasha had a genuine friendship, so he took the money and went to a store and bought a dress for Violetta and a shirt and tie for Sasha.

Their relationship reestablished, Sasha began once again to make inquiries about the identities of CIA personnel at the embassy in Vienna. Lonetree said that at first, "I told him since I was new at the embassy I did not know everyone on the staff or where they worked." But he admitted that at a later meeting, "I gave Sasha pictures of three employees I thought were probably CIA that I had taken from embassy files on Post One. I would consider that these pictures were classified anywhere from confidential to secret."

In November 1986, Sasha's requests began to pick up intensity. He asked a series of questions about the Austrian ambassador's secretary, and hinted that Lonetree should try to begin to date her. He asked detailed questions about other Marines in the guard detachment, and in particular he wanted to know which Marines had problems with alcohol or drugs or were homosexual. He asked about the embassy alarm system.

At a late-November meeting Sasha told him that he was ill and was not going to be able to continue traveling between Moscow and Vienna. He said that he was going to turn this thing over to his friend in Vienna who was a KGB officer, and a meet date was set up for December 5, 1986, at seven in the evening.

By now, Lonetree said, he'd become tired of the whole thing and wanted it to end. Upon hearing that Sasha was going to pass him on to a KGB officer, he also felt angry. "That's when I thought of getting a gun and killing him. One of my friends at the Marine House collected World War II souvenirs, and I'd talked to him about getting a pistol—a Luger or a Walther P-38— and some ammunition."

But he didn't do that. Instead he missed the next date intentionally, and agreed to meet again only after Sasha called.

This was a meeting he dreaded. They met at a church but moved to a restaurant, where Sasha talked about leaving the next day. Eventually the friend showed up, and Sasha introduced him as George. "He reminded me of the National Security Adviser during the Carter administration, Brzezinski," Lonetree said. George also had cold and humorless eyes, and a piercing stare that made Lonetree squirm.

With few preliminaries, George began asking questions about the ambassador's office. He was also interested in the cleaning personnel at the embassy and wanted Lonetree to get him a list. "But the biggest topic of conversation was how I was going to get to the Soviet Union. George said we would finalize plans at a meeting on the twenty-seventh of December."

George gave him a piece of paper with the directions, said goodbye, and left. Then Sasha said he had to leave too. When they shook hands, Sasha whispered, "Whatever you do, don't play with this person," before he turned and walked away. Lonetree said it was the last time he saw Uncle Sasha.

Thinking about the meeting afterward, Lonetree said, he had the impression that George would be a very different person to deal with than Sasha. That he would have to deliver or else he would be exposed or killed. And as he reflected on the trouble he was in, and how his involvement just kept getting deeper and deeper, Lonetree said, he felt he could no longer go on living like this. He knew he had betrayed not only his country, but everything he cared about. The Marine Corps. Other Marine security guards. His family.

To stop it, he said, he considered taking his own life, and almost did. But when he realized he was incapable of pulling the trigger, he decided to approach the CIA station chief at the annual Christmas party at the ambassador's residence.

The bulk of Clayton Lonetree's confession ended there. But there was one more paragraph on the statement sheet that appeared to be tacked on as an afterthought. In fact it was NIS policy when interrogating a suspect to always leave them a way out at the end. To allow them to provide an explanation for their actions that made them feel somewhat justified. To give them a chance to put their crimes in a context that made them seem more comprehensible.

In this paragraph Lonetree addressed his motivations for doing what he did. "I would like to say I feel no hatred for Violetta. I was not involved in this incident to protect her. She really had nothing to do with it." He went on to say he did not get involved in this for the money, either. "I guess some of my actions were based on my hatred for the prejudices expressed in the United States against Indians. What I did was nothing compared to what the white man and the United States government did to the American Indian one hundred years ago."

Clayton Lonetree signed his statement after it was typed. But he also penned in a very last sentence: "I still have a great love for my country."

4

Over the course of his interrogation Sergeant Lonetree had displayed a range of emotions. When he made a very damaging statement concerning his involvement with the Soviets and was asked if he realized he had been betraying his country, he would turn quiet, his eyes would go down, and he would clearly appear to be foundering on shame and remorse. Then there were moments when he was able to find some humor in his situation and the chances he took, or he would chuckle over something amusing that had happened with Violetta. At other times, when asked a pointed question, he would take an abnormally long break before answering, during which a kind of half smile would form on his face, almost as if he were doing a mental damage assessment about what he was about to say and how much it would hurt him.

It was this last impression, coupled with several elements to his story that didn't ring right, that made the NIS agents suspect there was more to the story than what Lonetree had related. He said he'd repeatedly been asked to provide various documents and pieces of classified information, but claimed he refused to comply. So why had he received various monies from the Soviets? The KGB was not known as a fiscally generous organization. Nor was he voluntarily admitting that the Soviets were interested in information that any smart hostile intelligence service would want to know from a Marine security guard: What was the easiest access to the building? Where were the alarms and cameras in the Moscow Embassy? How could they be shut down without alerting other security systems?

Furthermore, based on their experience, the NIS agents could not conceive of the Soviets' sending one of their agents from Moscow to Vienna with all the intricacies involved in moving a nondiplomat from Moscow to another country, as many times as Lonetree said Sasha had come and gone, and then brought a senior KGB case officer into the picture, unless they considered Lonetree a more valuable asset than he had admitted to being.

When they told Lonetree they thought he was withholding, omitting, maybe lying, he got that little smile on his face and remained silent.

So they brought in a new NIS agent, Tom Brannon, who was the regional polygrapher. Brannon had a legendary reputation within the organization for getting confessions, and the congenial Irishman led the interrogation that commenced on the twenty-ninth of December. He employed a variety of interrogatory techniques. He rephrased questions, looking for discrepancies and implausibilities in Lonetree's story and highlighting them. He played up to Lonetree's intellect: "Come on, Clayton, you don't expect us to believe that. You're an intelligent guy. Give us credit. Tell us what's really going on." He commented on body language: "Why are you so nervous? Aren't you telling me the truth?"

The outcome was a second statement, which began with an explanation by Lonetree of why he left out certain information in his first statement. "The reasons are various. They include fear of entrapping myself and also I wanted to protect the Russian girl, Violetta."

What he said he failed to report in his first statement, and parted with now, were the kinds of things the NIS agents suspected. Things like the fact that Sasha asked him, while he was in Moscow, to place a bug in the ambassador's office space, which he said he refused to do. He did, however, say he supplied Sasha with floor plans of the entire American Embassy, going over them and marking the spaces according to who worked where. He also admitted to hand-writing out and signing a statement that read: "I am a friend of the Soviet Union, I will always be a friend of the Soviet Union, and will continue to be their friend." He said it was no big deal to him to do that, he had done it at Sasha's request, and it evidently pleased him, because after that Sasha offered him the opportunity to defect to the Soviet Union if he desired. Lonetree said he told Sasha he did not want to defect, but he did hope to return to Russia someday after he was out of the Marine Corps.

The gravest admissions in this second statement concerned his efforts to help the Soviets identify CIA personnel in both the Moscow and Vienna embassies. They were much more extensive than he had previously acknowledged.

At the end, Lonetree elaborated on his motives: "In conclusion I wish to advise that I became involved in activities with the KGB due to the intrigue of it. After I got involved I was unable to get out and was afraid of being compromised. . . . I regret that I ever got involved with the KGB and am sorry I did so, because I totally disbelieve in the Soviet system."

After his second statement was typed and signed, Lonetree was asked if he would be willing to take a polygraph test.

"Sure," he replied. "I have nothing to hide."

The polygraph was set up and calibrated. Brannon then explained the examination and how the instrument worked, before asking Lonetree a series of four questions.

Other than discussed, did you provide anything to the Soviets that you have not told us about?

His response was *"No."*

Other than discussed, did you receive anything from the Soviets that you did not tell us about?

His response was *"No."*

Did you place any listening devices in the embassies?

His response was *"No."*

Other than discussed, while in Moscow, did you provide any classified documents to the Soviets?

The response was *"No."*

The examination portion of the process took approximately twenty minutes, after which Brannon went into an adjoining

44

suite, where the results were printed out on a computer. Deception was indicated on all four questions.

Brannon came back out shaking his head. "The machine tells me you're not giving us the truth."

"But I am telling the truth, Mr. Brannon," Lonetree protested.

"I believe you, boy. But you gotta convince this machine."

A second test was administered, and this time the same first two questions were asked and the results checked. Deception was indicated again. A third polygraph was then given, asking the third and fourth questions, and once more deception was indicated.

The interrogation that followed was much more intense than anything that had gone on before. Up until then, Lonetree had been treated with relative gentleness. After the polygraph registered deceptive three different times, with national-security issues at stake, Brannon bore down heavily on him.

"Come on, Clayton. If you don't cooperate, we're going to burn your ass. We know you're holding back. Now, tell me the truth."

When Lonetree said he'd told them everything, Brannon shouted, "Well, tell us more!"

At first Lonetree tried to keep up with him, responding, "There is no more." But Brannon found his answer unacceptable. "You couldn't meet twelve times with the Soviets without giving them something more than what you've said. Tell me what it was. Did you pass them any classified documents?"

Lonetree continued his denials, but soon became overwhelmed by Brannon's demands and turned nonresponsive. He seemed almost to go into a trance—staring straight ahead with his arms folded, a scowl on his face, refusing to answer Brannon's questions. But under Brannon's battering, tears streamed down his cheeks, and as Special Agent Moyer would testify later, "He looked like a person who wanted to say something but couldn't quite get himself to come out with the words."

In this context, to get Lonetree talking again, Brannon initiated an exchange that would be pivotal not only to this interrogation but to the entire NIS investigation that would follow.

"Talk to us, Clayton. Come on, talk to us."

Reentering real time, Lonetree cried, "What do you want to hear?"

Brannon emitted an exasperated sigh. "Say something. Say anything. Say you're sitting down, the walls are green, whatever. Just talk to me."

"Do you want me to lie to you?"

"Okay. Make something up. Tell me a lie."

This statement—"Tell me a lie"—appeared to break through the last of Lonetree's resistance. Sobbing, he then admitted to obtaining the combination to a secured office and safe in the Vienna embassy, removing three documents marked top secret, and hiding them in a drainpipe on the roof of the Marine House before turning them over to the Soviets. He said he also examined the contents of a classified "burn bag" and removed one hundred secret documents concerning Mutual Balance Force Reduction, which he turned over to his handler at the next meeting.

On a legal scale of zero to ten, before these admissions his espionage case was probably about a three. It had just jumped to a six.

Lonetree was weeping openly and having difficulty breathing and trying to talk at the same time. The agents gave him several moments, and when he was at last able to be coherent, it was to deny everything he'd just said. "It's not true," he told the agents. "It's a lie."

Brannon roared, "Clayton, look at me!" And he pointed the question like a gun: "Did you in fact steal and give those documents to Sasha?"

Lonetree seemed almost to be hyperventilating now. "Yes," he said, reversing his story once again. "I did. It's the truth and I'm so ashamed. I've never been more afraid in my life for what I've done."

It was an extreme moment, relieved when Moyer said, "Why don't you go in and wash your face, Clayton, and calm down."

Lonetree took the advice, going into the bathroom, where he splashed cold water on his face, toweled off, and sat on the edge of the tub for a few minutes. When he had collected his composure, he returned.

"How do you feel, Clayton?" Moyer asked. "You want to continue? Want to see a lawyer?"

Lonetree sniffed. "I want to stop. Yeah, I want to see a lawyer."

A third statement was drafted off the information he'd provided during the emotional session, but Lonetree refused to sign it. "It will only get me into more trouble," he would be quoted as saying. Both Moyer and Brannon were irritated because they felt he had only just begun to be honest with them. But they also knew their law.

In handcuffs, Sgt. Clayton Lonetree was driven to a U.S. Air Force base sixty miles outside London, where he spent the night in the brig. The next day he was picked up by a different NIS agent, James Austin, a quiet but shrewd assistant director of counterintelligence at NIS, who had come to London to provide support and guidance to the investigation, and to escort Lonetree back to the States.

The next day the two of them boarded an Air Force plane that was already scheduled to make a transatlantic flight. It was manned by reservists, one of whom, noting that Lonetree was wearing cuffs, made a point of letting Austin know that he was armed if there was trouble.

They talked very little during the flight, in large part because it was a huge cargo plane, so noisy inside they had to shout to be heard. But at one point Lonetree did ask Austin if he was really an expert on Soviet intelligence.

"My boss considers me one," Austin replied.

Lonetree thought about that, before asking what it took to become a double agent.

Austin was not inclined to talk shop. "You'll have to talk to somebody else about that."

The plane landed in Dover, Delaware, where they switched to a smaller plane that flew them to National Airport in Washington, D.C. There, two more NIS agents in civilian clothes walked them to a waiting car and drove him the forty miles south to the Marine Corps Development and Education Command (MCDEC) at Quantico, Virginia.

Lonetree was silent the entire ride, but as they entered the main gate to Quantico, passing a replica of the famous Iwo Jima monument of Marines raising the American flag on Mount Surabachi—one of them the legendary Pima Indian, Ira Hayes—he would later say that in his mind he was comparing this drive to the last time he'd passed this way. It had been after his graduation from Marine guard school, when, prideful of his accomplishments and savoring the anticipation of standing duty in the enemy's capital, he had departed for Moscow. It would have been inconceivable to him then, just as it was unbelievable to him now, that he would be returning in two and a half years in chains, charged with being a trophy of Soviet espionage.

MOONLIGHTING
IN MOSCOW

5

From eight at night until nine the next morning someone drawn from the officer ranks at the Marine base at Quantico would act as the base representative in place of the commanding general. His duties ranged from summoning the military police to handle barking-dog calls and listening to complaints from the civilian community about artillery rattling their houses, to handling medevac flights. The assignment was handed out on a rotating basis, and the night before Sgt. Clayton Lonetree was delivered to the brig, Maj. David Henderson was the acting duty officer.

Henderson was a laid-back six-footer, full of homespun anecdotes. He gave the impression he would rather be hunting or fishing than anything else. When visitors called on him in his office, as often as not they would find him sitting with his feet propped up on his desk, and he'd wave them in and start talking about his hunting dogs before he got around to asking, in a drawl that all but drew his home state of Oklahoma in the air, "And what was it you came by for?" Nothing much excited Henderson, but it was a mistake to underestimate him, because he didn't miss much either. President of his junior and senior classes in high school. Captain of the debating team. Graduate of the University of Oklahoma and its law school. Nomination to the Order of the Coif, which consisted of the top ten percent of law students in the nation. He was your classic country lawyer who kept his IQ under wraps as he outsmarted his adversaries, dressed in a Marine uniform.

Whatever else happened on this particular evening, what Major Henderson remembers today is the phone call he received from the staff judge advocate, Col. Patrick McHenry.

"What's your security clearance, Henderson?" McHenry asked straightaway.

"SBI," Henderson replied. An SBI was a Special Background Investigation clearance, which authorized recipients to see top-secret material.

There was a silence on the line that Henderson suspected could be attributed to the fact this was not a secured line. "Can I assume, Colonel, that you won't tell me why you're asking over the phone?"

"You're right," McHenry said. "Meet me in my office tomorrow morning."

The briefing Henderson received the next day was short and to the point. There was a heads-up at Quantico. NIS agents were flying in a Marine that evening. It looked like spy charges. Lonetree was going to be held incommunicado in the brig. As chief defense counsel, Major Henderson had been detailed to represent the accused.

By the luck of the draw, Henderson was duty officer again on New Year's Eve, and as it was an unusually slow evening, around eleven o'clock he decided to pay his client a visit. Leaving the duty office at Lejeune Hall, he slid behind the wheel of his two-tone El Camino and negotiated the mile and a half of turns that took him past the air station, past Officer Candidate School, and to the brig. He'd been warned that this was a case affecting national security and that any conversations that involved a discussion of classified material must be conducted in a specially secured area. His intention was merely to introduce himself and reassure his client that he was not alone in this.

The brig guard led Henderson to D-seg, a wing where six isolation cells had been designed with terrorists in mind. All the others had been vacated, so the entire wing was dedicated to Sgt. Clayton Lonetree.

Henderson's first impression of his client was dominated by the prisoner's pathetically frail appearance. His eyes were glazed with the astonishment of someone locked into a set of headlights who realizes he is about to be flattened, and he was shivering in a bare-bones cell in just his underwear.

"Why are you in your skivvies, Sergeant?" he asked.

"They said I was a suicide risk, sir," Lonetree replied.

"Why did they say that?"

Lonetree shrugged. "I don't know."

Henderson turned to the duty warden, who simply said, "Orders."

Any prisoner who came in with high visibility, either because of notoriety or because of severity of offense, went to D-seg. And if there was any indication—underline *any*—that the individual could be a suicide risk, he was stripped of all things that could assist him: shoelaces, socks, down to his underwear. Henderson didn't feel he could fault the brig personnel, because the NIS agents who brought him in might have said something that justified the precaution. But he made a mental note to call McHenry in the morning, because if there was no just cause, he would file a motion.

It was a short visit, during which Henderson did his best to put his apprehensive client at ease. He told him what he'd told a lot of clients, before and since. "Listen, I get paid to worry about this, so don't you bother. You see this gray hair? That's where it comes from. Just take it easy and trust me."

It was hard for him to tell by Lonetree's reaction what he was thinking, and whether he believed him. After all, Henderson was wearing the same green pants and khaki shirt as those who stood guard over him. He just hoped Lonetree would be somewhat relieved to know that there was someone on his side.

Afterward Henderson returned to the office. He did not have any paperwork about the case to look at; he knew only that the charge was espionage, and he was anxious to find out what supportive evidence had been gathered. But he would have to wait for that, so all there was left for him to do now was wonder. And that was what he did for the rest of the night. About the only thing he did not speculate on was what was going to happen when news of this case was released. He knew that a Marine charged with espionage was going to hit the press in a big way.

The next day Henderson got on the line and straightened out the skivvy business. But he had to wait for several days before the first batch of papers on the case was delivered. Compared with a normal military case, this one proceeded slowly, because nobody knew how to handle it. The Naval Investigative Service was classifying everything that had anything to do with the case, and even though Henderson had the proper security clearance, the defense was the last to receive material once it had gone through a classification review.

When at last Henderson received what he'd been anxiously waiting for, he read the summary of admissions: failure to report contacts and fraternizing with Soviet nationals; sexual liaisons with a Soviet national; contact with KGB personnel; theft of classified material; providing classified information to KGB officers; compromising identity of CIA officers; providing recruitment assessment data on other USMC personnel.

Then he turned to the three statements Lonetree had made to the NIS agents in London, describing in detail interactions with Soviet intelligence. The first two confessions struck him as serious but of minimal impact on national security. The third statement, however, was extremely damaging, for in it Lonetree admitted to providing the Soviets with top-secret documents he'd stolen from an embassy safe.

It didn't look good for his client, but Henderson wanted to hear his side of the story. Their first meeting about the case was held in the Secure Classified Information Facility. Known as the SCIF, it was a windowless room in the basement of Hockmuth Hall that was as safe as a bomb shelter. As they went over the confession and Henderson asked questions, Lonetree complained about the circumstances under which his statement had been taken.

"They'd ask me a question and I'd talk for fifteen, twenty minutes, they'd be jotting notes, then they'd get up and go in and show them to this secretary, and she'd have them back for them in two or three minutes. They left out a lot."

Henderson listened. What Lonetree was suggesting was that what remained was a rough cut of his actual statements.

"Did you read all the statements before you signed them?"

"No, not really. I glanced through them. But by that time I was so tired I didn't care. I wanted to be done with it all."

Henderson turned to the third statement. He'd noted that the first two were initialed and signed by Lonetree, but the third, the most damning one, was not. He asked about this and Lonetree said he refused to sign it because the things the interrogator had made him say weren't true. "They told me to tell them a lie, so I did. That's all a bunch of lies."

Henderson had been a defense counsel long enough to suspect that most of his clients were fibbing if their lips were moving. He just assumed they were going to dissemble while trying to make their side of the story sound as good as they could, and leave it up to him to decide where the truth lay. So when Clayton Lonetree told him that the NIS agents who interrogated him had instructed him to tell them a lie, and that was the basis of his third statement, Henderson filed it in his mind as one more false denial.

Most guys in law enforcement didn't like gals in law enforcement, and the Naval Investigative Service was no exception. It too was a male-chauvinist organization, which was why eyebrows had gone up when Angelic White had been transferred from Guam to NIS headquarters and put in charge of monitoring national security investigations for Europe and the Middle East. She came from a law-enforcement family, her father having been a special agent in charge in Orlando and London. While running the counterintelligence program out of Guam in the early eighties, she had been outstanding, exposing corruption and Chinese infiltration of the government of Guam. So she deserved the promotion. But still, it was unusual to see a woman on a fast track at NIS.

A.W., as she was called within the organization, was a blue-eyed blonde in her early thirties whose prettiness lay buried in a weight problem. She stood five eight and was as strong as a man. She'd been assaulted by a Guamian once, and not only had she repelled her attacker, she'd hurt him. But she dressed with class, wore expensive dresses and jewelry, and was cultured and literate. She was part of the new generation of agents at NIS, which at the time was top-heavy with the old guard, and by virtue of her position in Counterintelligence Investigations, she became the case officer on the Lonetree case.

A desk officer's job in a federal law-enforcement agency was essentially administrative in nature with little operational input, but A.W.'s role in this investigation took on a larger dimension than was customary. Because so many different agencies had a stake in its outcome, it would span the globe, and every directed lead and document would be prepared and transmitted by her. Most case files can be carried in a folder, this one would require file cabinets and a forklift.

Although this was the first espionage case that the NIS had been handed that involved a military person at a foreign embassy, the unique set of difficulties the case presented were immediately apparent to all. Problem number one was endemic to espionage cases in general: they tended to be elusive crimes, tough to fact-find. Unless the suspect was caught in the act of meeting with agents of a foreign power, his crimes were extremely difficult to prove. The criminal justice system had a far easier time with crimes where the facts were hard and could be presented without reasonable doubt.

Problem number two: In the military a man could not be prosecuted on his word alone. Regardless of the apparent validity of a confession, it could not be admitted as evidence against an accused unless sufficient independent incriminating evidence was available to corroborate its essential details.

Problem number three: Coming up with the proof of Lonetree's treasonous acts was going to be no simple task, because unlike normal investigative procedures, NIS would be compelled to work back from his confession to perfect a case for prosecution.

Problem number four: By virtue of the hostile environment in which the crimes occurred, they would be hindered from an examination of the crime scene, surveillance of the subject and observation of coconspirators, collection of evidence, timely interviews of critical witnesses, analysis of travel patterns, and other normal investigative actions.

Problem number five: The standards of proof in an espionage case were tricky to meet. If Lonetree said he stole top-secret documents, it had to be proved that such documents existed, that they were properly classified, that he had had access, and that they weren't accounted for. If he said he had a meeting with a Soviet agent, his presence at the appointed time and place had to be established, and the only ones who would know about that for certain were Soviet intelligence officers.

Prosecuting espionage was a job that no one did particularly well. Success, when it came, was often a matter of getting the breaks.

Given the passage of time, no one at NIS deemed it necessary to launch a team of agents on a Moscow-bound plane in hopes of retrieving hot pieces of evidence lying on the floor of the American Embassy. It had been almost a year since Lonetree had left the Soviet Union. The most promising grounds for a search party was in Vienna, and NIS agents already had recovered a good deal there.

When Agent Hardgrove had gone to Lonetree's room in the Marine House in Vienna on December 24, he'd found in Lonetree's locker a number of rough drafts of letters he'd written to Violetta; a pocket planner in which were written meet dates and places, and, conveniently, a note that read "Meet S"; pieces of paper on which contact instructions were written, apparently from Uncle Sasha; a publication entitled *The Complete Spy;* the enameled jewelry box Lonetree said Sasha had given him as a present before he left for Vienna; and, under the mattress, a list of names Lonetree said he had compiled in response to Sasha's request for the names of CIA agents stationed under cover in Vienna.

And that wasn't all. During the interrogations in London, Lonetree had indicated there was additional evidence in another room located on the same floor of the Marine House, and Hardgrove had gone back to Vienna on December 29 to collect it. This time he found more letters and photographs; a pair of ladies' black high-heeled shoes, apparently intended as a present for Violetta; and an excerpt from the book *The Essentials of Leninism.*

While there, Hardgrove had also gone through the Marine House records at the embassy and found a special liberty request from Lonetree for the period of January 5 to January 22, 1987, which coincided with the time he said he was planning on returning to the Soviet Union.

Added to that, A.W. had received confirmation from the CIA that "George" had shown up at the meeting place at the scheduled time. The actual document the CIA sent her was a lot less impressive than she would have liked. She was expecting and hoping for a detailed report containing information the CIA had about George, background on Soviet efforts to recruit American personnel in Vienna, detailed observations of the meet. What she got was a one-paragraph memo that read: Agent John Doe went to the designated place at the appointed time and visibly observed the Soviet agent identified as George. Period. It was nevertheless a critical piece of corroborative information, and its significance was enhanced after an unexpected turn of events.

When Special Agent Moyer returned to Vienna on New Year's Day to try to reconstruct what Lonetree had admitted in his third statement, nothing checked out. When Moyer attempted to confirm that Lonetree had had access to the communications unit in the Vienna embassy, upon checking the procedure for obtaining manual keys to secured rooms, he was informed they were kept in tamper-proof containers. When Moyer looked at the embassy logs, he determined that Lonetree had not even been on duty during the evening he said he'd stolen the classified material. Furthermore, after interviewing all persons in the embassy who would have had contact with the documents Lonetree had described in detail—down to the color of the paper, the number of pages, the location of the staples, the placement of the "Top Secret" markings—no one had seen or heard of documents of this nature. Even a tracer to the Department of State in Washington, D.C., came up negative.

Following the footsteps of the investigation where they logically led next, Moyer had gone up to the roof of the Marine House, where Lonetree said he had secreted the material in a drainpipe. Lonetree had even drawn a sketch of the location where he said the documents were hidden. And there was nothing there. Nothing to indicate anything ever *had* been there. No sign of disturbance in the dust and debris.

The only admission in that third statement that could not be ruled out was Lonetree's claim that he had removed secret documents from the burn bag. One of the security responsibilities of Marines at the embassy was to burn classified material in a rooftop incinerator at night, where all accountability was lost. If Lonetree had rifled through the contents, taking the most sensitive communications to his room and passing them to his handler, no one would know he hadn't done his job unless the documents surfaced at a later time.

This startling development generated a tremendous amount of consternation at NIS headquarters. To have a statement admitting to espionage crimes, and then, in the process of fact-checking, to determine that some of the admissions did not occur, with all that was already known about Lonetree, was alarming. It threw open the door to the infinite unknown. What other portions of the statement were false? Where did truth end and fiction begin? If he didn't do it, why did he say he did it? Was he playing some game? Was he trying to discredit everything he'd said before by making wild claims that could be proved to be untrue? Under what conditions was the statement taken? Was there agent misconduct? And what should the NIS do now? It had already committed itself by disseminating Lonetree's statements to interested agencies, some of whom had gone to general quarters because of potential losses and damage.

A.W. knew it was a rare investigation that proceeded faultlessly, but this was not something that could be blown off as a minor kink. At the very least it created a defense counsel's dream, and a prosecutor's nightmare.

Although a host of specters had been raised, White did not feel the situation was catastrophic. Indeed, she thought it could even mean that in the process of fitting the key into Lonetree's lock, they might open up greater crimes than he had yet confessed to.

6

At the Quantico brig Sgt. Clayton Lonetree was kept in a five-by-ten-foot cell that had three cement walls and a fourth of iron bars. His every move was monitored night and day by a closed-circuit camera. He was given no access to television or radio, he ate his meals in his cell, and every two or three days he was taken outside and allowed to run. But exercise is difficult when you're wearing leg irons, a belly chain, and handcuffs.

He was told not to engage his jailers in conversation, and the only time they addressed him was to say things like "Here's your chow, traitor," and "Haven't they lynched you yet, Indian?" As it was explained to him, he was in lockdown for his personal safety. For having dishonored the Marine Corps, there were any number of Marines who would take him out if they had the chance. It was made known to him that boot-camp drill instructors were invoking the name of Clayton Lonetree to fire up trainees at bayonet practice. Already two letters had arrived from citizens expressing outrage over his actions and recommending he be executed. One suggested it be done on national television.

Once in a while he was given a newspaper, but anything related to his case was cut out. When he tore a picture of a farm scene out of the paper and hung it on the wall just to remind himself what the out-of-doors looked like, it was taken down.

One day he was escorted to the brig library, which was a closet full of old paperbacks. He returned with a book written by the Russian author Dostoyevski, *Crime and Punishment*.

He had two regular visitors during those first few weeks. One was a Navy lieutenant commander in the Medical Service Corps by the name of Forrest Sherman. The brig psychologist, Sherman had been called in to evaluate Lonetree for suicidal impulses. But after spending several hours with him, Sherman had decided that while Lonetree's behavior could easily be seen as self-damaging, he was not, at least at this point, going to kill himself. What he was was a very confused young man.

So Sherman had gone to the commanding officer and said he felt it was important that Lonetree have someone to talk to during this period. Someone not involved in the process, who had no stake in the direction of the court-martial. The commanding officer agreed, and it was set up so that Sherman would visit Lonetree privately on a regular basis.

As Sherman saw his role, he wanted to provide some positive valuing of Lonetree as a human being. Certainly nobody else was. And Lonetree seemed to want to talk to someone. About himself. About what he'd done.

At that stage Lonetree seemed almost shellshocked by the events that had engulfed him. What would stand out in Sherman's memory of their early conversations was Lonetree's description of himself. When Sherman began by asking Lonetree about his name and his racial heritage, assuming there would be some comfort to be found in his cultural background, or a sense of identity, Lonetree shook his head and referred to himself as an "apple."

Sherman had been unfamiliar with the term at the time and asked, "What do you mean?"

Lonetree's answer was, "You know, like there are blacks who are Oreos."

Sherman still didn't catch it. So Lonetree proceeded to explain that his Indian heritage was not an important part of who he was. While he appeared to be a red man on the outside, on the inside he thought and felt like a white man, and that's what was known as an apple.

Lonetree also expressed a profound ambiguity regarding his loyalties. On the one hand he acknowledged that he had been manipulated by the KGB, but he also felt he had been set up by the CIA and betrayed by the NIS. At this point he didn't know who his friends were and who his enemies were. People on both the Soviet and the American side appeared to have befriended him only to take advantage of him.

The other person who called on Lonetree daily was Major Henderson. In the two weeks since he'd met his client, Henderson had come to a new appreciation of him. Initially Henderson had found Lonetree so lacking in guile, so slow and dim, that the possibility of retardation had occurred to him, or perhaps some kind of learning disability. There were times when Henderson would ask a question that was answered with what seemed like a non sequitur, or a response the exact opposite of what he expected.

But as they began to establish a rapport, Lonetree's thought processes gradually seemed to become more focused, and after getting to know his client better, Henderson had come to the conclusion that Sergeant Lonetree was a deceptively intelligent guy. Yes, he was someone whose attention drifted. And he certainly evidenced an emotional immaturity that resulted in questionable judgment. But Henderson saw indications of native smarts that he likened in his mind to those of a coyote. Nobody would call a coyote slow and dumb. Take them out of their element and they couldn't add two and two. But in their own element coyotes were crafty as could be.

His client's credibility had also been enhanced when the NIS released a report saying all of the assertions in Lonetree's third statement had proved to be demonstrably false. This told Henderson that Lonetree had been voicing the truth when he'd said an NIS agent in London had encouraged him to lie.

The overall result was that Henderson's thinking about this case had begun to change. Where at first it had sounded like a serious security breach, now he was beginning to think an overreaction might be taking place. And this was his frame of mind when the chief prosecutor at Quantico, Maj. Frank Short, raised the idea of a plea bargain.

"Dave, there's all these intelligence agencies who want to talk to your guy," Short said. "And I'm having trouble getting material and releasing it to you because it's classified. What do you say to a deal?"

Henderson was willing to listen. "What's the case worth?"

"If Lonetree admits to minor security violations and disregarding the Intelligence Identities Protection Act, and he's willing to cooperate with an intelligence debriefing, we're talking in the neighborhood of five years."

A defense counsel never measures success by acquittals. Effective representation was a matter of getting the best deal for the client, and Major Henderson had a reputation for recognizing early on when going to trial was a lost cause and negotiating a favorable deal. So he was tempted. His client was a Marine who had committed serious violations. He had confessed and was even now not denying most of what he said had happened. The government did not want the case to become a public spectacle, nor did it want to go through the risk of having national-security information divulged. This trial was also going to be expensive to conduct if witnesses had to be brought in from around the world. And as Short had said, Lonetree was in demand by a list of government agencies who wanted to talk with him. Added up, that made a persuasive case for accepting a pretrial agreement.

But for the time being, Henderson decided to pass. Under the Uniform Code of Military Justice a suspect had to be brought to trial within ninety days of confinement or the charges had to be dropped. Officially Lonetree had been taken into custody on December 24, so they were almost a third of the way through that period. At the rate the government was collecting evidence, and given the slowness of the classification process, he doubted the prosecution would be ready to proceed before the deadline. He was hoping either they would be unprepared to go to trial, which would give him added leverage to make an even better deal, or they would rush their case and make a mistake that would constitute grounds for dismissal.

At the very least Henderson wanted to wait until the Article 32 investigation was held. Often referred to as a "military grand jury," an Article 32 was a hearing to determine whether enough evidence existed against the accused to refer the case to a general court-martial. Witnesses were called and statements considered, all of which offered the defense an important discovery opportunity. Waiting would enable Henderson to see just how strong the prosecution's case was. And he was certain the deal would remain on the table for a while longer.

With these thoughts occupying Henderson's mind, he received a telephone call at home one Saturday evening, and on the line was William Kunstler, the flamboyant civil-rights attorney who had made a name for himself defending minorities in high-profile cases. Kunstler said he had been contacted by Clayton Lonetree's father and asked if he would participate in the defense of his son at the upcoming court-martial. He was calling to see if the major had a problem with that.

Though the call was unexpected, Henderson was not completely taken by surprise. He knew that the military justice system, in addition to providing a defendant with a military defense attorney, allowed him to request civilian counsel; in cases that generated notoriety this privilege was frequently invoked. And at first blush the idea of working side by side with a legal legend intrigued him. He even allowed the possibility that there might be an advantage to having Kunstler aboard, for just as he had suspected, the charges against Clayton Lonetree were making national news. There being a disciplinary rule that prevented military lawyers from using the press to influence a case, having an experienced, big-name attorney around who was willing to sound off in the press could be useful.

So Major Henderson had replied, "If it's okay with my client, it's fine with me. I'll speak with him tomorrow."

They talked a while longer—Kunstler asked a few legal questions, Henderson advised him to look into obtaining a security clearance because of the classified nature of the case—and the conversation ended on a pleasant note. But afterward, when he had more time to think about William Kunstler's reputation for trying cases in the press and how that would play in a court-martial setting, the major began to experience second thoughts.

Abruptly he reached for the phone and dialed the number of the deputy staff judge advocate. Lt. Col. David Breme had been a military judge at Camp Lejeune in North Carolina, and Henderson recalled that Kunstler had once tried a case in front of him. He wanted to hear whether Breme thought Kunstler would be an asset or a detriment.

The deputy SJA was not one to mince words. William Kunstler did not so much put up a fight for his clients, he said, as put on a show for them, and the trial at Camp Lejeune was a case in point. It was a straightforward unauthorized-absence case—a black Marine deserted when his unit was sent to Beirut—but when William Kunstler entered the picture, it became something else. The Marine was now a Black Muslim who had refused to go for religious reasons.

"The government put on a prima facie case for his guilt, and Kunstler used the judicial system as a podium for his political beliefs, and I convicted the guy. Immediately afterward, on the steps of the courthouse, Kunstler announced to the press, 'This only proves that a black man can't get a fair trial from the United States military.' That's how he plays the game, Dave. And if he can't be kept under control, you're going to have a hell of a mess on your hands."

That was enough good advice for Major Henderson. The next morning he visited Lonetree in the brig and explained what had happened and talked to him about this options. "It's your call, Sergeant," he summed up, "but I'd be less than honest if I didn't tell you that I don't think your best interests will be served by having Mr. Kunstler as your advocate in a military court."

Lonetree listened carefully and in the end agreed. He authorized Major Henderson to decline William Kunstler's offer of representation, and as far as the major was concerned, that was the final word regarding Kunstler's involvement in the case.

The first Clayton Lonetree's mother heard about any of this was when the phone rang in her Tuba City, Arizona, trailer a week into January. It was Craig, Clayton's younger brother by two years, and he was calling from St. Paul. "You got a chair there, Mom?" he asked. "Well, you better have a seat."

She thought he was joking, even when he enlarged. "It's about Clayton. He got picked up for spying in Russia."

"What are you talking about?" she demanded to know. "Who told you that?"

"A journalist called me this morning for a comment."

After a silence during which the line seemed to go dead, Craig said, "Brace yourself, Mom. It's going to be all over the news."

Sally Tsosie was a full-blooded Navajo woman in her early forties, with a broad face, slightly slanted brown eyes, a wide mouth with full lips, and hair that was naturally black and thick, who had been born to the Two Waters Flowing Together clan in a hogan near Big Mountain, Arizona. It was a remote part of the Navajo Reservation, home to some of the most conservative members of the tribe, and she had been raised traditionally—helping her father, a stockman, move the herds and flocks with the change of season; babysitting her nine younger siblings while her mother wove rugs; learning the family history from her grandfather while brushing his long gray hair. But it was the U.S. government's policy of moving young native people off the Reservation and into urban areas where they could be more easily integrated into the general culture that had determined her destiny.

She'd been eight when she was enrolled in a Reservation mission school run by evangelical Protestants, and three years there were followed by four more years at a boarding school in Brigham City, Utah, where she was occupationally trained as a film librarian. Upon graduation, she'd been given a train ticket to Chicago, where a job awaited her at Esquire-Coronet Films repairing documentary films, and where she shared an apartment with a Navajo girlfriend in a rooming house on the North Side of Chicago that was nicknamed Hillbilly Heaven for the white trash from Appalachia who shared the neighborhood.

Within a year she had met Spencer Lonetree, Clayton's father. He was a Winnebago Indian, descended from an orphan who had been named after a solitary white oak tree that still stood in a field in Wisconsin; but although his heritage was native, the extent of his Indian upbringing had been the summers he'd spent hoop dancing at the Stand Rock Indian Ceremonial in Wisconsin Dells, a tourist trap and center of attraction for millions willing to pay to be entertained by Indian singers and dancers. He was an urban Indian raised in St. Paul and living in Chicago, where he was employed as the director of youth activities at the Indian Center.

Under ordinary circumstances Sally would not have been attracted to someone like Spencer Lonetree. Whereas she was bashful, he was brash, and they were worlds apart in their thinking. A revealing moment for her had been the weekend afternoon they sat together under a tree along Lake Michigan and she tried to tell him about Navajo mythology, and how the Dineh came from an underworld and at one time could communicate with the animals. Having left the Red Path for the White Way, Spencer saw Indian beliefs as quaint notions of little value in the modern world, and commented, "You sound like somebody out of a cartoon."

But there was an independent streak in Sally. After a sheltered upbringing and a strict education, it was fun to let go of all the don'ts. For a girl who had grown up riding a donkey to the nearest trading post, it also felt like royalty to be escorted around the Windy City in Spencer's two-tone pink-and-white Cadillac. And after all, these were the sixties. . . .

Just seventeen, Sally was sexually naive and did not know the ways of making love without making a baby. She and Spencer were living together when she discovered she was pregnant, but she did not want to get married because their relationship was stormy, and she moved in with a girlfriend to have her baby in peace.

It was a difficult birth. She was in labor for two days before Clayton John Lonetree weighed in, on the morning of November 6, 1961, at six pounds, thirteen ounces. But for Sally it was the most joyous occasion of her life.

Remembering it now, however, filled her with sadness. Her lament was the same as every parent whose child ended up in trouble: Maybe if she had been a better mother, none of this would have happened.

This sentiment led her, in turn, to another memory. Shortly after Clayton was born, she and Spencer argued over how they should raise their son. The Winnebago being patrilineal and the Navajo matrilineal, their views naturally differed. By the time Spencer left, Sally was in tears, and their raised voices had upset Clayton enough that he too was crying. As they wept together, it had seemed to Sally that somehow her son sensed her unhappiness and was crying for her sake, and cuddling him in her arms, she had whispered a promise against his tiny wet cheek that should the day ever come that he needed her, she would be there for him.

The remembrance of that vow became the grain of sand around which a plan of action formed, as Sally recognized that this was her son's hour of need. She had no idea where he was being held and thought he might still be in Russia until a relative called the *Los Angeles Times* and discovered that he was being kept in the brig at Quantico, Virginia. She tried to reach him by phone but was unable to talk directly to him, so she left the message that she was coming. Her current husband—she had long ago separated from Spencer—drove her to Albuquerque, where she caught a flight to Washington, D.C. Once she arrived at National Airport, she didn't know how to get to Quantico, so she took a subway into the city and walked to the Navajo Nation office. From there she was directed to Union Station, where she bought a ticket and boarded a train headed south.

"How far is it?" she kept asking the conductor restlessly.

"I'll tell you when we get there," he assured her.

Passengers stared. She was certain it was because they knew whose mother she was and why she had come.

It was dark when she arrived at the right stop. Anticipating her arrival, several military men came up and told her they would escort her to the guest house.

"That's not where I want to go," she told them.

"Are you hungry? There's a restaurant—"

"No. I want to see Clayton before I eat or sleep."

So they took her to the brig. It was the first time she had seen him in over three years, and her tears flowed uncontrollably. She said she had been praying for him, and she would stand behind him through everything that happened.

To her surprise, he seemed almost nonchalant. Grinning at her, he said, "Mom, it's no big thing. This will all be put behind me soon."

At first she couldn't comprehend why he was so casually dismissing the charges against him. But as soon as she started telling him what was being said about him in the press, by his amazed reaction it became clear: He'd had no access to newspapers, radio, or TV, so he was in the dark as to what was going on on the outside.

"They are blowing it out of proportion. That's not how it is," he protested.

Sally looked into his eyes and she believed him. But she also believed that he did not realize the gravity of the situation.

After a sleepless night at the guest house, she met with Clayton's military attorney, Major Henderson. She had many questions about Clayton's case, but when she asked them he answered her circumspectly. Much of what she was asking involved classified information, he told her. She became frustrated and angry. She was convinced that her son had been telling her the truth when he said what he'd done wasn't that bad, just as she now became certain that the reason Major Henderson was so evasive was that he was part of a military conspiracy against her son.

Throughout the long journey back to Tuba City, Sally Tsosie thought about what was happening, and by the time she arrived home she had drawn a straight line from the conquest of the Navajo tribe in 1864 by federal troops commanded by Kit Carson to the imprisonment of her son by the military in 1987. She saw the United States government as not only the enemy of her people but her family's personal enemy as well. The way she figured it, they were part of the same system: the U.S. Cavalry who had boxed the Navajo people on a reservation and the Marine Corps who had incarcerated her son. In her eyes, they were all Bluecoats.

Thirty-seven years of age, sporting wire-rimmed spectacles and a mustache, his stocky frame perennially balanced on a pair of western boots, Michael Stuhff had yet to establish a prominent name for himself in the city where he currently practiced law—Las Vegas—but he was well known on the Navajo Reservation. After graduating from the University of Utah Law School in 1973, fired with the idealism of the times, Stuhff had decided to devote a year helping the hard-pressed Navajos. He stayed thirteen years and was involved in everything from defending Navajo Tribal Chairman Peter MacDonald on corruption charges to investigating allegations of a connection between the car-bombing murder of reporter Don Bolles in Phoenix and a scheme to get a new tribal chairman elected who would cut a uranium-mining deal favorable to corporations. He had also represented Navajos arrested by tribal police for protesting the boundaries drawn by the court in the Navajo–Hopi land dispute. The ownership of Big Mountain was part of that controversy, and when the Hopis had undertaken a fence-building project in the ancestral lands of the Navajo, many traditional people in the area had opposed the action and were arrested for interfering. Sally Tsosie had been one of those jailed, and Michael Stuhff had defended her.

It had been several years since he'd spoken with Sally Tsosie, and when his secretary told him she was on the line, he had no idea why she was calling. But at the top of the conversation she came to the point. "Mr. Stuhff, you've got to help me," she pleaded.

"Why? What is it?" he asked.

Sally let the words tumble out, telling all she knew, up to the fact that she didn't think Clayton understood what he faced and including her distrust of the military's intention to give her son a fair trial.

She finished by saying, "I try to picture it like they say, but I can't believe it, Mr. Stuhff. I know my child. I know when I look into his eyes that he is telling the truth. It's not like they are saying it is."

Stuhff recognized the seriousness of her son's predicament and matter-of-factly said, "Clayton needs a lawyer who's not part of the military."

Sally agreed. "I know. That's why I called you."

Michael Stuhff let out a big sigh. His specialty was racketeering, homicide, smuggling, and narcotics cases. He didn't know anything about military law, much less espionage. Pro bono, he had just worked the Judge Harry Claiborne impeachment trial, the first judicial impeachment to go before the U.S. Senate in fifty years, and it had drained him emotionally and financially. And he knew crusades on behalf of an oppressed minority group rarely turned a monetary gain, and were frequently costly.

"I need a day to think about it," he said.

Over the next twenty-four hours Mike Stuhff came up with a dozen more reasons not to take on this case. But even as he thought of the commitment in time, emotion, and money, he knew it would be hard for him to turn Sally down. The next afternoon he called her back and told her he would be willing to represent her son.

There was silence on the other end of the line.

"Hello? Sally? What's wrong?"

Apologetically, Sally said that since their conversation she had received a phone call from Clayton's father, who had informed her that William Kunstler had been contacted and *he* was going to represent Clayton.

Stuhff was hugely relieved. Not only did this let him off the hook, he knew the veteran Kunstler was the right man for this job. Indeed, as a passionate advocate for civil rights himself, he had been a longtime admirer of William Kunstler. Among his cherished memories was an exchange the two had had back in the early seventies. After Kunstler had delivered a speech at the University of Utah Law School, at a reception in the student lounge Stuhff had approached him and expressed the opinion that following the precedent of Nuremberg, he thought a war-crimes trial ought to be held and General Westmoreland and President Nixon, among others, ought to be tried for prosecuting the Vietnam War. An amused Kunstler had chuckled and said, "You're being too radical, my friend."

Since the remark was coming from a fire-breathing radical, Stuhff had taken it as a compliment. And now he took the opportunity to have another conversation with his legal hero, calling Kunstler in New York to wish him well.

"You have been misinformed," Kunstler replied. "I am not representing Clayton."

"Why not?" Stuhff asked.

"I'm not sure," Kunstler answered. "What I was told by his Marine lawyer was he did not want civilian representation because he thought it was in his interest to go through this without any publicity."

Stuhff was dismayed. It seemed more than a little suspicious that a Marine confined in the Quantico brig would not wish to be represented by someone free of military control. As for wanting to avoid publicity, it was too late. A cursory check of media stories had revealed that the adverse-publicity mill was already churning. In a session with a group of reporters at the Pentagon, Defense Secretary Caspar Weinberger had even made a statement to the effect that in his opinion if Lonetree wasn't hanged, he ought to be shot.

A second time Mike Stuhff called Sally Tsosie. He related the essence of his conversation with William Kunstler and said he was still willing to take her son's case. But for that to happen, he said, "Clayton is going to have to make up his mind that he definitely wants independent civilian counsel."

Sally said she would talk to Clayton, and the way she said it left little doubt which way her son would go.

After hanging up the phone, Mike Stuhff found himself thinking about his grandfather. Stories about the old man's involvement in the international protest of the French army's espionage conviction of Alfred Dreyfus because he was a Jew had been handed down in the Stuhff family as an example of social idealism to be emulated. From all that he'd read so far, the case against Clayton Lonetree sounded like a similar rush to judgment.

7

When the physical evidence confiscated from Lonetree's room in Vienna arrived at NIS headquarters, included were a batch of photographs. Angelic White spent several days sifting through them, culling the obvious ones—photos of Lonetree and his family—from those that were not immediately identifiable. Midmorning on the second day, a fellow NIS agent by the name of Ron Larsen dropped by her cubicle to help out. As he shuffled through the unknowns, he stopped on one of Lonetree in a white polo shirt and blue jeans, standing in front of a building beside a brass plaque.

"This is San Francisco," he remarked.

A.W. craned to see which one he was talking about.

"San Francisco? That's odd. There's nothing about San Francisco in his background records. I wonder what he was doing there."

Larsen looked more closely at the photo. He was familiar with the Bay Area because he had spent a lot of personal time there, but it was as an NIS agent that he was familiar with the foreign consulates. "I don't know, but that's the Soviet Consulate he's standing in front of."

"Get out of town!" A.W. exclaimed.

Larsen handed her the photo, and A.W. stared as if seeing it for the first time.

"This came from a stack taken during the time he was at

Camp Pendleton," she observed. "Where he was stationed before he went through Marine guard training."

The photo immediately took on the charge of a potentially case-breaking piece of evidence. Everyone had assumed Lonetree's downfall began in Moscow, when he met Violetta. The big question now was how far back all this went: Had Lonetree entered the Marine security guard program with the *intention* of betrayal?

Leads were immediately sent to NIS agents in the Bay Area, who were given the task of tracking every step of Lonetree's San Francisco trip. Within a week they reported back. Lonetree had purchased a plane ticket from San Diego to San Francisco in 1983, while stationed at Camp Pendleton. He had come up on a Friday, remained Saturday, and returned on Sunday. The hotel where he stayed was located and its records revealed that he had rented a single room. There was no record of any outgoing calls.

As for who took the picture, there was no way of telling at this point. He could have stopped some tourist on the street and asked for a favor. On the other hand, this was a guy who kept copies of his meet instructions in Vienna.

Had he just posed out front or actually gone inside? A.W. went to the FBI for the answer to that question, because they maintained twenty-four-hour visual surveillance of the Soviet Consulate. But apparently there had been a camera malfunction on that particular day, and for reasons never explained, no backup logs describing entries and exits had been kept. Lonetree could have gone in and out, but there was no way of knowing.

For several weeks Angelic White could not get the lead out of her mind and continued to try on various meanings. It proved he was there—so big deal, you could say. San Francisco's a popular vacation spot, lots of people go there. But from her position at the time she thought it was unusual for someone on Lonetree's salary to jet up to San Francisco for such a short trip. And presumably he shot a whole roll of film, but what was the one picture he saved? Not Fishermen's Wharf. Not the Golden Gate Bridge. Himself in front of the Soviet Consulate.

The ante was raised when a tantalizing results-of-interview was filed by an NIS agent on the Camp Pendleton interview beat who had located a Sgt. Scott Howard, a Marine assigned to the same company as Lonetree in 1982, who remembered him well. "Howard said subject was quiet, intellectual, and always reading books on World War II and the Soviet Union. Subject was current on world events and would sometimes talk with Howard about going to the Soviet Union and the activities of the KGB. Howard said that subject was fascinated by the world of espionage. . . ."

Angelic White didn't know what to make of the fact that Lonetree had apparently been absorbed in thought about the Soviet Union and the KGB at this stage of his Marine career. Her familiarity with KGB policies regarding walk-ins led her to believe that if Lonetree had initiated contact himself, it was unlikely they would have welcomed him. More probably they would have suspected he was a dangle or a crank, opened a file on him, and done nothing more. But even if Lonetree had not made an actual approach, she thought at the very least this indicated he was already fooling around with the notion of hooking up with the Soviets. Just in his head, maybe, but nevertheless he was thinking about it. Which put him on the road to espionage before he ever got to Moscow.

As provocative as the San Francisco lead was, when it went no further, A.W. turned her attention back to other investigative issues that were proving to be equally frustrating. Headquarters wanted NIS agents to speak with every Marine security guard who had come into contact with Sergeant Lonetree while he was dealing with Soviet intelligence. Thinking the Marine Corps was the logical place to go for that information, she had submitted a formal request asking for the name and current location of all MSGs whose tour of duty overlapped Lonetree's. When a week went by and she had yet to receive a response, she called for an update on the progress. This time she was informed that she had come to the wrong place. The Marine Corps didn't have those records because Marines on embassy duty technically belonged to the State Department.

"Terrific," she muttered to herself, clearly perturbed, and that very day put in an identical request to the appropriate people at the State Department. And when the much-awaited report did not show up in a timely fashion, she made an exasperated phone call demanding to know what was taking so long.

"Be patient," she was told. "It's going to take time for a list of names to be assembled."

"Why? Can't somebody just go to a computer and jet off a copy?"

It was at this juncture that she learned about the Diplomatic Security Service's outdated method of record keeping. Incredibly, its files on Marine security guards had yet to be computerized. MSGs were indexed by name only, they weren't differentiated by duty stations, and the State Department's tracking device consisted of going by hand through hundreds of three-by-five cards kept in a cardboard box.

Eventually ten names were turned over to A.W., which prompted another round of bickering. She wanted an open field: the right for NIS agents to interview Marine guards, to expand the conversation into interrogations if it seemed appropriate, to administer a polygraph examination if it was called for, and to conduct property searches should they be warranted. To her, these were the basic materials with which you built a case.

But the State Department didn't see it that way. When Angelic White notified officials that NIS intended to begin their interviews with those Marines in these locations on this day, she was reminded that the regional security officer was responsible not only for implementing overall security at U.S. diplomatic missions overseas but also for investigating all matters of criminal interest.

A.W. had assumed that even though embassies were not the Naval Investigative Service's natural jurisdiction, because the investigation of counterintelligence activities involving Marine Corps personnel belonged to NIS, full cooperation on the part of the State Department could be taken for granted. In any number of other investigations involving military personnel, a simple call to the primary organization was all it had taken, and where there had been concurrent jurisdiction, accommodations were usually made to let NIS take the lead.

This being the first inquiry of this nature, however, no established mechanism existed for coordinating this kind of counter-intelligence investigation, and the State Department was not inclined to relinquish its authority. So out of its own counter-intelligence shop went interview requests, which were received by security officers at the Moscow and Vienna embassies as well as embassies where other MSGs of interest to the NIS had been transferred. And when the first results came through, the weaknesses of the State Department's criminal investigative abilities were apparent. There were glaring omissions, obvious questions unasked or not followed up on.

When they arrived on A.W.'s desk, in disgust she kicked them back. "I can't use these. If a Marine said he attended a Thanksgiving luncheon with Lonetree, I don't want to hear what was on the menu. I want to know who else was there, and what they talked about."

Not until the State Department realized how extensive and detailed NIS wanted this investigation to be conducted, and the embassy security officers recognized the amount of work it entailed, did things finally loosen up and was the NIS invited to participate. But by this time several precious weeks had passed, and A.W. was beginning to hear the tick of the ninety-day clock.

The initial reports filed by NIS agents let A.W. know they were not investigating the good soldier. Sgt. Clayton Lonetree, it turned out, had had a history of significant personal problems while on post. His fellow Marines remembered that he could not hold his liquor, he was loud and obnoxious when he had too much to drink, and this had led to several disciplinary actions. He also had a lengthy rap sheet for minor misconduct: showing up late for duty, falling asleep on duty, standing guard in civilian clothes, losing his nightstick. And after he'd been counseled, when he did not shape up quickly enough, the detachment commander had even tried to get him relieved from the security guard program.

But there were surprisingly few hits that connected Lonetree to the elements of offense in his case. He was described as a loner who kept to himself, someone whose name defined him, so few Marines could say they knew him well. To no one had he confided his relationship with Violetta, much less his meetings with Uncle Sasha. Several did comment that he was openly enamored with the Soviet system, as evidenced by living quarters that were decorated with large pictures of members of the Soviet Politburo, a five-by-eight-foot Russian flag, and a blown-up photograph of a Russian tank. And it was mentioned that when he was inebriated, you could count on his going off on a tangent about how Indians were the low man on the totem pole in American society, but it wasn't like that in the Soviet Union, where everyone was equal. But no one thought much about it at the time because a lot of Marines collected Soviet military memorabilia, and everyone in the Corps had some gripe or other. Besides, other than those quirks, Sergeant Lonetree was a regular Joe. He responded to occasions for carousing as though they were a fraternity initiation, and got up the next morning and jogged ten miles in combat boots. While some of his barracks mates would jokingly call him Comrade Lonesky and refer to him as a "Red" Indian, he was more widely known by the nickname Running Bear.

The most inculpatory information turned up by NIS came out of the Moscow logbooks. The buddy system was in effect in Moscow, requiring Marines to travel in pairs whenever they left the embassy, but an inspection of the logs showed that Lonetree had signed out 104 times, and 73 of those times he had gone out by himself. The problem from an evidentiary point of view, however, was that even though it could now be confirmed that he had checked out on the days he said he met with Violetta and Sasha, there was only his word as to where he went.

By no means were the Marine interviews unproductive, however. To the contrary, although NIS agents were finding very little additional evidence against Lonetree that went beyond what he had turned over in Vienna, they were collecting a startling amount of contextual information about the Marine guard detachment at the American Embassy in Moscow. And what they discovered in this regard was as disturbing as it was enlightening.

The rule book said that Marines stationed in Moscow were not allowed to date Soviet women or women from any other Eastern Bloc country. They were not even supposed to associate or converse with them on a one-to-one basis outside the embassy. To reduce the possibility of interaction between Marines and Soviet women, certain hotels, bars, and discos were also declared off-limits. The rationale for these restrictions was that this would reduce the likelihood of Marines' getting sexually or personally involved with Soviet women and potentially setting themselves up for entrapment, because that was the way the KGB operated.

But in the overwhelming majority of the interviews, Marines admitted to NIS agents that their superiors looked the other way when it came to policing the nonfraternization policy. Virtually every one of the Marines who served in Moscow with Lonetree acknowledged having violated the nonfraternization regulation on at least one occasion. They had gone to a "dollar bar" and danced with a Soviet hooker, or they had picked one up and taken her back to their room in the embassy. Some confessed to having Soviet girlfriends and switching duty so they could check out and sleep over. One Marine even admitted smuggling a Soviet girl into the Marine House, where he kept her hidden away like a love slave for several days. Several accused the assistant detachment commander of having a bevy of Soviet prostitutes that serviced him like a harem.

When information about massive fraternization among the Marine security guards began to come out, no one at NIS headquarters wanted to jump to melodramatic conclusions—but the implications were unavoidable. Throughout the Cold War the Soviets had repeatedly demonstrated a bold proclivity toward the use of clandestine listening devices with legendary success. They had given a hand-carved replica of the Great Seal to U.S. Ambassador Averell Harriman. This masterpiece of art and ingenuity, constructed with a wireless resonant cavity, was given a place of honor on one of Harriman's walls, where it hung as an invisible witness to U.S. foreign policy in the making, monitoring the ambassador's conversations for several years, until located. (Later a U.S. diplomat was quoted as saying they went to the middle of Red Square for their private conversations, while in the embassy "they spoke for the mikes.")

In the years since, the KGB had bombarded the embassy with microwaves to pick up the vibrations of voices on the windowpanes; it had slipped an elaborate eavesdropping antenna in the embassy's chimney, stolen the embassy's electronic typewriters and rigged them to transmit every letter; and it had sprinkled a powder that was invisible to the human eye but glowed under certain lights as a way of tracing the travels of suspected agents. Not to forget the extensive list of foreign diplomats and officials captured "en flagrant" on KGB audiotape and film, these were just the efforts that were known.

So it was against this historical tapestry that a new threat had to be evaluated. Fraternization in the Soviet Union was more than a violation of regulations. From the viewpoint of Soviet intelligence, any American who agreed to an unofficial and personal relationship with a Soviet woman and concealed the fact from his superiors had already taken a first compromising step. While there was as yet no hard evidence linking fraternization to spying, in light of previous efforts by the Soviets to compromise the American Embassy, agents of the NIS were forced to consider the possibility that in the process of investigating a single Marine gone bad, they might have stumbled across something far bigger. Because everywhere they scratched, it was starting to bleed.

On January 30, Mike Stuhff, accompanied by a friend and private investigator by the name of Lake Headley, flew to National Airport in Washington, D.C., rented a car, and drove south to Quantico, where they checked into the Quality Inn motel across from the entrance to the Marine base. The next morning Major Henderson's legal assistant, Capt. Andy Strotman, delivered the unclassified NIS files to the two Las Vegans, which kept them up most of the night reading. The following morning all four men met for breakfast and discussed the case.

Henderson said that, bottom line, he thought a plea agreement was the way to go, because Lonetree had confessed and parts of his confession had been corroborated. If there were any promising aspects to the case, he said, he thought they would be procedural rather than factual, and he told Stuhff about the military's speedy-trial provision.

Mike Stuhff smiled privately, keeping his suspicions about Major Henderson's conflict of loyalties to himself. All he said was that while he recognized that the major's expertise on the procedural intricacies of military law was greater than his own, he felt that Henderson might be overstating the promise of the speedy-trial tactic. He found it hard to believe that the military would allow a case of this magnitude to be dismissed simply because the government wasn't ready to try the case; but this was not a decision that needed to be made this minute, and certainly not before he'd had a chance to meet his client.

A half hour later Major Henderson, Mike Stuhff, and Lake Headley were joined in a small conference room at the Quantico brig by Clayton Lonetree, who wore camouflage utilities and a yellow plastic badge with his name and photograph. Lonetree seemed to recognize that his fate rested in the hands of these three men, and he expressed his gratitude, indicating a ready willingness to answer all their questions openly and honestly. He was polite and addressed them as "sir" and "Major," and when he was asked by Stuhff to tell him what happened, he replied, "Where do you want me to start, sir?"

"At the beginning."

"When I was born?"

"No. Begin with Violetta."

The first time Sgt. Clayton Lonetree saw Violetta, he was standing at the window of the Marine House, and she was walking down the sidewalk toward the American Embassy. He thought she might be Swedish, she was so pretty, so sleek, and dressed so fashionably. She certainly wasn't typical of the Russian women he was accustomed to seeing since he'd arrived in Moscow almost a year earlier. The kind, he had heard at MSG school, who could be identified as Russian by their bad breath and big breasts.

When he asked around, he learned that he was not alone in his reaction to her. Other Marines commented on her provocative beauty. Later he would observe the way their heads craned whenever she bent over. He also discovered that only recently had she begun work at the embassy as a translator, which meant she spoke fluent English.

After that he went out of his way to cross paths with her. Post One was a glassed-in booth at the front door of the embassy where the Marine guards verified the identification of everyone who entered, and whenever she passed he would conduct a badge check just for the opportunity of talking with her. He obtained her work schedule and juggled his to be at the same place at the same time. He wanted to get to know her better, and he dared to believe, from their friendly exchanges, that maybe she wanted the same.

To put the next scene in perspective, Lonetree said that ever since arriving in the Soviet Union he had taken an intense interest in the country, its history, the culture, the people. He had read books, hired a tutor to teach him the language, collected Russian memorabilia, and traveled around the city visiting national historic sites. He had admired the domes of St. Basil's Cathedral that floated above the bricks of Red Square like hot-air balloons. He had watched the solemn changing of the guard in front of Lenin's mausoleum. Mentally he had scaled the turrets and the battlements of the Kremlin wall like a Mongolian invader.

But his favorite activity was joyriding in the Moscow metro. Even though Marines were instructed to travel in pairs outside the embassy, often he couldn't find anyone to go with him, so he would sign out and by himself ride the underground trains to the end of the line.

The Moscow metro was another world, he said. Built in the 1940s as a monument to the revolution as well as an air-raid shelter during the Great Patriotic War, it had no graffiti, no lurid advertisements. Many of the stations were veritable museums, with grand marble halls, frescoes and sculptures, gilded chandeliers, and bas-reliefs and ceiling mosaics depicting the brave new world of Soviet heavy industry and idealizing the rural lifestyle and traditions of Russian peasants. He enjoyed getting lost, just to see where a particular line went, coming up in the outskirts of the city and getting his bearings by searching the skyline for the ruby stars atop the tallest buildings in Moscow.

There were periods when he rode the metro almost daily, just to get out of the embassy, where he had made no friends, and to escape an environment that was dreary and, he felt, increasingly unwelcome to him. He had come to consider himself an expert on the Moscow metro and would fantasize that his knowledge of the metro system would one day be important. He envisioned himself guiding a U.S. Marine Corps general through the subway system of Moscow during a U.S. occupation.

So it was appropriate, in a way, that the first time he actually had a conversation with Violetta was on the metro. One day he followed her out of the embassy, down the sidewalk that bordered the Garden Ring boulevard, across Uprising Park with its hedges and benches, and beneath the shadow of the enormous granite-block skyscraper Stalin had built to prove to the world the might of Soviet architectural accomplishments, before arriving at the Barrikadnaya Station, named for the workers who had built barricades there in 1905 to protest the czarist regime. As she moved through the crowd of commuters and descended the escalator, he almost lost her, but he caught up in time to board the same train, the same car. And when the number of passengers thinned out, he approached her with an "Oh, hi," as if their being there together were an accident.

That first conversation consisted mostly of small talk. She said it was unusual to see an American on the Moscow subway, and he told her how much it fascinated him. They discussed her job in the General Services section of the embassy, and she said she had been previously employed as the receptionist at Spaso House, where the American ambassador, Arthur Hartman, resided. They were still talking when it was her stop, and she exited with a luminous smile and a "Goodbye. See you tomorrow."

"I couldn't believe it," he told his interviewers. "She was so beautiful."

A week or so later, Lonetree said, he again followed Violetta to the Barrikadnaya metro. This time they became so involved in conversation during the trip that she missed her stop, which he took as a good sign. But when she got off, she made a reference to going home to her "family," which made him wonder about her status. Was she married? He was reluctant to straightforwardly ask her, and in fact was distressed that he was even asking the question. He recalled thinking, I can't believe it. I'm jealous about a Russian girl.

When he realized he was developing feelings for Violetta, it was not something he accepted heedlessly. He was fully aware that Marines were supposed to avoid contact with Soviet women. They were advised to seek female companionship primarily from nannies, the young foreign women employed by Western residents to take care of their children. But he was also aware of Marines who frequented the off-limits bars and picked up Soviet "night butterflies," as they were called, and it seemed to him that everyone was getting away with *something* in Moscow, which made it easier for him to rationalize this.

"I started thinking, Okay, but play it safe. You can see her, but not as much or often as you'd like."

In the weeks following, there were numerous incidents of causal conversation at the embassy but no planned meetings. Then in October, after he became angry about some MSG matter the nature of which he could not recall, he left the embassy to ride the metro and spotted Violetta on her way home. He entered her car and did not speak to her or sit with her initially. He did approach her eventually, but not with the usual cheerful greeting. She could tell something was bothering him, and upon arriving at her stop, she asked him if he wanted to get off and go for a walk. He shrugged and said, All right, he was planning to go for a walk anyway.

Her stop was named Tekstilshiki, for a textile plant. A broad boulevard passed a park and a lake on its way to a cluster of apartment buildings the size of cruise ships, and as they walked along it together, their conversation centered on his background, his perceptions of Moscow, and Violetta's inquiries about the American way of life.

He told her he was a Native American but had never lived on a reservation. He'd spent most of his life in St. Paul, which had a climate similar to Moscow's: humid in the summer, freezing in the winter. He told her that before coming to Russia he'd heard about the long queue lines and the drunks in the street, and had mostly negative impressions about the country. For example, he'd been told that Russian people didn't think for themselves, and when asked for their opinion would repeat the official propaganda they'd been indoctrinated into believing. He also said he wanted to hear for himself what Radio Moscow had to say about Americans, and it was "a bunch of crap." Everything was anti-American. Anti-Reagan. He said that at the Marine House they would tune in and laugh because it was such a joke. Ninety percent of what was said just wasn't true.

"I know," she said, and then she answered his questions. She said she was also a member of a minority, her ancestry being Ukrainian and Jewish, and she spoke too of a lonely childhood. She denied that she had ever been a member of Komsomol, the Communist youth organization, but she did try to explain the thinking of most Russian people about America. Yes, it had been stamped into their heads that America was the Number One Enemy, but that was because if anybody was a threat to their country, it was America. It was the only other superpower. And after Ronald Reagan had become president, his rhetoric had been aggressively anti-Soviet. So there were good reasons for the Soviet people to be fearful of America.

That said, she admitted that her own experience of Americans as individuals had led her to believe that most of them were good, friendly people. She particularly admired their openness. On the news, when Americans were interviewed they spoke their minds as freely as children, and she liked that. It was something unheard of in her society.

Their discussion moved to culture: the Russian books he'd read, the American books she was familiar with. Contrary to what he'd understood was Soviet taste in literature, which was not supposed to distract from the proletarian struggle and was supposed to inculcate correct principles and glorify Soviet life, Violetta's taste was remarkably similar to his. She said her favorite American book was *Gone With the Wind*.

Ultimately they arrived at her apartment building, which was one of the so-called Khrushchev Boxes, a five-story prefab housing complex built in the late 1950s that was unattractive by all standards Americans were familiar with but provided Russian families with separate apartments. She invited him in, and he followed her up a narrow stairwell, entering a tiny, cluttered apartment but remaining close to the door. Violetta's back was to him, and she was talking to a woman in one of the rooms when he saw a little girl peer around the corner at him. She was extremely shy and wouldn't return his smile, but she was also curious, ducking her head back only to peek again. He thought it was neat. He was also relieved. The girl was probably around ten years old, making her too old to be Violetta's daughter.

After putting on a scarf, Violetta said she was going to shop for groceries and on the way she would walk him back to the metro station. This time, as they walked, she advised him of her living situation. She said her parents were divorced and she lived with her mother and younger sister.

Listening to her talk, he was struck by the similarity in their circumstances and interests. He was an Indian, she was a Jew, each relative outcasts in their respective societies, each the product of a broken family. He was a student of Russia, she was curious about the West, so they both had an interest beyond the national borders of their respective countries.

On the ride back to the embassy, Lonetree thought long and hard about what was developing. "I knew it was going to be difficult as hell and could only lead to trouble," he admitted to thinking, because it was common knowledge that the FSNs (foreign service nationals) who worked at the embassy were required to report back to some person, either in the foreign ministry or the KGB, about the habits of Americans they observed and any conversations they had. For that reason he had been wary of the questions Violetta had asked him, anticipating loaded inquiries. If she had delved into areas he thought were inappropriate to discuss, he told himself, he would have pulled back immediately and cut things off.

But she hadn't. He described their conversations as "pure innocent talk." Besides, there was nothing really to report.

Still, he was thinking that maybe it would be best for him to cool things when, the next day, Violetta approached him and said they needed to talk. Her manner was cautious and she seemed worried. When they met later, he learned that she was having some of the same concerns.

"You have to understand my position," she said.

"Tell me," he replied.

She looked away. "I can't tell you."

He implored her. "You can tell me a little bit about it. I won't say anything."

He was serious. His own security was at risk here too.

Her response was deliberately vague, but he interpreted it to mean that she didn't trust the other FSNs working at the embassy not to report on her activities with him if they found out. And she also was unsure about who he really was. Maybe he was just posing as a Marine guard and actually was CIA.

Her apprehension meant a lot to him. It meant if they continued, she would be discreet. And it meant she too cared and was willing to take risks to be with him.

They decided not to break it off but to "keep it low-key."

Over the next few weeks they carried on a clandestine relationship that consisted of meaningful glances and casual pleasantries, and the complicty involved in the game of limiting their exchanges and keeping their friendship a secret actually had a strengthening effect. That fall he was selected for temporary guard duty at the summit meeting in Geneva, and when he wasn't keeping an eye out for terrorists, he went shopping for Violetta, buying her Western fashion magazines, including *Glamour*.

Then came the Marine Corps Ball on November 9, 1985, at the ambassador's residence back in Moscow. It was the social event of the year, and among the guests cleared for invitations were most of the FSNs who worked at the embassy. Marines were not allowed to escort dates, but they did form a reception line to greet the guests, and it was their job to take the arm of each woman attending the ball and walk her onto the dance floor. Lonetree and Violetta danced once together that evening, and with exaggerated formality she shook his hand and offered "birthday congratulations," because she knew his birthday had fallen on November 6. He made an effort to be cautious, fearing they might be under observation by the other guests, and was relieved to see many of the diplomats in attendance also dancing with Russian employees.

When he and Violetta had a private moment alone, he encouraged her to attend other MSG functions where FSNs were permitted so they could spend more time together. And it was shortly after that that Violetta attended a farewell party at the Marine House at the invitation of another Marine guard. This gave them the time together they both seemed to want. They had an extensive conversation, they danced together, holding each other a beat longer than the music, and they touched hands when they thought no one was looking. He found her electrically attractive. When he was around her, he felt a current between them that instantly transferred energy, lighting him up. And after this evening he believed the attraction was mutual.

Several days later he made his first solo trip to her apartment. She introduced him to her mother and younger sister, who were watching a color television, and they retired to her bedroom, where they talked and later viewed a family photograph album. On this occasion Violetta gave him a black-and-white photograph of herself, and he gave her a picture of himself standing in Red Square. When he showed her photos of Geneva, it initiated a conversation about travel. She said her dream was to visit Paris, but she spoke about it wistfully, as though she knew it would never happen. This led to her admission that she disliked the way her government was so restrictive, limiting the freedom of movement of its citizens and preventing them from visiting other countries.

Although he had come alone and taken measures to avoid KGB surveillance—changing coats and trains—Lonetree allowed her to walk him back to the metro, where she kissed him publicly for the first time.

November was almost over when Violetta broke the news that she was going to quit her job at the embassy. She said she could no longer stand to work around a particular Soviet employee, who treated her as though she were his mistress. And she said she had been offered a job at the Irish Embassy.

Her departure changed nothing. Their relationship proceeded as before, only now it took a decidedly romantic turn.

Routinely he would log out of the embassy, indicating he was going to the West German Embassy or for a jog when in fact he was leaving to meet Violetta. Sometimes they would stroll through Gorky Park hand in hand, stealing kisses behind trees. As they walked he would try his Russian out on her, and when she laughed at his pronunciation and corrected him, he would pretend to pout and refuse to say anything more—which forced her to have to make up to him.

But they were afraid to go to many places in public together; she because of the KGB, and he because his Marine career was over if the wrong person saw him. They tried to hide in the crowds, but they were always nervous and often they ended up going back to her apartment and listening to her collection of records. She liked Michael Jackson, but he didn't. "I tried to tell her the guy was a homo. I said, Don't listen to him. But she didn't listen to me."

Once, while watching the news on TV, they saw an American aircraft carrier steaming into some world hot spot, and he commented, "Now, that's beautiful," meaning the ship. But she challenged him, accusing America of meddling in the affairs of other countries, and it resulted in their first argument.

Another disagreement they had was over whether the United

States and Russia had been allies against the Germans in World War II. She didn't believe it, which appalled him almost as much as when she vehemently denied the existence of God. He asked her what made her so sure and she said, "Just take my word for it."

"It's gonna take more than that," he told her.

More often they would hold and caress each other, and it was in the privacy of her bedroom that they first made love. It was not a physically passionate act. It was more a tender, intimate union, hurried in case her mother came home and hushed out of concern the neighbors on the other side of the thin walls would hear what was going on. As he would describe the scene, "It was good for me. Better than for her, I think. She said, 'I just want to be close to you. That's better than the sex.'"

Afterward they had another argument. As he thought about what had just happened and how it had compromised him even further, he kidded her. "You are KGB, aren't you?"

It was an old tease, his accusing her of being a KGB agent, her responding with the accusation that she was just as much KGB as he was CIA. But the timing was off, and she ordered him out of the flat. Mumbling as he put on his clothes, he called her "a stupid broad," and she was so insulted she slapped him.

All the way back to the embassy he asked himself what he was getting himself into and vowed to break it off right there. But he returned to her flat the next day, and her first remark was she had expected him sooner.

As close as Lonetree was getting to Violetta, he was also becoming increasingly absorbed into her family. Now when he visited her home, her mother, who had been initially leery of him, welcomed him warmly. "You're too thin," she would say, and insist that he join them at the dinner table. Few Marines could ever say they had eaten a meal in the home of a Russian citizen, but now *he* could. Once, her father visited while he was there and they drank vodka together. Completing the impression that he was with a second family, Violetta's little sister, Svetlana, would crawl onto his lap with a picture book and want him to tell her the English names for things. Already she knew a little English, and this impressed him because he knew there were not many ten-year-olds in America eager to learn Russian.

This was all so different from anything he had expected. Before coming, he had read about the gulags and the brutality of the Communist system and that all Russians slavishly adhered to Marxist-Leninist beliefs. At MSG school, it had been drilled into him that the Russians were the enemy and you had to always be on your guard because no one could be trusted. But once here, after getting to know the Russian people, he'd come to find that many of them did not necessarily believe what their government told them and had been skeptical of the party line about many things for a long time. The majority of those he'd met were not anti-American but in fact wanted to know more about the West. They enjoyed talking to foreigners and expressed the hidden desire to someday travel outside their borders. And whereas Americans who came to Russia were primed for discussions of the differences between socialism and capitalism, most Russians, when you had genuine encounters with them, were put off by politics and would rather hear about you and your life. Or talk about the clothes you were wearing—sometimes as a prelude to trying to buy them from you.

At the same time that he was beginning to decide that the Soviet menace had been exaggerated and the Russians were decent people who were simply misinformed, he and Violetta began to discuss their feelings for each other. It was good between them; there was no one else he could talk to about what he was thinking and feeling; and their sweet collusion led inevitably to a conversation about what it would be like to share life together.

By this time he had extended his stay in Moscow for an additional three months but was scheduled to be transferred to Vienna in March. She said his upcoming departure distressed her. She told him she didn't want him to go. She said she loved him and wanted to marry him. She wanted him to stay in Moscow or she wanted to go to the United States, she didn't know, she didn't care, she just wanted to be with him. She expressed the desire to see New York and visit his hometown of St. Paul.

It seemed she truly spoke from her heart, and so he did not listen to his head but followed his heart and told her that was what he wanted too. He promised to immediately make inquiries at the embassy regarding U.S.–Soviet marriages and the prospects of acquiring a visa for her.

It was several days after they discussed the issue of a visa that Violetta told him she had an uncle in whom she had confided about their relationship and who wanted to meet him.

That surprised Lonetree. They had gone to great lengths to avoid anyone's seeing them together. To bring another person into the equation seemed dangerous.

"I don't know," he said. "Are you sure he's not a KGB agent?"

She laughed and he asked her what was so funny.

"He asked me if you were a CIA agent. No, he's my mother's brother, my uncle, and he's a lawyer. He's not a KGB agent."

Lonetree still wasn't sure if he should. As he described his thinking, "Then I figured, Hell, I'm already in enough trouble as it is. If they have photographs of me with her they could send them to the embassy and they'd say, What were you doing with this girl? And they'd send me back to the States."

It was in late December 1985 that he met her at the Moscow University metro, where they boarded a bus that took a long, circuitous route before reaching their stop. They entered an apartment building through what seemed like a hidden front door and took the elevator to one of the upper floors.

By the way Uncle Sasha greeted Violetta, Lonetree was convinced she was his niece. He kissed her on the cheek, she asked him how he was doing, he said fine, he complained about someone at work, and then he turned his attention to the Marine in their midst. His English wasn't very good, so Violetta translated, and he explained that he felt like a father to Violetta and her younger sister.

"Would you like something to drink?" Uncle Sasha asked. And before Lonetree could answer, Sasha said, "I have wine. Do you like wine?"

"Yes," he replied, watching to make sure nothing was dropped in his drink, as Uncle Sasha poured them each a glass.

The conversation that followed dwelt on Lonetree's Indian heritage. Uncle Sasha talked about the Russian fascination with American Indians, with whom there was an ancestral link because they were descended from the indigenous people of Siberia, and about how Soviet officialdom spoke out in behalf of the rights of American Indians at international human-rights conferences. He condemned the historical treatment of Indians by the American government and asked whether or not Lonetree felt he had been discriminated against because of his race. Lonetree said he had, but that was life, and Uncle Sasha indicated not in the Soviet Union it wasn't. Here everyone was treated the same.

At the conclusion of the meeting, as Uncle Sasha shook Lonetree's hand, he said, "You're different from what I expected. Prior to meeting you, I was planning on forbidding Violetta from seeing you again." His final words were that he hoped that Lonetree would come and visit him again.

A few weeks later he and Violetta returned to Uncle Sasha's apartment, and over another glass of wine Uncle Sasha, whose English had improved markedly, directed the conversation toward politics. He asked Lonetree his opinion about a variety of international issues, and the two talked about what was wrong with the world and how each would improve it if he had the power. No one in the embassy had ever expressed an interest in Lonetree's thoughts on foreign affairs, but now that his viewpoints were solicited he gave them freely. And Uncle Sasha listened attentively before expressing his own. He was pointedly critical of President Reagan, who had maligned Russia as an "Evil Empire," but saved his most scathing comments for CIA Director William Casey. He considered Casey the ultimate capitalist—dedicated to the destruction of the great socialist state—and opponent of world peace and cited numerous examples of the CIA's acting in ways that were intended to undermine the Soviet Union's internal security and destabilize the international scene.

As for the CIA's activities right there in Moscow, he talked about clandestine operations intended to recruit spies, collect information, and encourage Soviet dissident organizations, and about how the CIA tried to take advantage of the difficulties and hardships the Soviet people were undergoing. The intelligence agencies of the U.S.S.R. were merely standing guard over the security of the Soviet state, Uncle Sasha explained. The sole reason for their existence was to counter the aggressions of the CIA.

As Lonetree listened, he had to concede that it did look as though the CIA's agenda was geared more toward perpetuating American interests than toward fostering harmony in international affairs. And he thought maybe Uncle Sasha had a point when he argued that in the pursuit of its objectives, the CIA was subverting the desire of all the people of the world who were striving for a happier and better life.

They continued to drink, and to talk, until Uncle Sasha swerved the conversation in a disturbing direction by saying, "You can help, you know."

"How?" Lonetree asked.

"Do you know anyone in the CIA in the embassy?"

Trying to remember this pivotal moment from the distance of a year later and the thousands of miles between Moscow and the Quantico brig, Lonetree would be unable to organize his motivations for continuing with this whole business into a single conscious thought. He would recall that he had read with fascination many books about spies and the KGB, so he felt he was particularly well equipped for encountering intrigue in the real world. In other words there was a bit of game playing on his part going on. The adventure and the risk involved added a thrilling dimension to what had otherwise been boring duty.

At the same time, after engaging in political dialogue and hearing how the Soviets perceived America and the CIA, he half believed that what Sasha had said was right. The effect of this was not only to confuse his sense of patriotism, but to encourage him to want to make things right. He felt as if he understood something now that he had only seen part of before, and it drew him toward the idea of doing his part to improve understanding and reduce tensions by engaging in a freelance form of personal diplomacy.

And then there was Violetta. Of course it had crossed his mind that their relationship had been engineered by the KGB, but he just could not bring himself to believe it, in part because he had initiated it, and in part because he felt their bond was genuine.

"Why do you want to know those things?" Lonetree said he fretfully asked Uncle Sasha. "It's not for you to know, and I'll be honest with you, I don't have the answers you want."

Lonetree said he turned to Violetta, who was sitting at the far end of the couch looking away from both men, and made a silent appeal to her for help. Up until this point she had said very little, acting as if she wanted no part of this, but now she came to his defense. "Maybe he doesn't know anything," she suggested.

Everyone was quiet for a while, until Uncle Sasha asked Violetta to come into the kitchen with him and help him prepare some food. Lonetree could hear them talking in the other room in lowered voices, and while they were gone, even though he was alone, he began to feel that he was being watched. He looked at the walls, studying them for anything unusual. He gave the curtains a once-over, not wanting to give himself and his suspicions away if he was being observed through a hidden camera. Nothing confirmed his intuition, which he still couldn't shake.

When Uncle Sasha returned to the room, he appeared to have adopted a change in tactics. He apologized for making Lonetree angry. He said he was merely asking these questions on behalf of a friend who was a general in the KGB, who worked at the Central Committee, and who was in a position to get Violetta a visa if anyone was. And Uncle Sasha said that was his intention: to help Lonetree and Violetta with their "trouble."

Lonetree relaxed then, and as soon as he did, Uncle Sasha started in again about the defensive nature of the Soviet intelligence agencies, how some CIA agents had recognized the sinister objectives of their agency and were working with the KGB, and how there were other Marine security guards who had dealt with the KGB.

"You would be surprised who else is doing illegal things at the embassy," he said mysteriously. "No one is an angel."

Lonetree said he tried fighting it. Once more he was unhappily aware that he ought to stop right here, get up, and walk out. But even as he debated with himself, under Uncle Sasha's persistent questioning he began to uneasily deliver answers. And the way his mind worked, he now rationalized that all the while he cooperated he would stay alert for an escape hatch. As he delivered information he would also try to collect information, believing that at some point he would find a way to turn his dilemma around and use it to his advantage.

Although he allowed Lonetree to continue telling his story, what Mike Stuhff had already heard suggested a way out. Given its political charge, this was still going to be a tough case, and the odds were against them. But after listening to his client, he felt he'd recognized a plausible defense strategy that did not involve plea bargaining, nor did it rely on the speedy-trial provision.

The pressing issue now was that before Stuhff could begin to develop his defense he needed his client's absolute confidence, and it was apparent to him that Lonetree was still very GI. Why else had he turned himelf in? Why else had he voluntarily given such a long confession to the NIS? Why else had he turned down William Kunstler's services?

Leaning forward for emphasis, Mike Stuhff said, "Clayton, I want you to listen very carefully. They're after your ass." That was how he put it and it was exactly what he thought. "As we speak, Marines are volunteering for the firing squad. If I'm going to get you out of this, you're going to have to trust me and do what I say."

Late the evening before the Article 32 hearing was scheduled to begin, Major Henderson received a phone call from Mike Stuhff, who said, "We need to ask for a delay in the proceedings."

"For how long?" the major asked.

"Just until one o'clock."

It was scheduled to begin at nine.

"Why? What's the problem?"

"Our fellow defense counsel won't arrive until noon."

Until now nothing had been said to Henderson about a second civilian counsel, so he didn't have a clue as to who it might be until Stuhff informed him.

"It's Bill Kunstler."

Since following up their phone call with a letter officially declining his services, Henderson had not given William Kunstler another thought. Hearing that Kunstler was coming back on the case surprised him, but it didn't particularly bother him, because at this stage of the proceedings he felt that there was little to be done that had not already been done and that any rational lawyer who looked closely at the case would agree with his judgment.

Shrugging, Henderson said, "Okay. Bring him on in."

Ten minutes before they were due in court, Michael Stuhff and William Kunstler strode into Major Henderson's office at Quantico. Looking leonine and rumpled, his trademark glasses perched on his thinning gray mane, Kunstler was personable and cordial, but there was barely time to exchange greetings before they had to leave for the hearing.

On the way over, Henderson reminded them both that since most of the material that was going to be presented at the hearing was classified, without proper clearances it was doubtful they would be allowed to participate in the proceedings. Kunstler left Henderson guessing as to how he intended to handle this detail until they arrived at the concrete room in the basement of Hockmuth Hall where the hearing was to be held; and there, before Maj. Robert Nourie, the investigating officer, Kunstler made a motion to the effect that it was improper for the Article 32 to proceed at this point because civilian defense counsel had been denied access to the full range of evidence against their client. When he was told that military defense counsel had seen everything that the prosecution possessed, and that civilian counsel could see the evidence as well once they had received their required security clearances, Kunstler insisted that an attorney's right to represent his client overrode the military requirement of clearances.

An argument ensued that took up most of the afternoon and did little to dim Kunstler's reputation as a disputatious litigator more than willing to be aggressive before judges. The matter was settled when Major Nourie called a recess until the next day, at which time the hearing would go forward without the presence of civilian counsel.

Eventually a compromise would be worked out that would grant Stuhff and Kunstler a Limited Access Authority (LAA) clearance, which allowed them to see classified material pertinent to the case under gag-order conditions. But that would take several weeks, and in the meantime Kunstler and Stuhff were barred from the courtroom.

For his part, Henderson thought he saw what Stuhff and Kunstler were trying to do. To create an error in the proceedings that could form the basis of an appeal was one way of protecting a case. But he didn't think this one was going anywhere. No appeals court was going to bounce an espionage case simply because civilian counsel did not have their clearances at the start of an Article 32. So to hear Kunstler make opinionated motions that discounted the military's right to protect confidential information, and pile on scorn—referring to the military's anti-civilian bias and the unconstitutionality of denying the defense the right to know what it was defending against—Henderson thought, was a waste of everybody's time. More significant, it drew the focus away from the real issue, which was to pay attention to what the prosecution put on the table and point out the weaknesses of the government's case through cross-examination, giving the defense more leverage come time to plead.

But Lonetree had designated Mike Stuhff as lead counsel, and when he instructed Major Henderson not to take an active part in the hearings until they were present, Henderson was put in the awkward position of registering a daily objection to the proceedings on the grounds that civilian counsel were not allowed to be present, then sitting passively by and having to listen to the incriminating testimony of NIS agents who had interviewed Lonetree as it was paraded before the investigating officer by the prosecution.

If what was happening at the Article 32 alerted Major Henderson to civilian counsel's cynical attitude toward the military justice system, over the next few weeks, as he spent numerous hours with Mike Stuhff and Bill Kunstler discussing defense strategies, he realized that their distrust extended to include military defense lawyers. Fixed in their heads was the notion that military attorneys were not real lawyers because they were more concerned about advancing their careers than being forceful advocates for their clients. What they didn't understand was that in a military setting military lawyers were often a whole lot more effective than civilian counsels. What they were assuming was that Major Henderson would roll over on his client. What they failed to take into account, because they did not take the time to learn, was that Major Henderson's once-promising career in the Marine Corps had stalled precisely because of a history of bucking command influence. That was why he was in the defense command, which was attached to the staff judge advocate's office at

Quantico for administration purposes but reported directly to Marine headquarters in Washington, D.C. Major Henderson was a "passed-over Marine" who wasn't going anywhere in the Corps and knew it, and the only thing that gave him satisfaction was doing his job well.

Feeling on the outs with the rest of the defense team, Major Henderson nevertheless held his peace—until the day William Kunstler called his first press conference. This was a week or so after Kunstler and Stuhff had received their LAA clearances and had been allowed to return to the Article 32, and it was held on the lawn in front of Hockmuth Hall. Up until this time the 32 sessions had been closed to the public—none of Lonetree's relatives had been allowed to attend, nor members of the press. But there had been a strong representation of government spectators from the NIS, State Department, and agencies that did not wish to be identified but had the right badges to get in—so a horde of journalists and cameramen anxious for a progress report showed up, shouting questions and jabbing microphones. This being a first for Henderson, he was blinking at the cameras and paying more attention to the crowd than to civilian counsel when Kunstler's words filtered through.

"Despite the fact that I have participated in many controversial, and sometimes unfair, criminal trials around the country during most of my professional life, I am profoundly appalled and shocked by what is happening to my client, Sgt. Clayton Lonetree. As his civilian defense counsel I feel utterly compelled to publicize the savagery that is being practiced upon him in a Mephistophelean effort to insure that he is convicted. While I cannot hope to be his Zola [a reference to the French writer whose public defense of Alfred Dreyfus played a major role in reversing the injustice of his arrest], I can at least chronicle some of the evidence to support my thesis that his railroad is running on an express track."

Kunstler went on to link Lonetree's prosecution to this country's disgraceful legacy of racial discrimination against Native Americans, and to proclaim his client's ultimate innocence, which he, as an American engaged for most of his adult life in the defense of minority persons wrongfully accused of crimes, intended to prove.

Henderson couldn't believe what he was hearing. How did Kunstler expect to prove his client's innocence? What exonerating evidence did he have? If he really understood the case and the law, how could he say with a straight face that Lonetree was being prosecuted because he was an Indian? This was a Marine who had admitted to committing serious violations. The Marine Corps wasn't picking on him because he was an Indian. Let any Marine spy against his country and he was going to be prosecuted.

This was a turning point for Major Henderson. After that press conference he was unable to keep his tactical disagreements with civilian counsel to himself, and he went to the brig to talk the situation over with his client. But when he tried to explain his thinking, it was apparent that civilian counsel had successfully undermined Lonetree's confidence in anyone wearing a uniform. Civilian counsel had gone in and said, "You can't trust Henderson because he's a Marine. You've got to listen to us." And not knowing better, Lonetree had believed them.

Henderson felt like withdrawing from the case. He wanted to say, "Look, Clayton. These guys have taken over, go ahead and go with them. I'd like to be relieved of my duty." And he knew Lonetree would not have put up an argument.

But he had seen cases where that happened and clients were promptly sacrificed. And by this time he felt a loyalty to his client to the extent that he had to protect and help him in any way he could.

So he told Lonetree that he disagreed with what civilian counsel was doing. He said, "I don't believe their tactics are in your best interest. But it's up to you. It's your decision."

Lonetree's response was, "I'm sorry, Major Henderson, but I'm not interested in plea bargaining, because Mr. Kunstler has assured me I'm not going to be convicted."

• • •

When Michael Stuhff had shown up at the door of Kunstler's New York City office, 13 Gay Street in Greenwich Village, and said, "Clayton Lonetree has authorized me to invite you back on the case," William Kunstler had agreed to return for the same reasons he'd been interested in getting involved in the first place. In his eyes the entire American legal system was an enemy and a corrupt tool of the "haves." He believed that there was bias built into the American system of jurisprudence and that a different set of rules flourished for the rich and powerful in a criminal situation, while people without money or influence went underrepresented and overpunished. His résumé and the cases he'd handled—he referred to them as "professional achievements"— left little doubt the man was on a crusade. From his defense of Martin Luther King, Jr., Adam Clayton Powell, Jr., and Stokely Carmichael to his defense of Daniel Berrigan, he had waged a battle against the establishment, the system, those in power.

And standing shoulder to shoulder with these well-known defendants were some of the biggest and baddest names in Indian America: Dennis Banks and Russell Means, leaders of the American Indian Movement (AIM), arrested at Wounded Knee, South Dakota, in 1974 for conspiracy to take over the town; and Leonard Peltier, convicted of gunning down two FBI agents during that uprising. The case of Sgt. Clayton Lonetree, in William Kunstler's estimation, was just the latest in a long line of government persecutions of Native Americans. He had yet to inspect the evidence or review the legal issues, but as someone keenly aware of the politics involved in this kind of high-profile case, and a self-appointed authority on racism in the military, he trusted the instincts that told him what was going on here was the unwholesome habit of blaming an individual for the failure of a larger organization. He suspected that Sergeant Lonetree was being overcharged so the Reagan administration could show it was hard on spies, that the NIS was going to outrageous lengths to try to convict this man because his arrest had been an embarrassment to the Marine Corps; and he had no doubt that if Major Henderson had his way, the march to justice for

Sgt. Clayton Lonetree would be played out to a military drum-beat.

The one sticking point, of course, was that Lonetree had confessed. And that was something that Kunstler was unable to comprehend: why his client had walked up to the CIA at a Christmas party in Vienna and said, Listen, I've been sleeping with a Russian girl and, oh, by the way, I gave stuff to the KGB. Who did that? Nobody in his right mind. If Lonetree had kept his mouth shut, there would never have been anything to this.

Mike Stuhff also had his problems fathoming why Lonetree had voluntarily stepped forward. But Stuhff had been going to the brig and interviewing his client almost daily, and if he'd learned one thing from these visits, it was that Clayton Lonetree was not a simply understood person. His character was as complex as it was concealed. He experienced life in a very different way from most people.

Take what he'd said during an early conversation: "Mr. Stuhff, do you think you can get me out of this without my getting a dishonorable discharge?"

Stuhff had frowned. "Why do you ask?"

Lonetree was slow in answering. He liked to take his time before he responded to a question. Watching, waiting, Stuhff could only imagine where Lonetree's thoughts would stop before they came out as a statement. "I was hoping things would work out so I could still go to work for the foreign service. You know, I always wanted to serve in a diplomatic capacity. . . ."

Confronted with evidence that his client lacked normal reality checks, Stuhff wondered if, in addition to his unusual personality traits, there might very well be a psychological imbalance present that would be worth his knowing about. After all, Lonetree had made a number of damaging statements that were untrue and physically impossible. When told to lie, he had obeyed the command as if it were an order. Could it be that he was more susceptible to suggestion than the average Marine? Or prone to making false admissions?

The end of this line of thinking took the form of a request for a psychological evaluation, and the individual Stuhff went to was a psychologist named Tom Williams. Once before, Dr. Williams had examined a client of Mike Stuhff's and testified for him in court. The case involved an Arizona State Police officer who went berserk one night, barricaded himself in his house with his daughter as hostage, and threatened a shootout. After an interview and psychological tests, Tom Williams, who specialized in post-traumatic stress disorder, had concluded that the police department's precipitate actions had turned a domestic dispute into a reenactment of the officer's combat experience in Vietnam. The verdict had been favorable to the defense in that case, and Stuhff was hoping that, after examining Clayton Lonetree, Williams would be able to come up with something just as useful.

A bearded, even-tempered man who had gotten heavy since he left the Marine Corps after two tours in Vietnam as an officer and a teaching stint at Annapolis, Tom Williams was based in Colorado at the time he was contacted about the Lonetree case. Williams instantly knew why Stuhff was coming to him: As an ex-leatherneck he understood Marines and how the Marine Corps worked. Just as a mechanic could look at the receipts for work on your car and know everything that had gone wrong, he could glance at a military service record and derive a tremendous amount of information that someone else would miss.

Credibility was also added by the fact that Williams's father at one time had been a deputy director of the CIA.

What Williams did not know when he agreed to fly to Quantico and evaluate Clayton Lonetree was that William Kunstler was an attorney on the case. He didn't find that out until he attended a defense-organized fund raiser in a hotel in downtown Denver. Mike Stuhff showed up, and so did Samuel Lonetree, Clayton's grandfather, wearing a full headdress. Even AIM leader Russell Means was there. William Kunstler couldn't make it, but a tape-recorded statement from him was played before the crowd, and even though the distortion from the cassette player, coupled with a bad sound system, made Kunstler's raspy growl sound as though it issued from a throat not fully cleared of noises within, his inflammatory rhetoric came through loud and clear: "This is a dirty, dirty case, and the penalty is so severe that the Marine Corps ought to be ashamed of itself for the action it has taken."

As Williams sat among Indian activists and white liberals listening to Kunstler accuse the Marines of singling out Lonetree because of his Indian heritage, he became increasingly irritated. He considered himself pro-Indian. His father was one-quarter Cherokee. He'd been in the Marines for eleven years, so he'd seen the way Native Americans were treated. And he didn't believe for a minute that persecution of an Indian was what was going on here. Ever since the Navajo Code Talkers had distinguished themselves in World War II, Native Americans had enjoyed a decided prestige in the Corps. The expectation was that, coming from warrior cultures, they would even be special fighters: silent, efficient, dedicated.

Had he known Kunstler was part of the defense team, Williams would have thought his involvement over more carefully. Knowing what he did of the maverick attorney, and of the case, he did not think going for headlines was the smartest way to deal with an institution like the Marine Corps. It would only cause them to close ranks. But he had committed himself, and the truth was he was intrigued by the case. So he flew from Denver on to Washington, D.C., and drove down to Quantico for his date to evaluate Clayton Lonetree.

The Marine personnel at the brig were surprisingly cordial to Williams, but when one of the guards escorted him to the gun locker and asked him to leave his weapon there, Williams suspected that was because they did not know who he was and were mixing him up with a military investigator. In a comfortable office, with a guard posted outside who peered through the glass from time to time, Tom Williams met his subject and was immediately struck by Lonetree's demeanor. One of the possibilities he had considered beforehand was that Lonetree would be angry at the Marines. When he'd been a Marine officer, Williams had done a lot of legal work, and most of the Marines he'd dealt with who had gotten into trouble were pissed off at the system. He was expecting Lonetree to be like some of those Marines, but he wasn't. Stuhff had said he was basically a nice kid, polite, eager to help, and he was.

Williams began by introducing himself and explaining why he was there. He said he'd been a Marine officer so he knew how things went, and after they rubbed globes and anchors together and a rapport had been established, he shifted smoothly into an interview mode that directed without leading Lonetree through a detailed, thorough personal narrative, from birth to the brig.

Clayton Lonetree told his life story in a flat, quiet, matter-of-fact voice. He said he was born on November 6, 1961, in Chicago, and that a brother, Craig Lonetree, was born two years later, and a half sister, Valerie, several years after that. He said his parents were from two different tribes and they had never married but he had been given his father's name. He said his strongest memories from childhood were his parents' arguments. "Sometimes it got pretty vicious," he whispered softly.

When asked, Lonetree answered he was never really comfortable when he was young. Maybe it was because he was never in one place long enough to make friends. Or because he and his brother were continually passed back and forth between their parents. "My mom and dad didn't get along," he said in a way that underscored that it was an understatement. Whichever parent the children were with would try to turn them against the other parent. Clayton said he used to cry at school thinking about the terrible things his father said about his mother. During this time, he said, he lived in terror of his father because of his drinking. "It got so bad, just the smell of alcohol used to scare me."

The intense loneliness of his childhood was poignantly rendered when Lonetree admitted that to get away he would ride his bike, climb trees, and draw pictures.

As he took all this down on a yellow lined legal pad, Tom Williams found himself thinking how sociological it sounded. Clayton's mother would not have been the first young Indian woman to leave the reservation for the city and have a love affair with an urban Indian from another tribe, which led straight to an unplanned pregnancy, economic difficulties, and alcohol abuse, a separation and custody battles, with the kids caught in the middle and pulled in opposite directions. Often it ended in tragedy. In this case, according to Clayton, it ended in a kidnapping. Parenthood apparently not only highlighted the wrongness of the relationship, it turned the mother vindictive, along the lines of the woman who avenges herself upon a faithless husband by stealing his sons.

"In 1969 my mother stole us. We were living with my father and she came and got us and said she was taking us on a vacation to Canada. But it was a lie. She took us to an orphanage in Farmington, New Mexico."

Farmington was a border town near the Navajo Reservation. The orphanage, Navajo Gospel Missions, was run by evangelical Baptists who believed that time spent in Christian homes would go a long way toward healing the emotional scars that grew out of broken families. It catered exclusively to illegitimate and abandoned Navajo children, who were boarded in cottages and raised by Christian houseparents drawn to this kind of service. According to Lonetree, his mother stayed with them for several months, working at the orphanage as a cook until she lost her job, and when that happened she left, virtually abandoning them.

Clayton said he was eight years old and a shy and easily frightened boy at the time; and when he realized his mom was gone, he was devastated. For months he stumbled around in a depression, sulking, refusing to talk to anybody. Making things even more difficult for him, once his mother was no longer around, the older kids at the orphanage began to pick on his brother because Craig had a cleft palate. Even though he'd had an operation and spent hours in speech therapy, when he spoke his voice sounded as if it were coming out his nose.

At night the Lonetree boys would cry together, wondering what they had done that no one wanted them. When his grief became almost unbearable, Clayton said, he came up with a plan to get even. In an act of self-defense performed as consciously and deliberately as ripping their pictures out of a magazine and tearing them into small pieces, he disowned his parents in his mind.

For most of the interview so far, Lonetree had spoken in laconic, toneless phrases that were clearly intended to deny or disguise his emotions. But at certain times his voice quavered and his eyes would glisten, conveying enormous pain. This was one of those times.

Clayton and his brother remained at the orphanage for five years, and if nothing else they were five years of relative stability. He attended public school, where he was an average student. He received extensive religious training, and if he wasn't one of the "success stories" who would stand in front of an audience and deliver a life-transforming testimony about how God and Navajo Gospel Missions had rescued him and given direction to his life, he did come out of it believing in Christian principles. The exciting tales of missionary experiences in foreign lands had also created an intense desire in him to travel someday and see the world.

Other than that, Clayton portrayed himself as an ordinary boy who played Little League baseball in the summer, watched football on TV in the fall, and loved things military. He could play with toy soldiers all day. While still in elementary school he was talking about joining the service when he grew up.

When Clayton was thirteen, his life took another sharp turn with the return of his mother. So glad was he to have her back, he quickly forgot the business about disowning her. But his willingness to forgive was short-lived, for Sally had not come back to reunite their family; she was returning to the Southwest with a husband and two new children.

It was about this same time that his father, Spencer Lonetree, resurfaced. He said he had been searching for them for years and only recently learned where they were. And he invited Clayton and Craig to St. Paul for the Christmas holidays, sweetening the deal by promising to take them to a Minnesota Vikings football game. When they begged Sally to let them go, she was reluctant at first, but in a conciliatory gesture she gave in.

As it would turn out, the vacation package was just a ruse on Spencer's part. He had no intention of letting them return. He knew that once he'd retrieved his boys, Sally would not have the wherewithal to come and get them.

Spencer was married at the time to a white woman Clayton

said he actually took a liking to and who he thought liked him, until she issued his father an ultimatum: "The kids go or I do." After she left, Spencer and his sons moved into a third-floor apartment in a building that overlooked a junkyard and rail lines on the East Side of St. Paul, a working-class community of whites, blacks, Hispanics, and "reservation migrants" of Lakota, Ojibway, and Winnebago descent. There, under a rekindled sense of parental responsibility, Spencer set about undoing the harm he believed had been inflicted on his sons by their mother and Navajo Gospel Missions.

Likening himself to the fictional and movie character *The Great Santini,* Spencer was a strict disciplinarian who converted his home into a virtual boot camp. Church was for sissies, he said, and he forbade them to read the Bible. Physical discipline and conditioning should be a part of the daily routine, and each morning, in the predawn darkness, without regard to the frigid Minnesota winters, he would lead them on a jog around Lake Phalen. He expected them to pitch in around the house with the cooking and cleaning, and he insisted on perfect attendance at school and good grades. All this was part of the necessary preparation for a triumphant entrance into American society, according to Spencer, because they were Indians.

Clayton said that if he heard it once he heard his father say it a hundred times: "Whatever I have accomplished in life has taken blood, sweat, and tears. Education and work are the two most important things in life. If you are going to make anything of yourselves, you cannot use being Indian as an excuse. Indians have to work twice as hard as other people in this world to make it, because they only get half a chance."

For all his bluster about the importance of instilling a strong work ethic at an early age, Spencer Lonetree's personal behavior undermined his stated objectives. He was a father who was exceedingly demanding and insisted his sons make him proud; and when they did not meet his unreasonable standards, he put them down in a way that diminished their self-esteem rather than inspiring them to do better.

He was also a man who went back on his word. Spencer had

assured Clayton his drinking days were past, but they weren't. In fact, they were worse. "He would come home drunk and would yell and scream and go nuts over typical teenage stuff." He never beat them, Clayton said, but he often threatened to.

According to Clayton, as concerned as his father was about his education, he seemed even more worried that as Clayton approached sixteen he "did not drink beer and chase women." Spencer even expressed his fear that maybe Clayton was homosexual. As if to scare the very notion out of him, Spencer took to calling him "faggot."

Although Clayton Lonetree claimed he had always been an avid sports enthusiast, Williams suspected his father's needling may have had something to do with why Clayton went out for the high-school football team. As he gazed at the young Marine sitting across from him, Williams recalled the comments of Lonetree's high school football coach in one of the newspaper clippings he'd been sent prior to this meeting: "Clayton wasn't big enough to be a lineman, and he wasn't fast enough to be in the backfield, so he played quarterback. But he couldn't throw either, so he never got in any games. For the most part he was a stand-in as the opposing team's quarterback during scrimmages. I'll give him credit, though. He was the kind of athlete who made it to every practice, never complained, hung in there. But he was a 'backup player.' In fact, that not only is an accurate description, I'd say it defined who he was."

But while that may have been the picture of Clayton Lonetree his high school football coach was carrying around, inside Clayton a very different self-image was apparently taking shape. After a long silence in which he seemed to be debating how personal he should get, Lonetree revealed to Williams that beneath his stoical and apparently passive exterior, he had begun to nurse passions of hatred and fanaticism.

It all started at the Navajo Gospel Missions with a TV movie about Germany and the Third Reich, he said. While everyone around him thought of Adolf Hitler as a sinister figure whose name was identified with evil, when he listened to what Hitler said, it got him excited. On scratch paper he started drawing iron crosses. In his spare time he fashioned a makeshift Nazi-style uniform that included a cross-chest belt, a side bag, and an armband with a swastika on it.

So immersed did he become in World War II fantasies that they began to invade his nighttime dreams. One nightmare in particular he would never forget: He was traipsing across a muddy, cratered, body-strewn battlefield while bombers roared overhead, machine-gun bullets whistled through the air, shells exploded left and right . . . and he walked through it all as though he were invulnerable.

Sometimes these dreams seemed so real he thought they might be memories.

Lonetree didn't say exactly when or how he obtained a copy of *Mein Kampf,* but he did say that after reading Hitler's autobiography, he had been amazed by the parallels between his life and the Führer's. Hitler too had been raised in humiliating circumstances under the thumb of a drunkard father who was unsympathetic, hard to please, and short-tempered; who insisted on respect and discipline; who was dissatisfied with his son's school reports and made his disappointment clear. As a boy Hitler too had been awkward and reserved in social situations; had few friends, lived a solitary life, and spent much of his time brooding and dreaming. Just like Lonetree, Hitler had exhibited an artistic flair that was manifested in sketchbook drawings, and had developed an interest in warfare at an early age.

Clayton said that was when it first occurred to him he might even be Hitler reincarnated.

This fascination with Nazism started coming back in high school. He devoured German-history books, focusing primarily on accounts of battle campaigns and the biographies of war heroes. He found a store in the Twin Cities that catered to World War II buffs, started a collection of Nazi military memorabilia, began wearing combat boots to school, and even contacted the American Nazi Party about attending their meetings.

As he heard Lonetree's confession of "fascist-type thinking," Williams pronounced no judgments in his mind because he thought he understood what was going on with the young man.

This obsession with the Third Reich sounded like the syndrome of a minority member trying to fill a deep personal void by identifying with a dictatorial group that preached superiority. More probable than a genuine admiration for Nazi beliefs was that this was part of an unconscious strategy for achieving a strengthened sense of self-esteem. When Lonetree described how Hitler had overcome a boyhood of hardship and misery, he was no doubt seeing in the Führer's success a formula for prevailing over his own circumstances.

Over the course of his junior and senior years, Lonetree said, his readings brought him into the larger arena of foreign affairs and contemporary world events. Naturally, his political views were conservative, almost hawkish. "I started thinking about the Communist threat. I was angry about our retreat from Vietnam. I was ready to bomb Iran if they didn't return American hostages. I was also in favor of increased defense spending and the need for a first-strike capability with nuclear weapons."

A bit sheepishly he admitted as well to fantasizing about being president of the United States.

This last acknowledgment was a significant one for Tom Williams, and not only because it showed the magnitude and direction of Lonetree's active fantasies. It also revealed that Lonetree possessed a defiant streak and an exalted sense of his potential that was very different from the way other high school students of the day were thinking. In the late seventies the youth were into smoking dope, partying, and blaming the whole elusive system of authority, from the President to the principal to teachers and parents, for the country's social ills. If there had been a draft, the majority of them would have been dodgers and shirkers. But in this milieu Clayton Lonetree was an exception. He took his rebellion to the right instead of the left. He said he didn't drink, didn't smoke, didn't swear, didn't do drugs, and he spoke about himself with almost an elitist attitude, as someone who believed in destiny and felt he was meant for something special.

Halfway through his senior year, without parental knowledge or permission, Lonetree said, he skipped school, spent the day in the recruiter's office, and joined the Marines on the delayed-entry program that allowed him to graduate first. The reasons he gave were varied. To get away from an overbearing father who wanted him to go to college and become a lawyer. For the action, the adventure, and to see the world—the usual reasons. To uphold the Lonetree family's distinguished tradition of military service.

Lonetrees and their relatives had fought valiantly in every conflict from the Civil War to the Vietnam War. A great-uncle, Mitchell Red Cloud, had even been posthumously awarded the Congressional Medal of Honor for his exploits in the Korean War. Clayton said he had grown up listening to the story of Mitchell Red Cloud's stand on Pork Chop Hill: Mortally wounded, his arm wrapped around a tree, he had mowed down Chinese Communist troops with automatic-rifle fire, almost single-handedly keeping the enemy from overrunning his company's position.

The way Tom Williams saw the decision, joining the Marine Corps offered Lonetree a sense of roots and gave him an affiliation: As a Marine he would be part of a family, a tribe. Being a Marine would also help him define his self-image as well as project it to others. The Marine Corps would take care of him, fulfill his need for a macho image, provide him with security, and bestow honor upon him.

In civilian jails an interview like this would have been interrupted by now. A guard would have shown up and said it was chow time, count time, lockdown time. But at the Quantico brig there was no interruption, and Williams encouraged Lonetree to keep talking.

Clayton said he reported for active duty on July 29, 1980, at the Marine Corps Recruitment Depot in San Diego. He said he was not singled out for special treatment, favorable or otherwise, and liked the fact that the Corps seemed to make no racial distinctions. Although the spectrum of racial colors represented at boot camp included white, black, red, and yellow, once in uniform everyone was green. The Marine Corps color.

After completing his basic training, Lonetree said, his first duty assignment was Guantánamo Bay, Cuba. He admitted he was excited at being sent to one of the few places where the American flag flew on Communist soil. Where better to learn what war was about?

At first, he said, he enjoyed himself at Guantánamo Bay. His primary duty was walking point, and it was a rush knowing that this was no longer playacting in a field exercise with false bullets—it was the real thing. Even though there was never an exchange of fire, he would pause during his rounds along the perimeter fence to stare across the minefields separating him from the bunkers and guard towers manned by Communist Cuban soldiers, imagining the kind of assault that the detachment anticipated in its defense exercises.

But after eighteen months of hearing about and thinking about the enemy, watching the enemy from a distance but never once engaging the enemy, a strange thing happened. His idea of the enemy became so abstracted that his readiness to fight them was transformed into a curiosity about them. Who were those guys? he began to wonder. How did they really feel about their system of government? Sometimes he would even gaze across the minefields and see a Cuban guard looking back, and it occurred to him that *he* might be thinking the same thing.

Several other developments took place during this time that started him thinking differently about his life. He began taking correspondence courses through Old Dominion University, expanding his interest in world affairs. And since about ninety percent of the barracks were smoking pot and dropping acid, he decided to give it a try.

It was during this period that he put in for Marine security guard duty. It was a way of doing what he'd always wanted: to travel. He also saw it as an opportunity for career enhancement. Being a Marine was good, but being a Marine security guard was even better.

The only problem was that in order to qualify for the program a Marine had to score a minimum of 92 on the GCT exam, and Lonetree's 77 wasn't good enough.

Lonetree skimmed the next few years, but having seen his service record, Williams knew enough about what had happened to fill in the blanks himself. Lonetree had been transferred back to Camp Pendleton in San Diego, where he had been promoted to corporal; he had served time uneventfully; he had continued to read his fortunes in the MSG program; and eventually, through a series of events that Tom Williams would judge harshly, admission had been granted.

As Lonetree told it, his father had appealed to a U.S. senator from Minnesota, Rudy Boschwitz, requesting that he be allowed to retake the GCT exam on the grounds that the military testing system was culturally biased. The senator, in turn, had used his influence, and the Marines gave Lonetree another test, which he passed this time, but just barely. And even at that his acceptance was conditional: Since his four-year hitch was just about up, he would be admitted to MSG school only if he reenlisted.

Of course Tom Williams registered none of his thoughts when he realized what had happened. But privately he was outraged. They'd had no right on God's green earth to give this kid GCTs until he got a score high enough to go on embassy duty, he thought. That's why they have a minimum score.

Lonetree's account of MSG school was breezy. He talked about the classes in which he was given weapons training and taught riot-control techniques and evasive-driving tactics. He said he learned about the chain of command in the embassy, and the security responsibilities of an MSG. He said for some Marines the perspective shift from the Marine who was trained to kill it, shake it, and then find out what it was doing there in the first place, to the "ambassador in blue" that described a MSG, was difficult. "Here," he quoted an instructor as saying, "we are looking less for the John Wayne type of Marine than the Jimmy Stewart type."

But what Lonetree said he had had the most trouble with was the time-consuming uniform and clothing inspections. It seemed to him an obsessive amount of importance was placed on dressing sharp and looking good. Indeed, he admitted that he had once been put on probation for his lack of attention to detail. But the warning that he must square himself away or else he would be cleaning out his wall locker had woken him up. It was just a matter of getting his brain in the right gear, he said, and he eventually graduated with a final class standing of 87 out of 128, which put him in the upper third.

Lonetree said his first choice for duty post had been East Germany; his second, anywhere else in the Eastern Bloc, because of his interest in Euro-Communism. When he learned he was going to Moscow, having read quite a bit about Russia, he was glad for the chance to see firsthand what life was like behind the Iron Curtain.

Tom Williams already had read the statements Lonetree had given to the NIS and he'd been extensively briefed by Stuhff, so he was familiar with Lonetree's earlier versions of his experiences in Moscow and Vienna. Nevertheless he let Lonetree tell it one more time, and as far as he could tell they all meshed almost identically.

But this time around, Williams was less listening to what Lonetree said he'd done than he was looking for the causes behind his actions. And along those lines Williams thought he came up with enough insights to feel comfortable with his understanding psychologically of how it had all happened.

He did not believe that Lonetree had gone to Moscow saying, "Oh, boy, now I can sell my country out." Williams believed it was more a matter of a chaotic personal history poising Lonetree on the edge of his fate as though it were a hole, and the right combination of circumstances waiting in the Soviet Union to give him a shove. An emotionally needy person yearning for love and acceptance, Lonetree had felt friendless in Moscow and unappreciated by superiors he thought were prejudiced; he had fallen for an attractive woman who, he felt, recognized his worth as a person; and he had been skillfully manipulated by a paternal figure who preyed on his weaknesses.

As for Lonetree's ability to rationalize spying for the enemy, Williams could only speculate about how his mind worked that out, but if he had to venture a guess, it would have something to do with his Indianness. Although Clayton discounted his Indian heritage and said he'd had relatively little exposure to Indian culture, he was a Native American, and like any native person who tried to assimilate himself into white society, a certain amount of dissembling was part of life. In Clayton Lonetree's case, here was someone whose identity had been damaged by his upbringing, who felt torn between two cultures and was unable to find his own voice, who had no core sense of himself or strong set of values—and the spy business, with its requisite role playing and assuming of new identities, had given him a chance to remake himself.

As he closed in on an understanding of why Lonetree had done what he did, Williams wanted to hear why Lonetree had stopped doing it.

"I felt like telling, many times," Lonetree said. "Once, I wanted to tell my detachment commander—even went to his door and said, 'Sir, uh, is it okay if I take my language lessons?' But I backed out at the last minute. I even had a dream one time that everyone knew and the Marines surrounded my house and came to my door. At that moment someone knocked at the door to my room and I jumped up and cried, They're here! But it was just a guy down the hall wanting to know if I wanted to go out and get a pizza with him. I came close to telling him."

"So what made you finally come forward?" Tom Williams persisted.

As he cast about for the answer to that question, Lonetree rambled, touching on a number of explanations, none of which seemed to satisfy even him. Then, after a long pause, he recalled an incident that appeared to have pushed him over the edge.

"One day I was invited to this school in Vienna. A USIS class. They wanted to learn about Native Americans, so I said I'd be glad to come. So I went and there were all these kids who looked up to me. Admired me, because I was a Native American and because I was a Marine. They went crazy. A little girl came up to me and she wanted me to sign an autograph. I did it. All right! . . . But afterwards I felt terrible. Here there were these people who thought highly of me, and yet I was rotting away inside. There was only one thing I could do about it."

At this point Lonetree broke down crying.

• • •

When he had finished the personal-history part of the evaluation, Tom Williams administered a series of psychological tests. The Minnesota Multiphasic Personality Inventory. The California Personality Inventory. The Weschler Adult Intelligence Scale. He didn't put a whole lot of stock in the tests—he was only half-joking when he admitted that he often gave them just so he wouldn't have to answer questions about why he didn't—but there were certain things he was looking for. He wanted to know if Lonetree's IQ was consistent with the figure that had been reported on the second GCT exam. It was. And he also wanted to determine the statistical level of Lonetree's intellectual functioning. What he found was that it was low—in the range that would indicate he would have difficulty forecasting the future and projecting the ultimate consequences of his actions. Low enough for Williams to say, Yes, he was someone more susceptible to psychological pressures than the average person, making him easily exploitable. But not so low that Williams could honestly say Clayton Lonetree had mental deficiencies that excused him from responsibility for his actions.

Wrapping the session up with a few encouraging words, Williams walked out of the brig to his car and headed for Major Henderson's house in Fredericksburg, Virginia, where the entire defense team was waiting to hear his report. As a psychologist he considered it his job to try to explain why a subject behaved the way he did; it was up to the attorneys to figure out where that fit in. But he knew they were hoping for better news and that what he was going to say was probably not going to be of much help in the coming legal proceedings. Childhood traumas threw shadows over their client's life. Just as the Russians had relied on and taken advantage of his background, so had the CIA and the NIS. But even though Clayton had been an accident waiting to happen, he'd brought this tragedy on himself—the way a lone tree drew lightning.

9

In mid-March, Special Agent Dave Moyer, the man who had conducted the initial NIS interviews of Lonetree, returned to Vienna as part of the ongoing investigation and, while there, paid a visit to the CIA counterintelligence agent Little John in his diplomatic office in the embassy. Over the previous three months the two men had spoken on several occasions, so Moyer wasn't expecting anything new to come up, and their conversation this time began as little more than chitchat. Little John asked about the progress of the investigation, and Moyer said they had just about run out of leads on Lonetree, but in the process of corroborating his confession NIS was turning up widespread fraternization among the entire Marine guard detachment. Then, almost in passing, Little John asked if anything hard had been developed on a black Marine by the name of Arnold Bracy.

Moyer remembered the name. Arnold Bracy had served in the Moscow detachment and Lonetree had mentioned he was friendly with him. But he'd said that about several Marines, so Moyer had attached no particular significance to the name.

"What's interesting about Bracy?" he asked.

Little John shrugged. "Just that he admitted to Lonetree that he'd been the subject of a Soviet recruitment approach."

This was news to Moyer. "Tell me more."

"As I recall, Bracy was caught in some sort of liaison with a Russian girl who had worked at the embassy. I'm sure the report was filed with the State Department, because it led to his termination from the security guard program. Anyhow, when I asked Lonetree about it he said Bracy had told him about the relationship, and that he'd cautioned Bracy to be careful."

From the CPU in the Vienna embassy, Moyer sent a cable back to headquarters recounting his conversation with Little John. He recommended that Arnold Bracy be located and interviewed if he had not already been, and that prudence would dictate that Bracy be considered as a possible espionage suspect.

When the cable arrived on Angelic White's desk, she sat up straight. Over the previous month, in light of the rampant fraternization revelations, A.W. had refined her original request to the State Department. It had occurred to her that among the Marines who served with Sergeant Lonetree, of special interest would be those who had also stepped over the line, socialized with a foreign national, and been caught. After another go-round with the State Department she had finally received that list, and she had prioritized, instructing agents to concentrate on those Marines who had been bounced for frat first. But nobody at the State Department had asterisked Arnold Bracy for special attention.

Pulling that list out of her desk drawer, A.W. ran her finger down the names until she came to Arnold Bracy. It was at the very bottom. There were no details about his frat offense, nothing that linked him to Lonetree beyond overlapping duty.

The very next thing A.W. did was order a copy of Bracy's service record from the Marine Corps, and when it arrived she was astounded to find that although the details of his violation were brief, they confirmed Agent Moyer's report. Sgt. Arnold Bracy had been discovered in a compromising situation with a Soviet woman by the name of Galya Gallotina, a former cook at the embassy, and as a result he had been dropped from the MSG program, demoted to corporal, and reassigned to Twentynine Palms, California, where he was now stationed.

White was furious. The State Department had supplied Bracy's name back on January 16, two months earlier almost to the day. The outline of Lonetree's recruitment was common knowledge, so someone over there had to have recognized its similarity to

Bracy's fraternization offense. Yet not one word had been said to them. Had they been given this information, Arnold Bracy would have been interviewed a long time ago.

A.W.'s frustration and anger with the State Department boiled over to include the CIA. The Agency had been closely monitoring all of their investigative reports, so it had to have known that the NIS had not gotten to Bracy yet. Which meant it had been sitting on this information too. Why? Why bring it out now? And what else did they know but weren't saying?

A.W.'s personal contacts at Langley were limited, but she knew her direct superior in Counterintelligence Investigations, Mike Bruggeman, had a channel open, so that was where she went with her suspicions that the Agency might be holding back on other information that could be relevant to the investigation.

"I'd like to know what the hell else they know," Angelic White said.

"So would I," Bruggeman replied. And he assured her he would make a call and see what he could find out.

In the meantime A.W. had no choice but to put these feelings aside. She knew that kicking and screaming at the system would do no good. Besides, there was too much catching up to do.

There were three or four Marines slotted ahead of Bracy, but now he was moved to the top, and Angelic White concentrated on getting ready for his interview. Under ideal circumstances she would have liked more time to prepare, but the lack of interagency cooperation had put NIS in a real bind. It was the middle of March and the ninety-day clock was beginning to sound like a countdown.

Protocol within the Naval Investigative Service dictated that when headquarters had business to conduct within a specific region it went through the regional director of operations (RDO), but to expedite matters, and not wanting to take a chance on losing anything in translation, A.W. received approval from Lanny McCullah to contact directly the special agent in charge (SAC) at Twentynine Palms. Michael Embry was a tough, former vice detective on the Honolulu police department in his late forties whom A.W. knew because he had worked cases with her father and he'd been her counselor at Basic School. She called him, briefed him on what was happening, and told him an action lead sheet that distilled the essential information collected up to this time on both Lonetree and Bracy would be arriving the following day. She stressed that at this point Arnold Bracy should not be regarded as a suspect, but rather as a potential witness against Lonetree. "Find out first how much Bracy knows about Lonetree that we don't know. That's our focus. Once that's cleared up, then you can explore the area of his fraternization."

Meanwhile she initiated the proper requests for approval for the two best NIS polygraphers in the region to fly to Twentynine Palms, so that once Embry was done questioning Arnold Bracy his statements could be checked against a lie detector.

As chief prosecutor at Quantico, Maj. Frank Short had done the usual stuff—assault and batteries and unauthorized absences—but he had not had much experience with complex cases that required strategic planning. Given the high estimation around the base of Major Henderson's legal abilities, to which had now been added a civilian defense team that included William Kunstler, the staff judge advocate, Col. Patrick McHenry, instructed the assistant SJA, Lieutenant Colonel Breme, to see how the government's case was shaping up and report back.

"Need any help, Frank?" Breme asked when he strolled into Short's office in Lejeune Hall.

"Naw. I've got it under control."

Breme glanced around at the stacks of files, the papers strewn everywhere. It looked as if a thermite grenade had exploded in the place.

"Well, why don't we have a talk and you tell me what you've done, and what you're thinking."

After the meeting Breme reported back to the SJA. Major Short was working hard, he said. He was spending eighteen, twenty hours a day in his office. "But if he had to go to court tomorrow, he'd get his ass handed to him. He's in over his head."

Overnight, Maj. Frank Short became persona non grata. Confidence in his ability to prosecute went from a full tank to empty.

And the next day Colonel McHenry called Lieutenant Colonel Breme back into his office and said, "I'm going to relieve Short. Do you want the case?"

Breme didn't have to think twice. "Hell no, I don't want the case. I've got enough problems of my own."

"Okay. Have you got any suggestions for prosecutor?" Colonel McHenry asked.

While he'd been a judge at Camp Lejeune, Breme had met some sharp trial counsels who had prosecuted cases in front of him, and he mentioned several names. Among them was Maj. David Beck.

The book on Major Beck was almost too good to be true. He stood six feet tall, weighed one hundred and seventy-five pounds, and had sandy hair, bright blue eyes, and a healthy glow to his boyish face. At thirty-eight years of age, he rose each morning at the crack of dawn to run ten miles at six minutes a mile, followed by forty pull-ups without stopping and five sets of one hundred push-ups. He was a religious man who could quote Scripture, and a family man married to his high school sweetheart, with four daughters and a son. His father had been an Army Air Corps pilot who had been shot down over Northern Italy and spent a year in a POW camp, and Beck had joined the Marines in 1971 when he was a senior at the University of Tennessee after learning that a friend he grew up playing football with in a mill village had stepped on a mine in Vietnam and been killed. After going into aviation, where he was trained to fly attack helicopters and earned a reputation as a "hot stick," without a war to fight he had pursued his second ambition and entered the Marine Corps law program, graduating third in his class at the University of Tennessee Law School.

Beck's military law career had begun in defense, where he was very good. As a trial attorney, who you are can often be as important as what you say, and Dave Beck's integrity and sincerity, his strong sense of right and wrong, and his gift for expressing his beliefs in such a way that there really didn't appear to be any other possible conclusion won him so many cases that the Corps soon moved him over to prosecution, where he went on to compile a perfect win-loss record. Nobody had ever been acquitted at a trial Dave Beck prosecuted.

The first Major Beck heard of the Lonetree case was in early February. He and his wife were in their home on Parris Island, South Carolina, and were in bed watching TV when it came on the news. His first reaction had been surprise that an Indian was implicated. The only one he'd known personally was a lance corporal who did the three-mile run barefoot on asphalt about two minutes faster than anybody else, and who walked around in winter outside in a T-shirt, and until this he'd heard nothing but good about Indian Marines.

Race aside, Major Beck's response was typical of most Marines. His notion of patriotism did not allow for the idea that a Marine sworn to defend the national interests of his country would ever be involved with a nation that considered America its mortal enemy. To his way of thinking, after the Tenth Commandment, the Eleventh might have been *A Marine Shall Never Be a Traitor*.

Beck was no longer actively prosecuting, he was on a two-year assignment as battalion commander, but if he were still practicing law, this was a case he would have loved to take on, and he said as much to his wife.

Early the very next morning he was playing a pickup basketball game with several drill instructors when the staff judge advocate at Parris Island showed up. "Dave, you've got to come with me. The general wants to see you."

"Why? What's going on?" Beck asked.

The SJA shook his head. "Can't say."

Nor was anything more said in the car on the way to the commanding general's building. The first indication didn't come until Beck was waiting outside the general's office and the chief of staff asked him, "What's a redneck like you know about the Soviet Union?"

Tennessee to the core, Dave Beck shrugged and offered the extent of his knowledge. "It's cold over there."

The chief of staff grinned. "Well, then, you better get your cold-weather gear together. There's been some meetings at head-quarters, and it seems you've been picked to take over the Lone-tree prosecution."

It was a standing joke at Parris Island that the officers' housing was bugged with listening devices. Dave Beck had never taken it seriously until now.

Arrangements were made for Major Beck to fly to Washington on February 15, and after a series of briefings and meetings he understood better why he had been brought in. The prosecution's case was in disarray and confusion. There was a confession, and a substantial part of it appeared to be legitimate and confirmed by evidence collected by the NIS. But numerous factual and legal issues remained unresolved, and virtually no coordination had been established among the various organizations and agencies with an interest in the case.

Although this was a case that Major Beck had glibly expressed the desire to prosecute, now that it had been handed to him, he had personal reservations about accepting it. If it meant he would lose his position as battalion commander at Parris Island, he wasn't sure he wanted to make the trade. More important, within a matter of weeks of being offered the assignment, his father died suddenly of a heart attack while tending his mother, who was undergoing cancer treatments, and Beck was reluctant to get involved in something that would prevent his spending the time she had left with her. All of these matters weighed on him, but headquarters was in crisis mode, and when his mother told him his dad would want him to do his job for his country, Major Beck heeded her words and accepted the assignment to shore up the prosecution of Sgt. Clayton Lonetree.

After relocating to the officers' quarters at Quantico, Beck turned his full attention to the case. For starters he ordered a mental examination to determine whether Lonetree suffered from a mental disease or defect that would affect his responsibility for the offenses alleged or his capacity to stand trial. He did this not only because Lonetree's behavior, as expressed in his confession, struck Beck as bizarre, but also because he had learned that the defense had arranged for a psychologist to render his expert opinion on the relevant psychological aspects of the case.

Next, Beck requested a meeting with the Department of Justice. Although he was an experienced trial attorney, he knew absolutely nothing about espionage. He was starting from square one and wanted to know how an espionage case was built. Their prosecutorial experience in these kinds of cases made them the experts.

The men he met with—John Martin, head of the Internal Security Section, and John Dion, who was in charge of the Espionage Unit—were smart and helpful. They shared their knowledge of the espionage-case world, briefed him on such issues as the handling of classified material in court-martial proceedings, which were generally open to the public, and supplied him with trial records of previous espionage cases. They also offered to talk strategy and help him prepare witnesses as the trial neared. But perhaps most important, they briefed him on the difficulties he could expect to encounter when dealing with the CIA.

"The most important of all principles to remember when dealing with the Agency is their mission—it's an intelligence-counter-intelligence one," he was told. "Everything they say and do is always directed toward accomplishing that mission. Criminal prosecutions rarely assist them in this. In fact, criminal prosecutions often harm the accomplishment of that mission by revealing classified information or disclosing covert identities. The Agency doesn't have a clue what it takes to prove a criminal case and they're not interested. So you may think they're your allies, but they're not. In a case like this, after they have done their damage assessment and put in their own internal preventive measures, the next thing that is important to them will be denial."

The Justice Department also arranged for him to meet with several Soviet defectors from the KGB, who educated him about the Soviet intelligence services, their tradecraft, and their recruitment techniques. Although no one knew for sure Violetta's background and whether she had been trained as a professional agent before being assigned to the embassy, or whether she had been tasked specifically to sexually entrap Sgt. Clayton Lonetree, the consensus was that this was a classic KGB "honey trap" operation: Violetta performed in a virtuoso capacity as a "swallow," and Sergeant Lonetree had been "played like a violin."

Beck couldn't understand it. This was the oldest trick in the book. In such a way had the Philistines given Samson a haircut. Anyone who had ever read a spy book or seen a James Bond movie should have known better than to get involved with a Soviet woman. Why would a Marine knowingly dance with the devil? he asked himself.

At the same time that he was acquainting himself with the espionage laws, reading the records of previous espionage trials prosecuted by the Justice Department, and initiating a rapport-building effort among the various agencies whose cooperation he knew he was going to need, Major Beck put in a travel request. If he was going to effectively prosecute this case, he felt it was imperative that he visit the key sites referred to in Lonetree's confession. He wanted to go to the American embassies in both Vienna and Moscow and examine documents and conduct interviews, and he wanted to go to London, where the NIS had interrogated Lonetree.

It so happened Major Henderson had already made a similar request, so Beck merely added his application. And on March 12 the trial counsel and defense counsel, along with their assistants Capt. Andy Strotman and Maj. Frank Short, flew commercial out of Dulles Airport, stopping first in Frankfurt, for Vienna, where they were met at the airport by NIS agent Dave Moyer, who drove them to their hotel.

It had been a long flight, and after a light workout to loosen up, Henderson and Beck stripped down and entered the hotel sauna for a sweat. The two had not known each other previously, meeting for the first time at Quantico shortly before their trip, and even though they were opponents in the case, already they had come to a mutual respect that allowed for good-natured banter.

They were relaxing on the wooden racks, soaking in the heat, and Beck was kidding Henderson, saying that after their Vienna

1

2

(above) Sgt. Clayton Lonetree standing in Red Square in front of St. Basil's Cathedral.

(right) Official Marine Corps photo of Sgt. Clayton Lonetree.

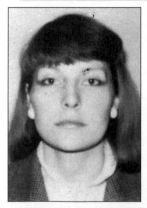

(above, left) Sgt. Clayton Lonetree standing in front of wooden Indian sculpture at Spaso House, Ambassador Arthur Hartman's residence in Moscow.

(above, right) Former American Ambassador to the Soviet Union Arthur Hartman, standing in front of Marine Security Guard Clayton Lonetree.

(right) American Embassy ID photo of Violetta Seina.

6

7

(above) Violetta Seina at age thirteen.

(top) Violetta Seina posing with a rose in photo sent to Clayton Lonetree while he was stationed in Vienna.

(right) Violetta Seina as she appeared on the CBS newsmagazine *Eye to Eye* in January 1995.

8

(above, left) CIA photo of "Uncle Sasha," who was identified as KGB agent Aleksei Yefimov.

(above, right) CIA photo of "George," who was identified as KGB agent Yuri Lysov.

(below) The editorial cartoon that infuriated Marine Commandant General P. X. Kelly.

12

13

(above) Sgt. Clayton Lonetree (second from right) being escorted into his court-martial by three Marine guards.

(right) Lanny McCullah, Director of Counterintelligence for the Naval Investigative Service at the time of the Lonetree affair, and the man who headed the espionage investigations.

(right) Major David Henderson, chief military defense counsel for Sgt. Clayton Lonetree at his court-martial.

(below) Press conference attended by Spencer Lonetree (lower left), William Kunstler (lower right), and Lonetree's grandparents Anne (upper left) and Sam Lonetree (upper right).

14

15

16

(left) Lieutenant Colonel
David Beck, chief prosecutor
at Lonetree's court-martial.

(below) William Kunstler,
Lonetree's civilian defense
counsel, speaks to reporters
after a pretrial hearing at
Quantico, Virginia, accompanied by fellow defense
attorney Michael Stuhff
(right).

Yozhik,

I got your letter. It made me feel the happiest woman in the world.

I do want to marry you.

The answer is YES.

I love you.

I miss you terribly.

Your Violetta.

A copy of the letter Violetta sent to
Clayton Lonetree in prison accepting
his proposal of marriage.

and Moscow excursions he was looking forward to visiting the hotel room in London where Lonetree had confessed to see if the chains and torture devices had been removed and the blood-stains on the carpet cleaned up, when the door opened and a woman entered. A gorgeous blonde, wearing only a towel. Which she promptly removed.

On the drive in from the airport, while pointing out landmarks and giving them an overview of Viennese customs, Agent Moyer had mentioned that the bathhouses here were coed. Yeah, right, they had thought. Now, with a beautiful blonde sitting beside them without a stitch of clothing on, like this is the way it goes, they came to a new appreciation of cultural differences.

The woman was obviously more comfortable with her nudity than they were, because after she took a seat, she gave them each a friendly smile and struck up a conversation. She introduced herself by saying she was a cosmetics representative from Germany.

"Really?" Dave Henderson said, hoping that small talk would relieve the sexual tension in the air. "My wife sells Mary Kay products. Who do you work for?"

The woman hesitated. "It's a new company," she said at last. "It doesn't have a name yet."

That struck Henderson as odd, and he shared a glance with Beck. Then he asked her several more questions, all of which she answered vaguely. Several times she responded with a question of her own, attempting to turn the conversation around to them and what business had brought them to Vienna. When the two men were equally vague, the conversation lagged, and a short time later the woman excused herself, leaving Henderson and Beck smug with the belief they had just flushed a Soviet swallow.

"That's enough action for me," Henderson said, and he too got up to leave.

Beck said he would be along shortly, but he wasn't alone five minutes before the blonde reappeared with a big smile, as though for a planned date.

Years later, when he would recall this incident and how he fled down the hall, Major Beck would chuckle and say, "My Marine and aviator buddies would have been ashamed of me." But from his own KGB come-on there was also something to be learned. Once he had asked himself, Why would a Marine knowingly dance with the devil? Now he remembered his Bible, and how it was told that Lucifer was one of God's most beautiful creations, and the devil's game was to masquerade as an angel of light.

From the start it was intended to be an investigative trip. While the two majors had slightly different interests—Beck was looking for corroborative details, while Henderson wanted to make certain Lonetree's third statement could not be substantiated—they both wanted to better understand the embassy world, to get a feel for the Marine security guard program and the role it played in providing security, and to ascertain the truth of what had happened. After two days of interviews in Vienna, during which neither man uncovered anything startling, they left for Moscow.

Major Henderson's first impression of the Soviet Union, formed during the drive into Moscow from the airport, was that this was a journey back in time. Motor traffic zigzagged around trams and trolley cars. Monstrous and shoddy apartment buildings rose into a gray sky with an unconvincing air of urban modernity. In America you saw people standing on the corners talking to each other, but in Moscow they walked straight ahead, coming and going with somber looks. He was reminded of black-and-white newsreels of a bad stockmarket year in the fifties.

What Major Beck would recall of the day they arrived was his footrace with a KGB shadow. After checking into his hotel room, he dressed for a jog and chose a route that took him along the Moscow River. He had just settled into a comfortable pace when he remembered where he was and glanced behind him. Sure enough, he'd picked up a tail. A man in a jogging suit was letting him set the pace. Nothing if not competitive, Beck picked up speed, and when he looked back again he saw the man was holding his own. Beck kicked into an even higher gear, and a two-man race was on. Perhaps a mile later he once again checked on the competition, and if he hadn't looked back at that moment,

he would have missed the satisfaction of seeing the Russian leaning against a car that had pulled up alongside him, holding his
side and gasping for breath.

After settling in, Henderson and Beck began a series of interviews, starting with the Marine detachment. And it didn't take
them long to recognize that a serious security problem existed at
what was supposed to be America's most sensitive diplomatic
post. Marine after Marine complained to them about the difference between what had been drilled into them at MSG school,
where they were told their job was to safeguard classified material and enforce security regulations, and the reality on post,
where political officers not only exhibited a cavalier attitude toward security precautions, they resented it when the Marines
tried to enforce them. Rather than being treated as an important
part of the security apparatus, the Marines felt the State Department "elite" viewed them as members of the domestic staff.

This lax attitude toward security went beyond personnel to the
technical, according to the Marines. Surveillance cameras to en-
trances didn't work. Alarms to secure areas malfunctioned.
Gates to the interior courtyard would stick in the up position.
And when they brought these failings to the attention of the
State Department's security officer, nothing was done to remedy
them.

Majors Henderson and Beck were appalled by what they
heard, but it also answered a question both had come hoping to
answer: How had Sergeant Lonetree been able to get away with
it? How could this have gone on and no one known about it? It
sounded now as though the State Department had tolerated
gross deficiencies in its security programs with a complacency
that was waiting for some external event to provide the impetus
for attention.

At this point Henderson and Beck went in different directions.
Major Henderson began to look for extenuating and mitigating
circumstances that would impact the case against his client.
While the State Department's lax approach to security certainly
set the stage, thinking as a defense counsel, Henderson realized
it wasn't going to help his case if it looked as though the Moscow

detachment were made up of by-the-book Marines and his client were the only one to step out of line. That was not how Lonetree had described the situation, however, and as Henderson dug deeper, nor was that what he found. He heard about a hedonistic mood in embassy quarters and a tolerant attitude by superiors that created a climate of easy sex, lots of liquor, and black-market profiteering. Making things worse, he found, this misconduct had apparently been covered by a conspiracy of silence. Heads were frequently turned away from infractions, and sex with Soviets was winked at. For all practical purposes, he was told, the Marine detachment in Moscow functioned as if it were an isolated outpost, answerable only to itself. There was a we-look-out-for-ourselves mentality, reflected in the belief that the only news to get out of Moscow was what the detachment commander wanted the outside world to know.

Henderson's conclusion was that while his client may have had his share of personal problems, he apparently wasn't alone in violating many of the regulations. It was also evident that what had happened with Lonetree very probably could have been prevented had the people in charge not been so involved in their own personal adventures.

Major Beck, meanwhile, was being educated to a different set of embassy realities, which bore out the earlier warnings of the Justice Department. After determining there was no chance of interviewing Violetta—he was told that swallows usually fly off well before the trap is closed—he focused on meeting with intelligence officers. He was fully aware of the official position that the CIA did not maintain a presence in the embassy. Nonetheless, to complete the process of understanding the character and magnitude of Lonetree's crimes, Beck felt he needed to know what impact his acts had had on the victimized Agency. It was going to be a significant part of his prosecution. Perhaps the most significant.

This was his thinking when he went to the regional security officer's office in the American Embassy in Moscow and made what he considered to be a reasonable request. There were people he said he wanted to talk to. He wanted to meet with agents, officers in the field, who could say to him, Yes, I work for the Agency. This is what I do, this is how it is done, and this is why it is important to the interests and security of the United States. This is why my identity must be protected, and this is how it hurts when it is revealed.

He wanted as well for someone to say to him, Yes, we have undercover Russians, defectors, in place, who are channeling crucial intelligence data to the West. This is what they have done for us, and this is what happens if they become compromised.

Finally, he wanted to be told what adverse effects the Agency had seen, *specifically* those that were a direct result of what Lonetree had shown and told the Soviets. If Lonetree had indeed confirmed the identities of CIA agents to the Soviets and afterward the agents found themselves followed by spycatchers to drop zones or rendezvous sites, that was damage. If the Soviets took that information and used it to wipe out human intelligence assets in Russia, that was even worse damage. Beck wanted someone to tie those things to Lonetree for him, and he thought that if Lonetree had done what he said he'd done, the Agency should be able to determine that.

But Beck was given none of this. All he got were generalities and cleared quotes. Yes, Lonetree had the potential to do damage of that nature. Yes, certain things were probably compromised by the information he gave up. Yes, during the period in question we lost some people.

Beck was white-hot. He felt that his position as prosecutor, representing the United States of America in a trial in which it was alleged that espionage laws that protected intelligence officers had been violated, meant something. He felt that by its actions the CIA was saying he was not important enough to be trusted. In the entire time he was in Moscow, Major Beck was never introduced to a single person who acknowledged an affiliation with the CIA. He was never even told who the chief of station was. He would leave Moscow thinking he'd have had better luck if he'd asked one of the Marine security guards who the intelligence officers were.

But before Henderson and Beck left Moscow, a development

would take place that would overwhelm these complaints. On March 21, the day before they were to depart for London, the regional security officer contacted Major Beck and indicated he had something important to impart to him. They rode the elevator up to the seventh floor, where they entered "the bubble"—a supposedly bug-proof room-within-a-room. There, the RSO said a top-secret cable had just come in from Washington, D.C., and he'd been instructed to share its contents.

Beck took the cable and read it. It said that a second Marine security guard by the name of Arnold Bracy had just signed a series of confessions to the NIS in which he admitted that he had conspired with Sergeant Lonetree to shut down alarm systems and allow KGB agents to conduct "moonlight tours" of the embassy. From this moment on, the memo indicated, the security of the ambassador's office, the CIA station, the code room, even the bubble, should be considered compromised. If what Arnold Bracy said was true, every classified conversation and electronic communication to and from the embassy was being simultaneously piped to KGB headquarters at Dzerzhinsky Square.

THE MARCH
TO JUSTICE

10

When the story broke that a second Marine security guard had fallen prey to the seductive charms of a Soviet woman and the two had regularly teamed up to allow Soviet agents to conduct midnight house calls inside the secure spaces of the embassy, what had previously been viewed as a surprising but limited security breach escalated into what appeared to be the most serious espionage scandal in U.S. history. Once the outpost for scholarly diplomatic and military attachés who mingled with their Soviet counterparts and then sent back to Washington telegrams containing political, military, and economic analysis, the Moscow embassy had become a vital intelligence platform for the National Security Agency and the technical side of the CIA, bristling with listening devices and sensors and receivers that were capable of intercepting top-level Soviet conversations and communications. If Lonetree and Bracy were guilty as charged and Soviet agents had been given hours to roam inside the embassy, it was conceivable that these agents had successfully performed the equivalent of safe-cracking operations and had entered secure areas behind combination-locked doors where secrets were stored. There was no reason to doubt that the Soviets had successfully been able to install equipment that allowed them to intercept and read virtually all coded communications between the embassy and Washington since 1985. If that was the case, it was even possible they had been able to break U.S. codes elsewhere in the world.

Even before a formal assessment of the damage had begun, government officials were expressing outrage and hinting at irreparable damage to the security of the Western world. Within the CIA there was conjecture that perhaps this accounted for the decimation of Moscow station. For several years the CIA had been experiencing significant losses in Moscow for which it had no explanation. A number of technical means of collecting intelligence information had gone bad. Equipment had been shut off or located and destroyed. As well, human assets that had been carefully cultivated for years inside the Soviet Union had been arrested and executed. Some of this had been attributed to Edward Lee Howard but not all, and the Agency had been at a loss and willing to consider any explanation, even that one of their own agents might be a traitor. But if the Russians had been given a chance to snoop, bug, and pore over CIA files identifying agents and informers in the Soviet Union, that explained everything.

The Reagan administration was forced to deal with the notion that for several years it had been playing poker with someone who'd had the benefit of looking at a mirror over the shoulders of their negotiators during discussions about arms control and space-based weapons systems. It was speculated that this might explain what happened at the summit at Reykjavík, Iceland, in October of the previous year, when administration officials had been disturbed by the Soviets' uncannily well-prepared responses to U.S. positions. Perhaps they'd had inside information derived from wiretaps on the communications gear.

In the days that followed, the Marine Spy Scandal dominated the headlines of every newspaper and periodical in the country, its seriousness ratcheted up by a succession of revelatory detonations. It was written that FBI counterintelligence experts had long ago warned the State Department about chinks in its security structure that enabled the Soviets to enjoy espionage opportunities, but diplomats had been more concerned about good foreign relations than the espionage threat and no action had followed the recommendations. Investigative articles about how Marines in Moscow routinely violated the "no women in rooms" rule, frequented off-limits bars, falsified logbooks, disregarded regulations, and took advantage of the lack of supervision were quickly followed by the announcement that so many more Marines had admitted to security violations with espionage implications that the entire twenty-eight-member Marine detachment in Moscow was being recalled to Quantico, which led to rumors of a Marine "spy ring." With the temperature dropping in superpower relations, Reagan administration officials acknowledged that security in the embassy may have been so compromised that Secretary of State Shultz, who was scheduled to make a trip to Moscow to discuss intermediate-range nuclear forces, might not be able to hold safe conversations or file confidential reports to Washington from the embassy without the Soviets' tuning in, so a special van, referred to as the "Winnebago," would be flown over for security purposes.

Just as newspapers loved a scandal because it increased sales, politicians welcomed one because it provided a great vehicle for partisan posturing, and congressmen on both sides of the aisle jumped into the fray. All but sputtering with fury, Senate Majority Leader Robert Byrd (D-W.Va.) delivered a speech on the Senate floor in which he gave the White House a severe dressing down. "While this Administration talks tough about combatting communism, about pouring our efforts into supporting freedom fighters wherever they may be found, American security is being compromised from the docks of Norfolk to the inner sanctums of our embassy in Moscow." No sooner had he taken his seat than two members of the House Foreign Affairs subcommittee, Rep. Daniel Mica (D-Fla.) and Olympia Snowe (R-Me.) leapt to their feet to declare their intention to fly to Moscow for a firsthand inspection of the embassy. Many people dismissed the congressional junket as political grandstanding, especially when Mica, at a press conference just prior to their departure, held aloft a red child's slate on which words could be written and then erased by lifting a sheet of cellophane, and complained, "After millions of dollars have been spent to make our embassies secure, we have been told that this will be the only safe method of communicating while we are in Moscow." But when Mica and Snowe released a report on their findings and asserted that not only had the American embassy been penetrated, but the *new* U.S. embassy building under construction in Moscow was honeycombed with electronic listening devices planted by Soviet builders and should be demolished, official Washington went into an anti-Communist frenzy not seen since the McCarthy era.

As director of counterintelligence, Lanny McCullah was kept informed of ongoing cases by his various department heads, and if there was a problem developing, he would sometimes ask to be kept advised, or if something appeared to be going astray or breaking big, he would sometimes stick his oar in. When Special Agent Mike Embry called headquarters from Twentynine Palms and reported that after failing a series of polygraph examinations Cpl. Arnold Bracy had copped out under intense interrogation and admitted that he and Sergeant Lonetree opened the doors and let Soviet agents into the embassy, McCullah had taken immediate acion. The first call had been to the CIA, and the second to the State Department, and by ten o'clock that night a man from each institution knowledgeable about the security systems in the embassy had joined a senior NIS agent on a red-eye flight out of Dulles bound for California. Their assignment was to evaluate the confession, formulate questions, and take the whole interrogation to a higher level—but they never got that chance. They were still in the air when Embry called back to say Arnold Bracy had terminated the interrogation and asked for a lawyer. So the embassy experts made a U-turn, flying back to Washington the next day with the original copy of Bracy's statements.

It had been a Saturday, but McCullah had come into the office anyway, where he was met by Jim Lannon and Gardner "Gus" Hathaway—the counterintelligence chiefs of the State Department and CIA respectively. Bracy had given NIS agents three sworn statements, and the three CI chiefs read them slowly and carefully, paying as much attention to the minutiae as to the major revelations.

In the first statement, Bracy had acknowledged knowing both Sergeant Lonetree and Galya Gallotina, but claimed he had not been good friends with the former, and that was all he'd been with the latter. Given a polygraph examination in which he'd been asked such questions as "Did you engage in any sexual activity with Galya?" and "Have you ever engaged in espionage against the United States?," when Bracy responded "No," deception had been indicated.

In his second statement, he revised his story, admitting that he had had intercourse with Galya and that she told him the KGB had been putting pressure on her to arrange for him to meet "Uncle Sasha," who was interested in learning the names of CIA agents. After failing a second series of polygraphs in which he was asked "Did you ever have a personal meeting with Galya's Uncle Sasha?" and "Did you ever give any classified information to a Russian?," Arnold Bracy appeared to at last be willing to tell the whole truth. He said that on several occasions when he and Sergeant Lonetree stood night duty together, he had shut down the alarm systems while Lonetree escorted Soviet agents around the embassy. "I could tell where he was by the alarms that went off," Bracy's statement read. "I know that he was everywhere, including the CPU on two or three occasions, and also into CIA spaces . . . and each time they were there for about an hour." The statement was signed, but that was the last cooperative act on the part of Arnold Bracy. Moments after reviewing his statement, signing each page, and swearing to its accuracy, he recanted and invoked his right not to be compelled to testify against himself. According to the polygraphers, he said, "I'd rather go to prison for false swearing than espionage."

For several hours McCullah, Hathaway, and Lannon discussed the significance of Arnold Bracy's confession. "Could they have done it?" McCullah asked.

Gus Hathaway had been a station chief in Moscow, while Jim Lannon was intimately familiar with the layout of the embassy and the systems that protected it. Both nodded grimly. Everything Bracy said he and Lonetree had done was feasible.

"What do you make of the retraction?" they asked McCullah.

"It's unfortunate, but not surprising," he replied. "Nothing hurts the truth like a good night's sleep."

By the end of the discussion it was apparent that both the State

Department and the CIA would have no choice but to accept the worst-case scenario. The operative question was not Could it have happened? but What if it had? A bug hunt of colossal proportions would have to be initiated. Coding equipment would have to be shipped back to the United States for inspection. No matter the cost, the security and communications systems in Moscow would have to be replaced.

As for the Naval Investigative Service, Lanny McCullah recognized that the investigation had vaulted beyond what could reasonably be expected from the investigative branch of his Counterintelligence Directorate. A much broader response was going to be required, and the following Monday he met with the deputy director of NIS, Brian McKee, to give him a status report and make a recommendation.

"The spy case that at first appeared to be an isolated instance of a lonely Marine being seduced into espionage has taken a more ominous turn," he said. "To corroborate everything Bracy said, hundreds more interviews are going to be required. Not only that, there's no reason to think this stops at two. Already there are several other Marines worth taking a close look at who may have been recruited by the Soviets, and before this is over we very well may discover more. We don't know how big this thing is, or how big it's going to get once we start looking into it, but to determine that will be the biggest thing NIS has ever been involved in. We're going to need a lot of people for this. We're also going to need office space, furniture, equipment, vehicles, phones. . . ."

Asked "What are you proposing?," McCullah replied, "I think we're talking task force."

McKee pursed his lips but saw the sense of it. "Okay. Do what you think needs to be done."

The NIS task force came together in an amazingly short period of time. Office space was found in a GSA building at Buzzards Point in Southeast Washington, the same building that housed the Washington Field Office of the FBI, and within a matter of days it was transformed into an office facility. As the investigation proceeded, there were going to be thousands of pieces of information that would have to be stored and cross-referenced, so an NIS reservist who had his own computer company was brought in to set up a database. McCullah wanted the top interviewers in all of NIS at his disposal—guys who could elicit information under difficult circumstances—so a list was drawn up and twenty of NIS's best agents were TDY'd (temporary dutied) to Washington, where they were thoroughly briefed, paired with the best polygraphers to form flyaway teams, and dispatched to specific locations to follow up on leads. He then contacted each agency with a special interest in the outcome of the investigation—the NSA, CIA, FBI, State Department, and Marine Corps—and asked them to assign someone with expertise to the task force who would examine and analyze information as it came in and would advise them as they went along. Of course, the whole campaign had to have a designated code name, so someone came up with Bobsled, and on April 1, 1987, the Bobsled task force was officially launched, with Lanny McCullah as its director.

With confirmation of Arnold Bracy's confession heading the list of task-force objectives, McCullah went after an explanation for why the State Department had played deaf, dumb, and mute and withheld critical background information on him from the NIS. His source was Angelic White, who had been told what happened by her counterpart on the Department of State's counterintelligence staff. Bracy had been booted from the MSG program in the summer of 1986, when he was discovered with Galya in an American diplomat's quarters where she was working as a maid. The embassy security officer had identified Bracy as a possible espionage suspect at that time and suggested he be debriefed in Washington, but somehow, when he returned to the States, the recommendation had been overlooked. When details of Lonetree's recruitment became known, the counterintelligence people at State, recognizing the similarities to Bracy's story and realizing a potentially embarrassing oversight on their part, had dropped Bracy's name to the bottom of the list of Marines bounced from the program for frat, and ordered one of their debriefers to go to Twentynine Palms and talk to Bracy.

They were hoping to buy time, but had not gotten around to Bracy when the NIS came up with his name on their own.

McCullah was livid. To save face, the State Department had obstructed their investigation. When he called Jim Lannon and confronted him, all attempts to be friendly and professional were off. "I'm not going to put up with any more of this shit. How many more other Bracys do you have sitting on your shelves?" he demanded to know.

Within a week he had his answer. A document appeared in his in box titled "Marine Security Guard Program Disciplinary In-fractions, 1980–1987." It listed 579 incidents involving MSGs whose assignments had been prematurely curtailed for a variety of violations, only a fraction of whom NIS had been aware of be-fore.

There were no words to describe McCullah's reaction. He couldn't believe that the State Department had not shared this information with them, because NIS had jurisdiction over these people and a substantial number of the offenses would have been of interest to them from a criminal or counterintelligence view-point.

In the first thirty days of its existence Bobsled proved its worth, as investigators turned up the names of new and more Marines who admitted to involvement in a range of infractions—unreported sexual encounters with Soviet females, currency violations, black-marketing, unauthorized travel—that were the favorite recruitment ploys of hostile intelligence services. In rapid succession three more espionage investigations were opened, and NIS agents appeared to find the corroboration they were looking for when another black Marine, by the name of Robert Williams, who had served with Arnold Bracy in Moscow, told agents that Bracy had confided to him that he was intimately in-volved with Galya and that she had recruited him to engage in espionage, for which he had been paid thousands of dollars. In support of his statement, Williams said there had been another Marine present who overheard this admission, Sgt. Vincent Downes, and when Downes was interviewed by NIS agents, he acknowledged that the events as reported by Williams were true.

It was still a mystery just how extensive the Soviet infiltration of the Marine security guard program was, but it was growing before Lanny McCullah's eyes when he learned through confidential channels that a "sensitive source," having heard through the media about the Marine security guard investigations, had reported that on three separate occasions, three different and senior KGB officials had made specific references about the phenomenal successes they were having in the recruitment of American Marine security guards.

The way the memo was worded, McCullah knew the source was a defector and not an electronic intercept, and he called Gus Hathaway and asked about their source's credibility. "Has anything he said ever been proven to be wrong? Or disinformation?"

"No," Hathaway replied. "Everything he's reported to us has either been corroborated, or we have been unable to establish it as untrue. The reliability factor we place on him as an informant is high."

"Then I'd like to have a face-to-face with him," McCullah said.

Several days later he drove to a remote northern Virginia location and met the defector. The man's true identity was disguised—his death in an auto accident had been staged because he had left family behind and did not want his previous employers to know he was in U.S. hands—but it was established that he had been a senior intelligence officer from an Eastern Bloc country. An interpreter was available but unnecessary, for the man spoke passable English. Chain-smoking an acrid, foreign brand of cigarette, he elaborated on what had been written in the memo.

He said all three occasions took place during a trip he'd made to Moscow for a training seminar. The first was a social setting, over dinner with wine, when a general bragged, "You wouldn't believe what the American Marines have done for us." The second was a remark made in passing by the aide to a different general, who said essentially the same thing, except he mentioned that in addition to succumbing to the use of women to co-opt them, the Marines had compromised themselves with black-market violations and the like. The third reference came in a classroom setting, when a KGB colonel who was an expert in operations aimed at Americans said their successes were not limited to the Soviet Union but were widespread and included countries all over the world. And he named several.

McCullah left the meeting feeling slightly overwhelmed. Until now the task force had been aimed at Lonetree and Bracy and a few of their cohorts. Factoring in this defector information, he knew the scope of Bobsled was going to have to be amplified. If NIS was going to be thorough in its efforts to determine the extent of MSG recruitment by foreign intelligence, it was going to have to look well beyond the Marines who had served in diplomatic missions within the Soviet Union. It would have to proceed as though the Soviet intelligence services were not only engaged in a full-blown worldwide effort to penetrate U.S. diplomatic missions but, with the help of the Marine security guards, had been hugely successful.

NIS had always thought of itself as a never-say-no, can-do outfit, and with the seeds of an epidemic diagnosed, McCullah jacked up the NIS response. To handle the increased workload, he brought in a deputy on the senior management level: Goethe "Bud" Aldridge was a tall, silver-haired, physically and mentally tough former Marine, a previous director of Criminal Investigations at NIS with twenty-five years in operational field assignments worldwide, known to be a troop handler and someone with a low tolerance for malingerers and bureaucrats. Then McCullah doubled the number of agents assigned to Bobsled. And knowing he did not have the resources to adequately cover virtually every embassy in every country served by MSGs, he asked the CIA and NSA to grade a list of countries from an overall threat posture: Which contained the largest number of KGB agents? How active were they? What were America's national interests in those countries? Adding those to the five or six countries singled out by the defector, and throwing in some others from a cover standpoint, the NIS was able to narrow the number down to a manageable figure and then prioritize.

The task force was putting in seven-day workweeks, often fourteen to sixteen hours a day, arranging interviews, receiving results, cross-checking information and looking for patterns and connections between people, and sending out the latest data to agents in time to prepare them for upcoming interviews. But there existed a sense of euphoria among the members, because this was a front-page case and all knew they were involved in the biggest event of their professional lives.

There was also a vindication factor at work. It was a commonly held notion within law enforcement that the Naval Investigative Service was a second-rate investigative agency. Its agents were occasionally maligned—it was said those who didn't make the FBI cut settled for NIS. There had been allegations that some of its investigations had been diverted or thwarted by command influence, and critics had made the NIS walk the plank for not detecting the Walker family spy ring before Mrs. Walker disclosed its existence to the FBI, and for not terminating the security clearance of Jonathan Jay Pollard in view of his known character flaws, although it had been the NIS that had first suspected Pollard of spying and it was the NIS that captured him on video stealing classified documents. While NIS officials felt most of the bad press that darkened its reputation was unfair when it wasn't downright mistaken, there was no denying that a good part of the adrenaline that drove the members of Bobsled came from the knowledge that this investigation gave the NIS a chance for a big win for a change.

Up until now, just about everything NIS had done had been blessed by the other counterintelligence agencies in town. Every step NIS had taken had been viewed by representatives of the FBI and CIA, who had also been invited to sit in on the brainstorming sessions, and not once had NIS been criticized for the way it was doing things. Not once had any of its esteemed colleagues said, You're overlooking this, or You might want to consider that. Not once did anyone say this investigation was beyond NIS's abilities.

Indeed, as director of Bobsled, Lanny McCullah was being accorded the respect you would expect of an FCI czar. He was in

great demand as a speaker around Washington by people wanting updates on the progress of the investigation. In the first two weeks of April alone, he spoke before the Senate Select Committee on Intelligence, the House Armed Services Committee, the Defense Counterintelligence Board, the President's Intelligence Oversight Board, and the House Permanent Subcommittee for Intelligence. All wanted status reports on the investigative results: How many people have you talked to? How many violations were admitted to? How many DIs (deceptions indicated) on espionage questions?

Essentially everyone was interested in the same thing—the numbers, which McCullah provided like a box score. "We talked to five yesterday, and three admitted to infractions: five and three." But when you brief a committee, you aren't there just to provide information, you're there to tell a story and send a message. And the members wanted to hear McCullah's personal assessment of the significance of the numbers.

Each time, he sounded the caution that the figures could be misleading because the evidence that would allow them to prosecute, much less convict, had yet to be collected. That said, when he described his vision of what had happened and how bad he thought it was, the way he spoke gave everyone the impression that when the NIS was done flushing out all the spies, this was going to be the biggest espionage case of the century.

The slant was alarming. The speculations sensational. People came away awed. And at the time it didn't seem like much of a leap to believe that Bobsled would prove McCullah right.

In none of his statements had Sergeant Lonetree ever said anything about letting foreign agents into the U.S. Embassy, and when Mike Stuhff asked him about it, Lonetree emphatically denied anything like that had happened. Yes, he knew Arnold Bracy, but he had no idea why he was saying these things. They were not true, they did not happen.

Mike Stuhff believed his client. He didn't know what was going on with Arnold Bracy, but with five additional espionage-related charges filed against Sergeant Lonetree based on Bracy's

allegations, and with his client now confronting capital offenses, Stuhff knew he would need some time before he could effectively refute the charges. So at the next Article 32 session he requested a three-week continuance to give the defense a chance to examine the evidence.

After almost two months as lead defense counsel, Mike Stuhff had seen little that had caused him to reconsider his initial assessment of this case. Clayton Lonetree was no innocent. His head swimming in a tangle of espionage books, young love, and delusions of outwitting the KGB, he had done some very dumb things. But it also sounded as if there was a lot of blameworthy negligence to go around, and Stuhff believed absolutely that his client was being made into a larger villain than the facts supported.

As he put it together, for years people in the upper levels of government had been aware there were significant security problems at the American Embassy in Moscow and had failed to do anything to rectify the situation; the system that had allowed conditions to continue unchecked should be blamed for this whole sordid affair, not Clayton Lonetree.

Stuhff believed that the CIA—masters in deceiving and disrupting an enemy population, specialists in "disinformation"— was happy to be able to blame its intelligence losses on a Marine security guard, because it had been embarrassing to have them attributed to Edward Howard, a defector from its own ranks. He thought that the State Department, which had done little to improve its understanding of security problems or to take measures to protect U.S. missions and its employees from an identified threat, and was now feeling the heat from Congress for allowing the KGB to be the general contractors on the new embassy building, welcomed this opportunity to divert attention away from its gross dereliction. And he suspected that the Reagan administration, concerned about the widening implications of the Iran–Contra arms-for-hostages scandal and desperately searching for a newsworthy distraction, had seized on the Marine Sex-for-Secrets scandal as a windfall.

This was why his client was being abused by the system, he

thought. And if that did not add up neatly to a conspiracy, the configuration looked at least like a community of interests among a number of agencies and officials, all with their own reasons and motives, who had come together and decided to make this Marine a scapegoat for their own failings.

Given his faith in this scenario and the amount of prejudicial publicity that was mounting because of the Bracy allegations, Stuhff and Kunstler decided that, during the three-week recess from the Article 32 hearing, they should initiate aggressive measures to neutralize the hostility against their client. It was time to come out of their corner, swinging.

This was William Kunstler's bailiwick. He *liked* to try cases in the public arena. He felt it was important for all defense lawyers in highly visible and controversial cases to understand that sometimes their only escape, only help, was the press. In this case Kunstler felt that the prosecution had a big jump on the defense. No less an authority than the President of the United States, seconded by the Secretary of Defense, had made sweeping statements condemning his client before he'd had his day in court. *The Daily News,* the largest-circulation paper in New York, had run a front-page article, "Pentagon Claims Marines Led Reds on Spy Tour," with a picture of Sergeant Lonetree and Corporal Bracy.

In a series of interviews with wire-service reporters and major newspapers, Kunstler set out to recast the public image of his client as a "traitorous spy." While conceding that Clayton Lonetree did have unauthorized contacts with Violetta and Uncle Sasha, Kunstler insisted that he gave the Soviets nothing of value and did not believe he was betraying his country. He said he wasn't even sure that Lonetree's offenses rose to the level of espionage. And he initiated a series of actions and statements that were vintage William Kunstler.

In the best of all situations, he preferred to represent an angry, aggressive defendant who had a political agenda and took a strong interest in what was happening, but by this time he knew Clayton Lonetree was no Russell Means or Dennis Banks. Just how square Lonetree was struck Kunstler when he dropped their names and Lonetree gave him a blank stare. He didn't know who Kunstler was talking about. The one plus to having an uninformed and apolitical client, however, was he allowed his attorney to improvise.

Among the Indian militants he had defended over the years, Kunstler felt he had made a number of lifelong friends, and he got on the phone to some of them in an attempt to martial support for Clayton Lonetree from Native America. It was a logical place to go, and a certain amount of sympathetic activity had already been generated in Indian country. Clayton Lonetree defense funds had sprung up in hot spots around the country known to embrace Indian causes, where this was received as a familiar story of government persecution of Native American people and Lonetree was viewed as a political prisoner as undeserving of incarceration, in their opinion, as Leonard Peltier.

But the response from Native America, and Native American veterans in particular, was by no means unanimous or uncomplicated. In the minds of the patriotic Navajo Code Talkers, decorated for their actions in World War II, if Lonetree was not a traitor then at the very least he had disgraced their proud tradition of service. When Sally Tsosie asked the Navajo Tribe for money to help pay the legal costs of Clayton's defense, the Navajo Veterans Commission recommended she be turned down. And when Spencer Lonetree's sister, Kathy Lonetree, attempted to organize rallies to raise money for the financially strapped defense team, the turnout was a major disappointment. The rally in Denver produced $612, and one in St. Paul fared worse, netting $220.

Kunstler would have far better luck when it came to attacking what he perceived as a double standard in the superstar status accorded to Lt. Col. Oliver North. In an op-ed piece published in the *Los Angeles Times,* Kunstler drew a vivid picture of North as a renegade who hid behind the Fifth Amendment when testifying before the House Intelligence Committee about the unlawful diversion of arms-sales proceeds from Iran to the Nicaraguan Contras, who shredded pertinent documents, who publicly admitted to a number of serious federal crimes, and who yet was walking around a free man, "flatteringly portrayed by the press and his supporters as a dedicated soldier, a consummate patriot and loyal subordinate . . . a devoted husband and father." All the while this was going on, dramatically different and "medieval conditions of confinement" had been imposed on the other Marine in the news, Sgt. Clayton Lonetree, who had not been caught in the middle of any wrongdoing but who voluntarily had gone to the authorities with his story and yet had spent almost four months in captivity.

These issues were clearly going to be raised in the Lonetree defense come the court-martial, but in the meantime the defense team decided another culprit needed to be targeted, which is how they came to gang up on the Naval Investigative Service. In their minds the NIS was a besmirched organization looking for a way to polish its reputation, staffed by cowboy agents willing to go to any lengths to secure confessions. For the defense team, the telling moment in the investigation had come in London, when NIS agents, not satisfied with Sergeant Lonetree's voluntary statement, encouraged him to "Tell me anything, tell me a lie." That said to them that the Naval Investigative Service had already made a determination as to what was going on, and the interrogators had concrete ideas about what they were looking for even as they were in the process of formulating questions. And the way that translated in Kunstler's mind was that the NIS, rather than developing an espionage case against Clayton Lonetree based on the facts, had begun with a preconceived notion and was less interested in finding out what happened than in confirming their theories.

What was going on with Arnold Bracy? Kunstler was convinced that the NIS, in quest of a witness to assure a conviction, had contrived a case against another minority—a *black* Marine—thinking if they put enough pressure on him he would roll over and testify against Lonetree.

11

At Marine Corps headquarters (HQMC), Eighth and I Streets in Southeast Washington, D.C., where the commandant of the Marine Corps had lived and presided since President Thomas Jefferson picked the spot, the turmoil could not have been greater if Marines had been engaged in a military campaign. The Marine Corps was a proud organization that embraced a powerful code of integrity. Its lustrous reputation as the nation's truest warriors was based on each leatherneck's commitment to the hallowed concepts of honor, duty, and country. The Corps was supposed to be a tribal brotherhood as much as a military service, and loyalty was a religious vow with its members. For this reason the current commandant, General P. X. Kelly, had made a point of letting the military counterintelligence service know that Marines were not available for double-agent operations: He did not think any hostile intelligence service would believe that a Marine would ever betray his country.

It had been a strange and turbulent tenure for General Kelly. No sooner had he come into office in 1983 than a suicide-terrorist crashed a 5,000-pound truck bomb into the Marine barracks in Beirut, killing 241 Marines on a peacekeeping mission. It was a disaster that in retrospect had been both foreseeable and avoidable, and the general's handling of the crisis had drawn sharp criticism from Congress. Then had come the invasion of Grenada, where instead of reprising an Iwo Jima–like amphibious assault, the Marines had become mired in an interservice turf battle. To these frustrations had been added the image of a Marine lieutenant colonel by the name of Oliver North, wearing his medal-bedecked uniform and invoking the Fifth Amendment when asked about illegal plans to supply arms to the Nicaraguan Contras and his decision to misinform Congress about it. And now, on the verge of retirement, the general was forced to contend with casualties from a program that was supposed to harvest the best and the brightest from its overall ranks, casualties whose wounds were inflicted not on the battlefield but in the bedroom.

There had been a time when it was widely believed that General Kelly was on his way to becoming the first Marine to serve as chairman of the Joint Chiefs of Staff. Not anymore. Not with congressional committees convening with the expressed intention of ripping the covers off this scandal, dragging former and current Marine commanders before them and demanding an explanation for why a wheel had to come off before the Marine Corps realized there was something broken. Not when your troops were being ridiculed the way they were on a mock travel flyer tacked prominently on a bulletin board at CIA headquarters:

> Moscow Embassy Tours. See Ambassador's Office. See Latest in Communications Equipment. See Finest in Secure Rooms. Special Rates for Representatives of the Special Services. $$$$$$$$$$$$ Bonus. Burn Bag Souvenirs for First 10 Visitors. Pretty Girls Free. Contact: Local Marine Security Guard for details. And watch for our new offerings in: Leningrad. Vienna. Rome. Asia. Africa. Latin America.

Perhaps the crowning insult was delivered when *Time* magazine carried on its cover the picture of the square-jawed Marine normally seen on recruiting posters, except this leatherneck sported a black eye.

You could all but hear the commandant's teeth grinding each time he picked up the paper and saw another cartoonist making the Marine Corps the butt of an outrageous joke. One drawing in particular that was reported to have aroused his wrath parodied the Marine hymn:

From the halls of our own embassy,
To the girls of the KGB—
We pass our country's secrets,
To break the monotony. . . .
First to let them bug our offices
And to steal the codes they've seen,
You had better change the guard tonight
He's a United States Marine.

The way the Marine Corps was portrayed in the press was very important to General Kelly. Image was not just a matter of appearance. It affected budgets. Manpower. Morale. Missions. So it was painful beyond belief when media pundits, searching for unmistakable signs of the decline of American civilization, looked no further than the "utterly demoralizing spectacle of members of this country's most elite fighting force betraying . . . their fellow countrymen in a disgusting swap of sex for top secrets." Op-ed pieces were even referring to the scandal as a symptom of the Me Decade, a crime of cultural failure, and issued a call for a national commitment to rebuild character standards: "Our government, our churches and our civic institutions must reestablish a national curriculum that breeds honor, loyalty, respect for tradition, patriotism and individual and collective responsibility." Let's get back to *Semper fidelis,* in other words.

The official response of the Corps to date had been that a few "bad apples" will turn up in any large organization and the Marine Corps had never been in better shape. At a Congressional hearing the commandant asked that "the American people . . . judge this very unique institution not by the alleged actions of a few but by the patriotic and exemplary conduct that has been our heritage." And he assured the Senate that "our readiness to go to war today is the highest it has been in our peacetime history."

Unfortunately, given the climate, the commandant's comments sounded like so much bumper-sticker bravado.

In the face of mounting criticism that the Corps was "wallowing in complacency" and incapable of engaging in self-analysis, the senior legal people at headquarters drafted a memo to the commandant saying, in essence, it was time to get off the track and on the train. If this thing was as big as NIS was making it out to be, the Marine Corps needed to get more involved. Do we want to continue to read about it? Or do we want to help write it?

The particular action they recommended was the formation of a joint Department of Defense–Department of Justice task force to take over the investigation and prosecution of all future cases relating to security breaches at the U.S. Embassy in Moscow. Urging this would accomplish several things. It would put distance between the commandant and the investigation/prosecution process; it would blunt criticism that the Marines were not vigorously pursuing the cases; and it would serve as a preemptive strike. A big fear at HQMC was that the Department of Justice, which ultimately had jurisdiction over all cases related to national security, was going to step in and assert its prerogative, and the Marine Corps would lose all influence on the scope and thrust of the investigation—a politically unpalatable result.

The commandant signed off on the proposal, as did everyone in the Department of Defense chain of command up to the Secretary of the Navy, where it died. Justice wanted no part of this one, because every time it took on a case involving the CIA there were problems getting the suspects' statements into evidence. The CIA invariably used all manner of psychological ploys in their efforts to get a statement, which damaged the notion of a free and voluntary confession required by law. Justice was also candid in saying that after the lambasting it had received from the Secretary of the Navy for its handling of the John Walker case (Secretary John Lehman had been bucking for the death penalty and had accused Justice of being lenient in its treatment of Walker when it agreed to cut a plea-bargain deal without consulting him first), Justice was more than content to stand back and let the Navy go it alone this time.

The task-force concept did not die there, however. Headquarters decided the second-best idea was to go ahead on its own in a modified form. Create an "independent" Marine Corps organization that would provide the overall legal support necessary to make sure the military justice system worked properly and justice was done. And this was how the National Security Task Force (NSTF) came into being.

Selected to run the effort was a sharp deputy staff judge advocate from Camp Pendleton. Lt. Col. James Schwenk was blessed with the collegial manner required to facilitate such a complex undertaking, and in mid-April he, along with ten experienced Marine trial lawyers and five enlisted Marines from various parts of the country, moved into an abandoned floor of a building at Quantico that was scheduled for renovation and turned their attention to the business at hand. This involved setting up prosecutorial trial teams, making certain they had their cases totally prepared to go to court, orchestrating court-martials, clarifying legal gray areas as they arose, coordinating exchanges of information with various agencies, and arbitrating jurisdictional disputes.

Once the National Security Task Force was in place and functioning, General P. X. Kelly's advisors felt the time was right for the commandant to go public. His first press conference was held at noon on Friday, April 17, and it began well enough. Reading from a prepared statement, Kelly explained that he had made a conscious decision not to participate in media interviews "which could in any way jeopardize the ongoing investigation and subsequent judicial proceedings," and he thanked the press for its patience. Sounding a note of caution—"I cannot answer specific questions about the ongoing investigation . . . for obvious reasons"—he then launched into an exhaustive defense of "the patriotism, the courage, the selfless devotion to God and country, and honor of over four million Americans who have called themselves Marines," as a prelude to attacking those who would judge the institution by the sins of a few Marines in Moscow. After all, these were the first Marine prosecutions for treason in the Corps's 212-year history.

The media wasn't buying it, and the questions fired by reporters clearly annoyed the commandant.

"General Kelly, can you comment on reports that there has been interagency fighting . . . ?"

"Sir, how do you know that right now, what went wrong in Moscow is not happening at other diplomatic posts around the . . . ?"

"If I can follow up, how do you respond to some of your critics who say that the discipline problem in the Marine Corps goes beyond the spy scandal in Moscow . . . ?"

"One final question, General. If you are angry, and the Marines are a close-knit organization as you say, then how can you be sure that you'll be able to try people who you feel have undermined the reputation of that organization in a fair way . . . ?"

The commandant was aware that the media were normally liberal in their approach, skeptical of the military, and always looking for "the scoop." But by the end of the press conference he had come to believe even more than that might be going on.

Just what, he revealed in his next speech, delivered to the Commonwealth Club in San Francisco. The Soviets were attempting to use this case to degrade and humiliate the Marine Corps, he asserted; and going a step further, he accused the media of pernicious complicity.

"The press focus has not been on the alleged acts of individuals, but on the Marine Corps as an institution," he declared angrily, "and I have one agonizing question. Why?"

The explanation, he went on to suggest, could perhaps be found in a novel called *The Spike,* which implied that leftist elements controlled the media. "The KGB works around the clock," he said. "If they can seduce and exploit a Marine officer, there can be few in this country who cannot be exploited."

General Kelly's attempt to compare what had happened to Marines in Moscow with critical coverage of the Corps by journalists was roundly laughed off. If anything, it goaded the press. In the weeks that followed, the Marines, in particular Marine guards, continued to take media shots on the chin from both the left and the right.

The official Soviet news agency Tass, referring to MSGs in Moscow as "drunken Yankee brawlers," accused them of driving drunk in Red Square, harassing Muscovites on the street, tearing down Soviet flags, scuffling in bars, and luring women into the embassy compound for wild nights of liquor, drugs, and pornographic films. Editorialized *The National Review,* "With their red-striped trousers and white hats and gloves, they are an aesthetic treat when you see them in a foreign capital, and not least because they are a throwback to another era, rather like the red-coated guards outside Buckingham Palace, with their black fur hats. But let's be serious. This is the Twentieth Century. The Moscow Embassy should have been guarded by mature, professional counterintelligence squads, not by a couple of skirt-chasing enlisted men with room-temperature IQs."

There was even talk of disbanding the MSG battalion and replacing Marines with a civilian security force made up of retired military personnel; a CI-trained rent-a-cop service that would not be inclined to conduct foreign policy independently and in the nude.

While some of the critics were unduly harsh, even reasonable voices acknowledged that the job was self-contradictory. That the Marine Corps was a war-fighting organization whose primary purpose was to prepare for and conduct successful combat operations, and taking young, robust, adventurous, single men and assigning them to what was often excruciatingly boring duty in countries where they were forbidden either to fraternize or fight with the enemy made them vulnerable to those facets of intelligence operations that involved the manipulation and exploitation of human weaknesses.

Such talk was blasphemy at HQMC, where the Marine security guard program was considered a sacred cow. To be able to say the State Department chose Marines over all the other armed services to protect its embassies overseas was not only a source of prestige for the smallest service, it was good recruiting material. Marine Corps propaganda loved to emphasize the fact that its troops stood between American ambassadors and their enemies. That even when Marines were not storming beaches, MSGs were in combat in the sense that their presence at embassies was an active deterrent to terrorism.

But there could be no denying that something in the system had gone wrong. Troubling questions about how Sergeant Lonetree had gotten away with behavior that should have flagged him as a problem child continued to haunt the Corps. An examination of his military record book showed that he should never have been admitted to MSG school in the first place, should never have gotten through it, and certainly should not been sent to the most sensitive U.S. outpost in the world, where he'd been allowed to extend his tour of duty. Details from his career suggested that many of the traditional warning signs of a security risk were ignored in his case, and that Clayton Lonetree was as full of character flaws and vulnerabilities as a man could be. "We did everything we could to set him and ourselves up for what we got," concluded an internal report.

And then, just when it seemed things could not get any more confusing for the Marine Corps, the knot began to slip on Arnold Bracy.

From the moment he had terminated with the NIS polygraphers and asked for a lawyer, through his arrest at Twentynine Palms and transportation to the brig at Quantico, where formal charges capable of carrying the death penalty were preferred, Cpl. Arnold Bracy had continued to disavow everything he had said and signed. Even when confronted with the information that two other Marine guards who had served with him in Moscow, Cpl. Robert Williams and Sgt. Vincent Downes, had signed sworn statements implicating him in admissions of espionage, he denied his guilt. He claimed his statements were concoctions of speculative scenarios that NIS agents had asked him to advance, not admissions of things that had actually happened.

His retraction was not taken seriously, however, because even though some people under duress admitted to things that later turned out to be true, Bracy had not been locked in a room and grilled day and night; and contradicting his version of events was the testimony of two respected NIS polygraphers.

But when William Kunstler heard what Bracy was saying, having already decided on a strategy of attacking the credibility of the Naval Investigative Service, and recognizing that Bracy's accusations of NIS misconduct paralleled Lonetree's tell-me-a-lie experience, he seized on the situation, pointing to a pattern of coercive techniques and deception used in interviews and polygraphs, and launching a ferocious campaign of NIS vilification. Lonetree was "the scapegoat of a botched-up investigation," he thundered, predicting the case against his client was destined to fall apart because it was "unprovable."

Of course, it would only stay unprovable as long as Bracy steadfastly denied conspiring with Sergeant Lonetree, and out of concern that the young military attorney assigned to defend Bracy, Capt. Brendan Lynch, would cave under pressure and convince Bracy to take a deal and testify against Lonetree, Kunstler made a series of phone calls. One was to Benjamin Hooks, executive director of the NAACP, a personal friend from previous civil-rights cases; the other was to Arnold Bracy's parents. The picture he put out was that a black man was in danger of being sold down the river, and the upshot was that the NAACP decided there was a racial injustice in the making and it would get involved.

As it turned out, Kunstler was right in at least one respect: A deal was being offered to Bracy's military attorney. But being just a captain, Lynch felt he was in over his head, and instead of accepting or rejecting it, he put in a request for help from a higher-ranking judge advocate. This was how Lt. Col. Michael Powell, SJA at the 4th Marine Division, headquartered in New Orleans, came to be detailed to the case.

Powell had eight years as a prosecutor and two on the defense side. He was a top-flight trial attorney. He was also a maverick, more interested in enjoying his career in the military than he was concerned about rank. Brash, he had an exceedingly high opinion of his own judgment. As he explained in an interview with a reporter, "What happens is I am frequently in a position where I tell people in advance what's happening, but they don't believe me. Then it turns out I'm right and they get pissed off at my I-told-you-so grin."

Before he ever met Arnold Bracy, when he'd first heard about the case, Powell smelled a rat. He found it hard to believe that the KGB would trust Marines enough to risk sending an agent into the secure areas of the American Embassy. What were they going to do if he got trapped in there? Send in a rescue team? The potential for international embarrassment was too great, he thought.

After he had received copies of Bracy's three statements and read them, the odor in the air was even stronger. There were things in there that looked strange, shoddy, rushed. Specifically, there were misspellings and words crossed out. Normally when that was done, the suspect initialed the changes, but here the agent's initials were penned in. That was not necessarily an incriminating point, but it raised the question why Bracy's initials weren't there.

In the second statement, where Bracy allegedly said he slept with the Russian girl, it appeared to him that there were racial overtones to their interrogation. The agents seemed to be more interested in the fact that a black man slept with a white girl than anything else.

The third statement dealt with the espionage charges, and reading it Powell found himself thinking, Marine security guards don't have that kind of access. Not only that, there was something troublesome about Bracy's signature. Only when he stacked the pages together and held them up to the light did Powell realize what it was that bothered him. They lined up almost perfectly. Yes, Bracy had signed the bottom of each page, but the placement of his signature suggested to him that rather than reading each page and signing, the agents had been afraid he wouldn't sign them if he read what was written, so they had peeled the bottom corner back and told him to sign there.

Powell drove up from New Orleans, arriving late in the day. The minute he walked in the door of Lejeune Hall to report in, before he'd had a chance to meet with either Captain Lynch or Arnold Bracy, he was approached by Maj. Frank Short, coprosecutor on the Lonetree case. "We'd like to negotiate with Bracy. Nobody has a hard-on for him. The guy we want is Lonetree."

"Whoa," Powell said. "I haven't even met my client yet. I can't agree to anything. I won't close the door on the offer if it will help him, but give me a chance to talk with him first."

After visiting Arnold Bracy in the brig at Quantico and talking with him for hours, after learning more about his family background, and after hearing Bracy's version of what happened in the motel rooms at Twentynine Palms, Lieutenant Colonel Powell felt the case against his client was going nowhere.

Arnold Bracy had grown up in Queens, New York, but he was no street-smart kid from the projects who'd joined the Marines as an alternative to jail. He was a bright, articulate young man, college material, who had opted for the Corps because he didn't want to impose a financial burden on his parents. Until this, he had compiled an impeccable record.

As for his character, Powell would never forget the day he and Bracy had been talking in the secure facility for several hours, and they took a break. In the hall outside, there was a candy machine, and while Bracy bought a candy bar, Powell lit a cigar. As he was standing there puffing and swearing about something, he looked over and saw that after Bracy took the wrapper off he paused, closed his eyes, and murmured to himself. When he was done and had taken a bite, Powell asked him, "Corporal Bracy, what were you just saying to yourself?"

"I was saying the Lord's grace," Bracy replied.

Arnold Bracy, it turned out, had all but grown up in the Calvary Full Gospel Pentecostal Church, where his parents were Sunday school teachers, and his religious orientation prohibited him from drinking, smoking, swearing, or engaging in premarital sex.

When Lieutenant Colonel Powell asked his client to tell him the truth of what had happened in Moscow, Bracy's account admitted to a petty infraction and a mistake in judgment, but no more. He said he had been friendly with the female Russian cook at the embassy. He acknowledged that she had approached him and told him she was being pressured to seduce him. He even allowed that foolishly he had gone to the diplomat's home, where the cook worked as a maid, to see her and had not reported the contact. But he vehemently denied sexual intimacy was part of their relationship, and as for his alleged espionage admissions to the NIS agents, he said they were a mix of half truths, fabrications, and lies that he had been coerced into signing.

Powell believed his client. And over the following weeks nothing happened that would change his mind. To the contrary, the defense would benefit from independent investigative efforts by the Naval Investigative Service to assess the truthfulness of key parts of Bracy's allegations, because agents would determine that in every significant detail it was factually impossible. There were doors and devices, which Bracy never mentioned, that would prevent a Marine from entering the communications center. There were alarms that the Marines were unaware of that would have registered intrusions if Bracy and Lonetree had allowed Soviets to wander about inside the embassy; these alarms had not sounded. The logs were checked, and the guard duty assignments as recorded did not allow for the nighttime collaborations described in Bracy's confession.

But the most significant development was that Cpl. Robert Williams and Sergeant Downes, the two Marines who had given NIS agents statements implicating Bracy in espionage, had also executed retractions. Both men complained of unethical interrogation techniques. They said their words had been twisted and events changed. They said they had been harassed and browbeaten. They said they had signed their statements reluctantly, because they were tired of arguing and were told their careers in the Marine Corps, indeed their lives from this point on, would be ruined if they did not. In other words, tactics similar to the ones Bracy said were used on him had been used on them.

The next time Powell was approached, he didn't even make an effort to be cordial, because now he was absolutely convinced of his client's innocence.

"Look, Mike, we'll give you a deal. He gets a twelve-year sentence, does four."

"You don't understand. Bracy will walk."

"What have you been smoking?"

"This case is a loser. You heard it here first."

"This is your last chance. Go with us and we'll pin it all on Lonetree."

"You're still not listening. There was no penetration because of Bracy."

The Marines had to go ahead with an Article 32 hearing. There was probable cause, and you didn't just walk away from a confession. You aired it out.

Joining the defense team for the proceedings were two high-powered civil-rights attorneys supplied by the NAACP: Charles Carter, assistant general counsel for the NAACP; and a private attorney out of New York, George Hairston. Both men were commanding and formidable personalities, and the very presence of two distinguished black men on the defense side of the aisle sent a loud and clear message that they considered race to be a component of this case.

Character witnesses were brought in. On the stand, Williams and Downes testified that their original statements had been doctored. Then the NIS agents who took the statements from Bracy were grilled. The points the defense hammered home were that a DI on a polygraph did not necessarily mean the subject was lying; it could just as easily mean the question needed to be reworded for more clarity. A false positive could also be the result of hostility in the interrogation, which was why polygraph operators should be neutral. But Agents Jim Pender and Patrick Hurt had not been neutral, argued Bracy's defense attorneys. At an early point in their interviews they had become interrogators, and to administer polygraph tests repeatedly under hostile conditions was unprofessional and unethical, and the incriminating results should therefore be disregarded.

Polygraphers rarely came off well under tough cross-examination by informed inquisitors, and Pender and Hurt did nothing to help their cause. They answered Powell's questions as if they expected him not to believe them.

As the Article 32 began to lean toward the defense, the prosecution found itself in a quandary, which Maj. Dave Beck brought to a head at a meeting with the lawyers assigned to the National

Security Task Force. Asked about the Lonetree case, he said it was good and solid. Asked about the Bracy case, he said, "We have a confession and it's alarming. But as for corroboration . . ." and he reached into his right-hand pocket and pulled it out and there was nothing but the inside of his pants pocket. Then he pulled out his left one the same way and there was nothing there, either. "That's it," he said. "There's not a single piece of independent, corroborating evidence. We've got no case."

Everyone in the room was flabbergasted. The only known basis for the belief that Soviet agents were permitted into the American Embassy was the testimony provided under interrogation by Bracy.

No one involved in the investigation—in the NIS or in the Marine Corps legal command—was entirely comfortable with Arnold Bracy. There had been inconsistencies and contradictions in the various stories he'd told investigators. He denied sex was part of his relationship with Galya, yet the people who caught him with her said different. Bracy maintained he and Lonetree weren't buddies, but the logbooks showed they signed out together on seven occasions during the last month Lonetree was in Moscow. Before Cpl. Robert Williams complained that NIS agents had browbeat a false statement out of him about Bracy's espionage admissions, Major Beck had interviewed Williams in a Virginia hotel room, and there had been no NIS agents present when Williams recounted those admissions to the major. And if Bracy had nothing to hide, investigators just couldn't fathom why, when the interrogation heated up, he wouldn't have just said, Screw you guys. I want to see an attorney. Why would he end it by saying, Okay, I was a spy for the KGB, Lonetree and I did it? It didn't make sense. There were strange and troubling aspects to the Bracy case that remained unresolved, but without corroboration, without logical investigative leads, there was really no choice but to call it quits.

By now Lieutenant Colonel Powell had become so personally involved in this case that he was an advocate for Arnold Bracy. He was ebullient when he heard that the Marine Corps intended to drop its charges against his client, but that wasn't good enough. Powell knew from conversations with Bracy's parents that they wanted the people in their neighborhood, their community, to know their son was not guilty as charged. It was important to them that their son's name also be cleared. So Powell, along with the two attorneys from the NAACP, decided they would orchestrate a press conference. Powell got on the phone and called reporters, giving them the time and place, as well as tips on how to get past the MPs at the gate who might try to screen them out. He guaranteed them it would be worth their while coming.

The four attorneys—Carter, Hairston, Lynch, and Powell—agreed beforehand that there should be no laughing or smiling. Their demeanor would be serious—even grim—and they would not sugarcoat any answers to questions.

At noon on June 12, 1987, Arnold Bracy, his two military lawyers, and his two civilian counsels filed into a room in a building at Quantico that was packed with journalists and cameramen. Reading from a statement, Charles Carter explained his interest in this case—"For some seventy-eight years the NAACP has been fighting for justice for black people"—before taking the media itself to task. "Caught up in a hysteria of what they saw as a juicy sex scandal, it has in effect already tried and convicted this young man. In the minds of millions of people he is a treacherous Marine who was taken in by the Russians and betrayed his country. . . ."

It was left to Lieutenant Colonel Powell to affix the blame for what he perceived to be a travesty. "Corporal Bracy is innocent not because of any technicality or lack of evidence. He is innocent because the things the NIS said he did didn't occur. They did not happen. They were fantasies in the minds of Mr. Hurt and Mr. Pender. Fantasy."

Nor did Powell stop there in his castigation of the NIS. He proceeded to challenge their investigative techniques, calling them "shabby and unethical." He issued a call for the FBI to look into their methods of operation. He even went so far as to maintain that the Naval Investigative Service was responsible for "a worldwide wild-goose chase looking for spies in the Marine

RODNEY BARKER

Corps who helped Russians come into the American Embassy, which is not true."

Later in his career Lt. Col. Michael Powell would teach a course to defense counsels in how to deal with the press. He would always remind them, "You never know when the camera is focused on you, so you must always be careful how you behave." And to illustrate the point he would show them a videotape of his biggest boner.

After the press conference, he and Arnold Bracy had exited the building at Quantico together. "Corporal Bracy," Powell observed, falling into step beside his client, "this is the first time I've seen you outside the brig without handcuffs and manacles on."

"Yes sir," Bracy had replied. "And it feels really great."

Regetting profoundly the grief the young man had gone through, Powell had smiled and patted him reassuringly on the back.

It never occurred to him that at that very instant a telephoto lens was trained on them, until he saw the clip on the evening news. And the same footage would be repeatedly shown, night after night, for weeks to come: Arnold Bracy, appearing to be slapped on the back by his gloating attorney, the two of them looking to all the world as though they were beating feet to the nearest pub to celebrate.

168

12

Shortly after eight on the morning of July 22, 1987, Sgt. Clayton Lonetree stepped out of the white panel van that had brought him from the brig to Lejeune Hall. He was dressed in a khaki uniform and a fore-and-aft cap, and wore handcuffs linked to a waist chain. Staring straight ahead and appearing not to notice the battery of television cameras trained on him, Lonetree was marched by five MPs, two of them holding his arms, down the sidewalk and up eight steps, disappearing into the two-story red-brick building where his fate was to be determined.

The stringent personal security surrounding Lonetree extended basewide. Armed military police patrolled the walkways around Lejeune Hall, stopping and questioning unescorted visitors. Entry into the administration building was through a metal detector tuned so finely it pinged on belt buckles and shrapnel in a leg. Even military personnel had to present special ID to get inside. The precise threat was never officially declared—some said it was to protect Lonetree from a misguided patriot who might attempt a Jack Ruby–type assassination. There was even talk of an Entebbe-like KGB rescue operation—but when the press was informed that it would be barred from attending the courtroom proceedings, reporters knew immediately what was going on. Even though Public Affairs explained it was because of limited seating capacity (twenty), and that to accommodate the press a media center had been set up a few hundred meters away in a building equipped with a closed-circuit TV system, desks, phones, heads, candy machines, and convenient parking, in the wake of the commandant's criticism of the media for their excesses there was open skepticism and grumblings that this was payback time.

Immediate members of Lonetree's family were permitted to witness the court proceedings, however, and declaring an uneasy truce, Lonetree's parents put aside their differences and presented a united front on behalf of their son. Joining Sally Tsosie was Clayton's aunt from Flagstaff, Arizona, Mae Washington, who carried a single eagle feather in her hand, and his maternal grandmother, Alice Benally, from Big Mountain, who wore a traditional black velvet dress and turquoise-and-silver jewelry.

Spencer was the sole representative of the Lonetree side of the family, but enlarging the Indian presence were two groups of Native Americans who showed up at the invitation of William Kunstler. On the parade grounds outside the courtroom, in nearly hundred-degree heat, Floyd "Red Crow" Westerman of South Dakota pounded a drum and chanted a traditional Sioux spiritual song before a dozen or so sweating believers, while beneath the Iwo Jima memorial at the entrance to the base, Vernon Bellecourt, a Chippewa activist associated with AIM, led a rally attended by almost twenty Indians from different tribes.

"The second man in that statue who is raising the flag was a man named Ira Hayes, who died in six inches of water," Bellecourt told reporters who decided to cover one of the sideshows, since the main event was being televised. "Clayton Lonetree and Ira Hayes represent the reality of Native American Indians who fight for their country and then are taken advantage of while their lands are stolen. If this trial lasts two months, there will be hundreds of us at the gates."

By nine o'clock all the trial principals were assembled in the courtroom. At a long table on the right-hand side of the room, Lonetree sat stiffly between his military and civilian defense attorneys. On the other side of the room were the government attorneys, Maj. Dave Beck and Maj. Frank Short. Facing them all on a dais one step up were two rows of chairs that would seat court members (the military jury) when they were chosen. And perched in an elevated box, rather like a pulpit, was the presiding military judge, Navy Capt. Philip Roberts.

To no one's surprise, upon the completion of the Article 32 hearing, the convening authority at Quantico, Lt. Gen. Frank Peterson, Jr., had ruled that there was sufficient evidence to proceed with a court-martial. The Marine Corps had dropped its most dramatic charges, dismissing as inadmissible hearsay those based on Arnold Bracy's statement that Lonetree had allowed Soviet agents access to sensitive areas of the embassy, so in effect the case had reverted back to the original charges filed against Lonetree after his arrest in December. Peterson had also ordered that Lonetree's prosecution be on a noncapital basis, meaning the death penalty would not be sought. If convicted on all counts, he was facing confinement for life.

In a military setting, defense counsel was allowed to ask for a motion of voir dire against the judge, and although Major Henderson saw no advantage unless they had knowledge of specific grounds for dismissal, which they did not, Mike Stuhff and William Kunstler wanted to establish an assertive tone at the start. After introducing themselves, they opened up with a series of questions that were intended to scrutinize Judge Roberts's impartiality. They asked Roberts if he had been assigned to this case because of his reputation as a "heavy sentencer" and if he had any "preconceptions about Native Americans" because he grew up in Sioux Falls, South Dakota, a state with a large Indian population.

No judge was going to flunk questions like that, and Roberts fielded them easily. He said to the best of his knowledge he had been assigned this case because of his previous experience with national security cases, and he could only vaguely recall having known any Indians and had formed no lasting friendships with them. Although Roberts appeared unperturbed, and even slightly amused by the line of questioning, by the time it was over, while civilian counsel could claim they had successfully insinuated into the courtroom their belief that prejudice against Indians was a subtext to this trial, Major Henderson felt the only thing that had been accomplished was that when the defense needed a close-call answer to a question, they were going to be asking someone whose judicial integrity had been challenged.

Next on the morning agenda, Lonetree was given his choice of a court consisting of Marine officers (including enlisted members if he specifically requested them), or judge alone. In this area Major Henderson's opinion prevailed. In prior discussions with civilian counsel, he had strongly recommended they opt for just officers. His reasoning was based on what he had seen in previous courts-martial. When enlisteds were selected to sit on a court, they tended to be tough people—master sergeants and gunnery sergeants—who were especially hard on other enlisteds, particularly those who had had an opportunity to go on elite duty and screwed up. No one in the Marines was going to be particularly sympathetic to Lonetree, but with officers at least you could play the leadership card: *Had this young Marine been given the proper supervision—had you been his leader—this would not have happened.*

After requesting trial by officers and not enlisteds, Lonetree was asked, "How do you plead?"

Speaking softly, he replied, "Not guilty."

Then Judge Roberts went "in camera"—a legal term meaning the courtroom was emptied of all persons without security clearances and the plug was pulled on the closed-circuit cameras, because classified matters were about to be discussed.

While the reporters in the press room were cursing and throwing crumpled candy wrappers at the snow pattern on the TV monitor, under discussion was a motion advanced by the defense that "closed sessions," such as the one that was occurring at that very moment, should not be allowed. They wanted Sgt. Clayton Lonetree to be tried in "an open and public court." Citing both the First and Sixth Amendments, and referring to what he described as the "evil release of information by high government officials about Sergeant Lonetree," William Kunstler argued that considering the amount of negative pretrial publicity generated by government spokespeople, to close the trial now would be unfair. It would aid the prosecution by giving "the aura, I think sort of deliberately, that we are involved in big secrets here, instead of what is truthfully a relatively simple case of a mountain being created out of a mole hill."

Kunstler had yet to sit down when Major Beck stood up. "Can the government respond, Your Honor?"

"All right," Roberts replied.

Given William Kunstler's public statements denigrating military attorneys as essentially toy soldiers wound up to follow the orders of their superiors, those in the courtroom who were aware of Major Beck's reputation as a dynamic litigator observed the subsequent exchange with anticipation and curiosity. And if there were ever any doubts that Major Beck would be able to handle the flamboyant Kunstler's bombast without breaking stride, they were quickly dispelled.

Projecting absolute confidence and eminent rationality, Major Beck pointed out that while the defense complained heartily about government-generated publicity, in fact "much of the pretrial publicity in this case has come from defense counsels" themselves, who have "attacked unmercifully and unwarrantedly" various government organizations, especially the Naval Investigative Service. After setting that matter straight, Beck took the position that while the government certainly recognized the accused's right to a public trial, at the same time there were valid national-security interests that needed to be acknowledged. Given the classified nature of some of the material to be discussed, and a desire by certain intelligence agencies to protect the identity of their agents who would be asked for testimony, there were going to be times when it was appropriate for the proceedings to be blacked out. The prosecution was asking for nothing more than "a satisfactory balance," Beck said, and certainly nothing less.

Judge Roberts did not have to deliberate. He recognized the motion as a bid on the part of William Kunstler to switch the venue of the trial to a public channel that would allow him to play to the media as he performed before the members. Roberts also knew that the law was fairly clear on this matter. While trials were not to be closed, certain selected portions were allowed to be if justification was demonstrated. Noting for the record that going to a closed session did not mean the accused, his counsel, and the members would not get the benefit of hearing all the information that was presented, he denied the defense motion for an open court, but he did approve its request for a luncheon recess before proceeding to the next motion.

Hungry for news, reporters scrambled for a noon feeding. And on the lawn in front of Lejeune Hall they were treated to a feast. To the beat of a large wooden drum, Red Crow lifted a ceremonial pipe skyward and summoned spirits from the four corners of the universe "to have pity on all of us—red man, white man, black man, the court, and America." Clutching her eagle feather, Lonetree's aunt explained that it was a sacred symbol of peace that protected Indian people.

Next Spencer Lonetree stepped up to the microphone. For all his public posturing as a concerned parent trying to rescue a son who had been wronged, Spencer remained a controversial figure. His announcement that he intended to write a book about the case and news that he had already signed a movie deal strengthened the impression that he was using Clayton's plight as a vehicle to further his own ambitions; and the rambling, self-referential speech he delivered did little to change the way he was viewed. He said he knew his son was innocent because he'd raised Clayton "to excel," and he proceeded to describe how this ordeal had cost him "countless hours of sleeplessness, the loss of appetite, the agony and anguish of uncertainty. . . . Many times I have asked the Earthmaker: Why me? Of all the millions of parents in the world, why was I chosen to partake of this bitter cup?"

Then William Kunstler, his wild hair freaking in the Virginia humidity, apologized to reporters for not finding a way to include them but assured them that he had done his best. He said he had made an "impassioned plea" for the trial to be open so that the American people could see that the charges were unfounded, only to be overruled by the judge. And he reiterated his denunciation of the entire proceedings.

It was not the kind of scene you would expect to see played out at a military court-martial on a Marine base. But it soon became recognized for what it was: part of an orchestrated attempt to elevate the court-martial of Clayton Lonetree to a higher public stage.

The tactic of using an individual case to capture public attention, and then refocus the issues to a broader governmental or societal issue, had been used before with great success by the venerable civil-rights attorney. He had used it effectively in the trial of the Chicago Eight, portraying the radicals involved in the riots at the Chicago Democratic Convention in 1968 as responsible citizens who were exercising their right to civil disobedience in order to effect important governmental change. He had used it at the trial of militant members of the American Indian Movement who were involved in the shootout with the FBI at the Pine Ridge Reservation in South Dakota, turning the court into a forum to dramatize the grievances of Indians in America. And he was trying to do something of the same in this case—by presenting Sgt. Clayton Lonetree as a human sacrifice offered up by the U.S. government to camouflage "the criminal negligence of the State Department, the intemperate prejudgment of the Pentagon, the lies of the CIA, and the brutal excesses of the Naval Investigative Service." In Kunstler's estimation, Lonetree not only did little if any damage to the United States, he ought to be given a medal for bringing to light matters such as the flawed security conditions at the U.S. Embassy and the identities of two KGB agents.

Of course, expressing these opinions to reporters on the lawn outside Lejeune Hall was a lot easier than establishing them in a military court-martial.

Over the next several weeks, long, detailed written motions were submitted, dramatic oral arguments were presented, and in some instances evidentiary hearings were held that summoned witnesses from around the world, as the defense mounted an aggressive pretrial attempt to implement this broad-brush strategy.

One of the strongest motions argued was whether or not there had been improper command influence in the case. In support of its contention, the defense cited public statements by the Secretary of Defense, produced press releases by military officials, and held up newspaper clippings containing comments by assorted high-ranking individuals in the government, all of which indicated that in their minds Sergeant Lonetree was guilty as charged, and his offenses had done serious damage to the security of his country. Since these men were Lonetree's superiors in the military chain of command, the defense maintained that this couldn't help but "cause a chilling effect on anyone involved" in the court-martial; "jaundice the ability of the convening authority, military judge, and members as to their responsibilities in the case"; and "preclude Sergeant Lonetree from his constitutional right to a fair trial."

Judge Roberts was aware that unlawful command influence was probably the biggest single threat to the fairness of the military justice system. Indeed, every military court was subject to the same suggestion: Since everybody involved is on the same payroll, how can you ever get a totally impartial jury? But he would deny this motion, and his reasoning was that unless the entire court-martial proceeding was abolished, he didn't think you could ever get rid of the specter that a panel of officers may be influenced by the pressure of command influence. But in this case no one was overtly saying to them, Vote this way. There was enough uncertainty and variety in the press to cast doubts on the accuracy of some of the statements that had been made. And the individuals saying these things were so far removed from the people who would be making the decisions, he didn't think it would influence them to the extent that they could not hear the case fairly or impartially. He also knew that defense counsel would get the chance through voir dire to question the members about whether or not they felt they could do their job honestly. Although he could only speculate on what operated at the subconscious level, he certainly did not see this motion as grounds for dismissal.

The crucial motion for the defense concerned the damning statements Lonetree had made in his confession. If the confession was allowed, chances were good he was going down; if the confession was thrown out, he was home free; and they thought there were legitimate grounds for suppression. Under Article 31 of the Uniform Code of Military Justice, which was the military's version of a Miranda warning, as soon as someone with military status was believed to have committed an offense, prior to any interrogation by a person of authority and before any attempt to elicit incriminating responses, he had to be informed of his rights. But this was not what the CIA had done when Lonetree had come forward in Vienna. Little John had told Lonetree that his disclosures were "confidential" and it would not harm him to be forthcoming and truthful. Lonetree was even led to believe that the CIA would consider using him as a counterintelligence agent if he continued to cooperate. And meanwhile the CIA was sharing the substance and details of Lonetree's disclosures with other agencies, including the Naval Investigative Service, knowing that they would stack up for future use in a criminal investigation and eventual prosecution.

The second part of the motion to suppress challenged the impartiality and credibility of the investigation conducted by the Naval Investigative Service. The defense attacked Lonetree's statement to NIS agents on the grounds that it was not a verbatim transcript but had been constructed and selectively edited so as to get Lonetree to admit to offenses he did not commit, as proved by agent Tom Brannon's instruction to "Tell me a lie." And as further proof of NIS's malice, the defense wanted to introduce into evidence the allegations made by other Marines that NIS agents had tried to intimidate them into supplying false statements that would implicate Lonetree in an espionage conspiracy, with Arnold Bracy as the star witness.

Of course, the prosecution disagreed. While acknowledging that the CIA may have behaved in a manner that could be thought of by some as unethical, Major Beck pointed out that the CIA was not legally obligated to inform Lonetree of his rights, because it was a counterintelligence agency, not a police force. Furthermore, testimony taken from the CIA agents who had dealt with Lonetree showed that while they encouraged him to keep talking, they did not deceive him with false promises. Indeed, the NIS had gone to some lengths to make sure he was given the opportunity to sign the appropriate warnings and waivers when he came into its custody as a precaution against these very accusations.

Concerning the malicious attacks on the NIS, Major Beck declared, "Mr. Kunstler has made a lot of broad statements and a lot of broad accusations in this case, most of which are not only inaccurate, they're wrong."

Before he would make a ruling, Judge Roberts felt the importance of this motion and wide differences of opinion necessitated testimony. Both Big John and Little John of the CIA, as well as the NIS agents who had picked up Lonetree in Vienna and interrogated him in London, were brought in, and the scenes they described made a sound case for voluntariness on the part of Sergeant Lonetree. Little John even testified, "The only trouble I had was writing fast enough to keep up with him."

For the defense, none of this testimony mattered. They knew that cold cross-examination of CIA and NIS agents was only going to produce a recitation of their previously stated positions. William Kunstler was so disdainful toward the NIS agents who testified that as they answered questions he doodled on a scratch pad. At a press conference afterward, he distributed a poem he said was inspired by their testimony.

> The NIS's a very hardy bunch
>   Whose members go to any length to show
> The government's first instinctive hunch
>   Is nothing less than absolutely so.
> "Please tell us anything you want to say,"
>   They urge, "no matter that it is a lie."
> They like to question suspects night and day
>   In hotel rooms until their victims cry.
> They piously proclaim their every move
>   Is to protect the rights of everyone,
> While, in their hearts, they're only out to prove
>   That what the prosecution claims was done.
> It seems to be an awful crying shame
>   That this is how these minions play the game.

Judge Roberts would reject the defense team's argument that the confessions were improperly obtained, saying that even though at a later time Lonetree had apparently decided it had not been to his benefit to confess, from everything that had been testified to, it was apparent that Lonetree's statements were "completely voluntary" and legally obtained. The CIA had no formal obligation to inform Lonetree of his rights, and the NIS agents appeared to have obtained a statement in textbook fashion. Whether or not Lonetree should have been told to lie was debatable—the NIS defended the tactic as a technique the polygrapher used to encourage Lonetree to resume talking, not to solicit a false confession—but what was important from a legal standpoint was that as soon as the NIS determined that this part of Lonetree's confession was untrue, the charges based on what he'd said in response to the request to lie had been dropped. Furthermore, and perhaps most significant to Judge Roberts, there was no rebuttal from the accused. Lonetree admitted he had initiated these matters. He did not get up and say, Here is what they did to me and here is what was wrong with the questioning procedure.

Dealt a critical blow when Roberts ruled against the motion to suppress, civilian counsel were left with very little other than hoping that the prosecution would not be able to prove the elements of offense beyond a reasonable doubt. It was one aspect of the military justice system that could work for them: A confession had to be corroborated almost line for line.

No one knew this better than Major Beck, and all along it had concerned him, because he was not absolutely confident that the evidence collected by the NIS was sufficient corroboration. What if Lonetree suddenly claimed he made this all up? What if the defense decided to say the confession was a figment of Lonetree's imagination?

Beck felt he needed to have a witness, and the closest person to filling that bill was the CIA man in Vienna who had shown up at St. Laurentius Church in Vienna on December 27 and identified Lonetree's handler: Yuri Lysov, a.k.a. George.

Battling the Agency over this issue had just about driven Beck to resign as prosecutor. Criminal prosecutions were anathema to the CIA, because they threatened to reveal classified information or disclose covert identities. In this case, the Agency seemed to feel that what it had to learn had been fully disclosed to it, and it didn't have anything to gain by cooperating with the prosecution. When Major Beck first raised the matter of providing a witness, the Agency's response was typical of a bureaucracy that knew delay would serve it well: There was no response. Tired of watching sand fall through the hourglass, Beck asked again and received a curt no. He decided to appeal and went up the chain of command for help. This resulted in a series of negotiations with CIA attorneys, with whom he became so frustrated that at one point he said, "Look, the espionage laws that Lonetree is being prosecuted for were designed to protect not national security generically, but specifically intelligence officers operating overseas. If you people don't want your officers and their sources protected, then the heck with it. We'll just fold up our tent and go home."

A workable compromise was still a long time in coming, and the form it took was so constitutionally questionable it posed an entirely new threat to the prosecution's case.

In the vaguest of terms it was explained to Major Beck that the individual who had identified George was an important agent involved in a sensitive intelligence operation in Vienna. Beck was told that the only way this man would be allowed to testify was if acquittal was truly at stake, and then it would have to be under the condition that his identity be protected. He would enter the courtroom as a man with no name, no history; the scope of his testimony would be limited to the fact that he personally observed the appearance of an officer of the Soviet KGB at a time and place that had been identified by the accused as having been established for a clandestine meeting; he would not have to answer any questions about the planning, conduct, and techniques used in the surveillance of the meeting site; and then he would leave.

There were significant risks in calling a "hooded witness," the most obvious being the Sixth Amendment right of an accused to confront his accusers. And even though there were precedents in civilian courts with government informants, there was nothing on the military side. If he agreed to these terms, Beck knew, there was a good chance that the judge would not allow the man to testify; and an even greater possibility that even if Judge Roberts ruled in the prosecution's favor, an appellate court would rule an error had been committed and would overturn a conviction. But in Beck's view there was an even greater risk of an appellate court's looking at the record of trial and deciding each element of the offense had not been corroborated. And since there did exist a witness who from a legal perspective could provide incontrovertible corroboration, he was willing to gamble.

When the prosecution introduced the motion in the pretrial proceedings, the defense argued strenuously in opposition. The motion was flagrantly unconstitutional. The credibility of the witness was crucial to his testimony, but in order to determine that, they had to know who was testifying, what his qualifications were, and how reliable an eyewitness he was. If the judge were to allow this individual to testify unchallenged, he would be hampering the defense's ability to prepare and defend this case properly.

When Judge Roberts granted the government's motion, everyone was shocked. For Kunstler and company it revealed the military judge's pro-government bias. It convinced them a fair trial was impossible and their client was being railroaded toward a conviction. Even Major Beck was surprised. He wasn't sure that if he had been sitting on the bench, he would have ruled the same way.

Although he expressed no equivocation at the time, Judge Roberts himself wasn't absolutely convinced he had made the right decision. This was new ground in military jurisprudence. There were very few applicable precedents to guide him. Before ruling, he had done what he thought was appropriate in a case where the interests of national security weighed adversely against the rights of an accused: he had gone back to the classifying authority to determine whether they had valid concerns. And he had seen a top-secret affidavit in which the CIA maintained that the witness was involved in an ongoing operation; if his cover was blown, it would be dangerous to him personally and to other people involved, and if the flow of information he was providing was cut off, it would be detrimental to national security. Roberts, like Major Beck, was not sure his ruling would get past the appeals stage, but at the time he felt the immunities could be justified.

Not until now were Mike Stuhff and William Kunstler willing to consider a plea bargain seriously. They had lost all their legal motions. They felt nothing they said had made an impression on the judge. And all along Major Henderson had been saying to them, "Guys, we really ought to plead this case. The evidence is overwhelming. Our client is standing against a wall and there are fifteen police officers with guns pointing at him—it's time to surrender."

The meeting to discuss the terms of a pretrial agreement was held in the staff judge advocate's office at Quantico and was attended by senior Marine legal officers, the prosecution, and the defense. William Kunstler let it be known straightaway that he found this proceeding distasteful both personally and professionally. "I do not believe in plea agreements with the government, and I don't believe we should be pleading in this case," he said. "Our client has been grossly overcharged. If he is guilty of anything other than poor judgment, it is in bringing necessary attention to the weaknesses in the State Department's security system and the unclean hands of the NIS and other intelligence agencies. However, even though there are substantial issues, both legal and factual in this case, which very well could be resolved in Sergeant Lonetree's behalf if we were to continue with a trial, we would be willing to plead guilty to violating regulations regarding contact with foreign nationals and failure to report them, in exchange for dismissal of the espionage charges and a sentence limitation of two years."

It was clear to everyone in the room that William Kunstler was not just blowing smoke; he really did believe that two years was all this case was worth. What was not apparent to him, however, was that the Marine Corps viewed Lonetree's transgressions as a lot more serious than he did. In their eyes, for a Marine to co-operate and conspire with the enemy involved a betrayal of all the values—patriotism, tradition, *Semper fidelis*—that the Corps stood for, and was not just a two-year offense.

Moreover, although plea bargaining can take place at any time, its success depends on what the different parties bring to the table. Had the defense come up with an offer earlier in the process, as Major Henderson had advocated, the prosecution would have had something to gain. A deal would have saved the government time and the money it cost to bring in witnesses. At this stage the defense had nothing to trade, and the prosecution no incentive to accept.

"No prosecutor in the world can convict my client of espi-onage," Kunstler continued. "And even assuming one could, be-cause of the mitigating circumstances we can walk him in eighteen months or less. So really, the government is getting a bargain here."

At that point, Col. Patrick McHenry turned to Major Beck and asked him what he thought of the proposal.

In a show of deference that to all the room seemed genuine, Beck shrugged his shoulders. "I realize Mr. Kunstler is from the big city and has all the experience in the world and has tried some very important cases," he said. "And I have no doubt he knows a whole lot more than me. But Colonel . . ."

A beat later, displaying a dead-on instinct for timing, Beck fin-ished his thought. "I am absolutely confident the prosecution can get a conviction in this case. And any plea bargain that does not include pleading guilty to espionage, because that's what he did, with anything less than twenty to twenty-five years, should not be considered."

There was only one order of business left before the trial was to start: the voir dire process, during which both the prosecution and the defense were given an opportunity to question those se-lected for jury consideration. William Kunstler lodged a protest, saying basically that asking a jury of Marine officers to sit in judgment of a Marine accused of espionage was tantamount to trying a case of corporate malfeasance before its board of directors. But under questioning, each of the officers indicated he had no preconceptions about the defendant or the case. Every potential juror answered, "Yes, I could," when asked by Major Beck, "If at the end of the evidence on findings, you, sir, have concluded that the accused is guilty of the most serious offenses charged, and at the end of presentation of evidence on sentencing, you are convinced that the maximum punishment in this case was appropriate, would you be able to come back into the members box, look the accused in the eye, and have a sentence announced that includes confinement for life?"; and every one answered the same when asked by the defense, "If you felt there was some reasonable doubt, would you be able to come back, look government counsel in the eye, and announce a sentence of not guilty?"

13

The court-martial of Sgt. Clayton Lonetree officially began at 9:30 on the morning of August 11, 1987, and the prosecution went first.

Major Beck had given a great deal of thought to his opening statement. Most military prosecutors marched to the podium and dryly stated the list of offenses and the prosecution's intention to prove them beyond a reasonable doubt, but that wasn't good enough for Dave Beck. Not in a case that was being observed by the national media. Not when opposing him was an attorney notorious for bringing theatricality to the courtroom.

From the motions made by the defense in the pretrial stage, Beck figured the defense team was going to point the finger of blame at everyone other than their client, so at the very start he wanted to set the tone dramatically and emphatically for what he wanted the members of the court to keep in mind throughout the coming proceedings.

Pushing his chair back, he strode briskly over to the defense table, where he stopped, snapped to attention, raised his right hand, and staring Sergeant Lonetree fiercely in the eye, recited the Marine oath of enlistment.

"I, Clayton J. Lonetree, do solemnly swear that I will support and defend the Constitution of the United States, against all enemies foreign and domestic, that I will bear true faith and allegiance to the same, and that I will obey the orders of the President of the United States and the officers appointed above me, according to regulation and the Uniform Code of Military Justice, so help me God."

Some of Beck's legal friends had cautioned him against using this opening gambit. They were concerned the members of the jury would roll their eyes and think it was overly histrionic for a formal military hearing. But when Beck saw the entire defense team, including Sergeant Lonetree, leaning backward as if they'd just been blasted by a cold wind, he knew he'd made the right decision.

Swiveling on his heels to face the Marine officers in the jury box, Beck followed the script he had carefully prepared.

"The oath of enlistment is familiar to each of us, and I want you to keep it in mind throughout the course of this trial. Whatever sins of commission or omission by other organizations you may hear about, that is the oath this Marine swore to. And the evidence will show that he betrayed not only that oath, but his fellow Marines, and his country."

Major Beck was of the mind that whether the charge was espionage or robbery, for a trial counsel to be effective he had to capture the jury's interest right at the start. Then he had to keep them focused by reducing complex evidence to its simplest elements, and hold the jury's attention all the way to the end with the strategic ordering of strong and weak witnesses. Experience had also taught him that juries were no different from ordinary people in that they liked to be told a story. So when he tried a case, he did his best to organize it into a compelling narrative, which he would unfold like a storyteller.

The bulk of Beck's opening statement was devoted to previewing the evidence and highlighting the story the jury was about to hear—starting with Lonetree's clandestine love affair with Violetta, which was the formal beginning of the recruitment process of him as an agent for the KGB; moving on to his expanding involvement with Uncle Sasha as they entered a conspiratorial relationship; and ending with the passing of documents and information vital to the national defense, "with reason to believe that it would be harmful to the United States, and helpful to the Soviet Union."

Once he had hinted at the serious national-defense implications of Lonetree's betrayal, Major Beck appeared to jump track. His voice lowered and his manner became more personal, as if he were taking the jury into his confidence.

"It's only natural for you to ask at this point why a Marine, a Marine security guard with a top-secret security clearance, would commit such traitorous acts."

If the question had not yet surfaced in the minds of the members, now it was their foremost thought, and Major Beck stroked their curiosity, saying that even though the government was not required to prove a motive, he intended to present evidence that would establish clearly that Sergeant Lonetree betrayed his country for all the usual reasons—sex, money, compromise, ideology—plus one. Embittered by the U.S. government's treatment of American Indians, he sought revenge.

Wrapping it up, Major Beck predicted that by the end of testimony the members would agree with his conclusions. And "Justice and logic will demand a verdict that Sgt. Clayton J. Lonetree is guilty of conspiracy, that Sgt. Clayton J. Lonetree is guilty of espionage against the United States of America, that Sgt. Clayton J. Lonetree is guilty of all the other offenses on the charge sheets before you, in violation of the law, in violation of his oath, in violation of his duty."

When the defense lost the motion to suppress Lonetree's confession, the basic legal argument they had in the case was taken from them—or at least removed until the day it was reviewed by an appellate tribunal, where they felt it had a good chance of being reversed. But that didn't mean they were giving up. Indeed, to his client Mike Stuhff had likened the situation to a baseball game. "First base is the motions. Second base the trial. Third the Court of Military Review. And home plate the Court of Military Appeals. What you have to remember is just because the other team got a single, that doesn't mean the game is over."

In anticipation of just this setback, the defense team—primarily William Kunstler, Mike Stuhff, and their investigator, Lake Headley—had spent innumerable evenings discussing alternative theories of the "crime." It was a practice every defense team engaged in, and particularly appropriate in cases involving intelligence organizations, where, as a matter of course, one should always rethink the obvious. The range of conjectures they considered in their brainstorming sessions had strayed from the notion this whole thing was a Russian disinformation scam to distract State Department and CIA attention from someone in a much higher position who was providing the Soviets with compromising information, to the possibility that Lonetree was another Clifford Irving and this was all a hoax: He never had a relationship with Violetta, and he had concocted his confession because he realized he had no future in the Marine Corps and this would make him a celebrity and lead to a book and movie deal. The theory they settled on portrayed Clayton Lonetree as someone who had taken it upon himself to engage in freelance double-agentry.

"Things are seldom as they first appear. We all make snap judgments. But quite often there is something else beneath the surface that we don't catch at the beginning," Mike Stuhff told the members of the court in his opening statement for the defense. And after encouraging them to free their minds of any preconceptions they might have based on what they had heard or read about this case, and not to forget that so-called facts were always subject to interpretation, he introduced Sergeant Lonetree as somebody who never intended to betray his country but actually wanted to spy on the Soviets to help the United States.

The truth of this case, according to Mike Stuhff, was that Clayton Lonetree came from a family of war heroes who were held up to him as people to respect and emulate. He was somebody who felt he was in competition to be the star of the Lonetree family. And as a result he was always looking for a way to do something above and beyond the call of duty. In Moscow he found himself presented with an opportunity to give away little and score big. He thought he could match wits and outfox the KGB by giving them useless information and ensnaring a KGB general and his accomplices. All along he intended to expose the KGB's efforts and its agents to the CIA, and in that way become a hero.

"He made a mistake," civilian counsel admitted, "but he did not betray his oath."

Lonetree's error, as described by Mike Stuhff to the jury, was in having ambitions beyond his capabilities.

There was a corollary to this theory, which Stuhff introduced toward the end of his opening statement, a provocative explanation for the failure of Sergeant Lonetree's efforts. It drew on information that had come to his attention through the release of State Department cables that revealed the Soviet whom Lonetree knew as "Uncle Sasha" was in actuality a KGB officer by the name of Aleksei Yefimov, a man who as well as recruiting Lonetree had had regular contacts with an official at the U.S. Embassy in Moscow by the name of Shaun Byrnes. While those meetings were described by the State Department as "backchannel conversations" that went on all the time in the diplomatic community, to the suspicious defense counsel something a good deal more nefarious was implied. In Stuhff's mind it raised the possibility that at the same time Lonetree was conducting his private counterintelligence operation, the CIA was aware of his activities and allowed them to continue because they were useful to a larger scheme that it was running. And that was providing Uncle Sasha, who in reality was a double agent working for the CIA, with the kind of credibility and success he needed to secure and even advance his position within the KGB.

After the trial, when he was asked by a journalist if this spy-thriller scenario wasn't a bit of a stretch, Stuhff would shake his head and reply that the characterization was forthright. It complied with the facts as he knew them. He was convinced the CIA knew more than it was letting on. And even though it was admittedly "kind of a bank shot," he thought it would give the defense a fighting chance, over the course of the trial, at creating reasonable doubt in the minds of the jurors.

It didn't make any difference to Major Beck what strategy the defense decided to employ, because he had a clear and strong vision of how this case ought to be prosecuted, and he had blocked it out from opening to closing.

At the start, he wanted the jury members to know what training and instructions Sergeant Lonetree had received at Marine security guard school before he ever went to Russia. To provide them with that information he called on one of Lonetree's former instructors and a State Department official who gave courses at MSG school. He had them brief the court the same way MSGs were briefed, specifically about their responsibilities to safeguard classified information, and what to watch out for from hostile intelligence activities. By the time these witnesses left the stand, all in attendance felt a little as if they too had attended those classes.

The testimony they heard established that Marine security guards were warned they would be high-priority targets because they had access to classified material and because they controlled access to the embassies. Traditional methods of recruitment and exploitation were discussed. Specific examples were given about how women and alcohol were frequently used to compromise and recruit foreigners. A briefing specific to the Moscow post was also repeated, in which Marines were told to keep their distance from Soviet citizens working in the embassy, especially those who were overfriendly or inquisitive, because the only Soviet citizens who were allowed to commingle with foreigners in the Soviet Union were officers, agents, or co-optees of the KGB. They were told to expect that sooner or later they would be approached, and they were told to report the contact to their superior for counterintelligence purposes.

After establishing Lonetree's primary responsibilities as an embassy guard, Beck brought in Big John and Little John. They testified that when Sergeant Lonetree spoke with them in Vienna, he admitted that he had broken the rules, that he had failed to report his contacts with Soviet citizens, that he had become romantically involved with a Soviet woman, and that he had allowed his involvement to expand to include a conspiratorial relationship with a person she called her Uncle Sasha, and later Yuri Lysov, to whom, in the simplest terms, he passed information related to the national defense, all in violation of orders and ignoring training, common sense, and loyalty.

Having seen what can happen when a witness comes into

court who has not been adequately prepared and is hearing questions for the first time on cross-examination, Major Beck made a point of always interviewing his witnesses at least once before trial. In an effort to let them know what to expect, he would try to anticipate everything the other side would ask, and give them a more thorough cross-examination than they could expect to receive when they took the stand. That was why, before calling the Johns as witnesses, he had put them on the firing line. He had challenged their credibility, accusing them of all but beating Lonetree with rubber hoses to soften him up for a confession to the NIS.

"What do you mean you just meant 'confidential channels' when you told him you'd keep your conversations 'confidential'? What would you expect a twenty-three-year-old to think you meant? You knew he had an alcohol weakness—how much liquor were you giving him during these meetings?"

By the time he had gotten through with them, both Johns had been so stirred up they were ready to lunge across the table and grab him by the throat. But just when tempers were threatening to get out of hand, Beck had said, "Now, when you face Bill Kunstler, Mike Stuhff, or Dave Henderson, you'll be ready for anything they throw at you."

The defense did its best to rattle the Johns. It hit them on the promise-of-confidentiality issue. It accused them of manipulating Clayton Lonetree's passivity and malleability to keep him talking.

But both Big John and Little John fielded the cross-examination questions without an error. Lonetree had come forward spontaneously, they said. He'd been eager and willing to talk. The meetings were arranged at his convenience. He was told time and again they were in no position to promise him immunity. And when he admitted to providing information and material at the direct and repeated request of Uncle Sasha, for which he said he had received money, there was no question that he knew that what he was turning over was classified secret and confidential.

During the testimony of Big John and Little John—who later

told Major Beck that after the grilling he'd given them, the defense's cross-examination had been "a breeze"—Major Beck introduced as exhibits several important pieces of evidence that the two Johns said Lonetree had spontaneously brought to them during the ten days he was debriefed. These included photos of Violetta and letters he'd received from her in Vienna, and slips of paper on which the dates and descriptions of meet sites with Uncle Sasha were written.

After hearing from several of Lonetree's former barracks mates who testified that he often praised the Soviet system and the KGB over the United States and the CIA, that his room was so full of Soviet flags, posters, and books it looked like a shrine to Communism, and that he appeared to have such an obsession with Russians that he was jokingly called by some "Comrade Lonesky," the prosecution played its face cards. It called to the stand the NIS agents to whom Lonetree had admitted passing secrets to the KGB. And from direct examination of special agents Moyer, Sperber, and Hardgrove, Major Beck elicited the details of what happened once they took Sergeant Lonetree into custody—beginning with the issuance of rights warnings, through the interrogations in Vienna and London, to the result: two sworn statements that in Lonetree's own words described his criminal activities.

When it was the defense's turn to cross-examine the witnesses, the focus in the courtroom seesawed between two very different interpretations of Sergeant Lonetree's intentions and state of mind when he was meeting with Uncle Sasha. Mike Stuhff and William Kunstler tried to impeach the notion that what Lonetree said to the NIS agents was a pure confession of espionage, and maintained the position that in order to understand what Lonetree was admitting to, the jury should understand his actions in the light of his decision to play the role of a double agent. In support of their contention, they pointed to portions of the confession that could be read in such a way that it did appear Lonetree purposely misled Uncle Sasha and thought the KGB already had what he was giving them. They argued that NIS agents had guided the interrogation in a direction that supported their pre-conceptions and prepared a statement that omitted the mitigating statements Lonetree had made over the course of the time he was in their custody. Proof, they said, lay in comparing a 260-page transcript of the taped interrogation sessions that led to the confession, and the mere 15-page confession that the NIS agents had presented him to sign.

Major Beck knew that if his case had a weakness, it lay in the circumstances surrounding the taking of the statement, but his own reading of the unedited confession had brought him to a different conclusion about the way the NIS agents had condensed Lonetree's admission. After the defense was successful in putting before the jury the notion that it had been a document manufactured by the NIS, Major Beck put the NIS polygrapher Tom Brannon on the stand and asked him if he remembered Sergeant Lonetree's stating, "I thought of the ugliest Americans I could think of when I handed over the photographs [of American intelligence agents to Uncle Sasha]." Brannon said he did. Asked if that quote had been put into Lonetree's statement, Brannon said it had not.

It was apparent to Major Beck from Mike Stuhff's opening statement that at some point defense counsel was going to bring up the patriotism of the Navajo Code Talkers and invoke the example set by Lonetree's uncle Mitchell Red Cloud as a way of characterizing Sergeant Lonetree as a Marine who wanted to serve his country in a big way but whose plan backfired. This, in his mind, entitled him to bring on his next witness, June Dahl, Lonetree's American History teacher when he was a junior in high school.

Instinct had told Major Beck that by this time in the trial the members were probably beginning to wonder where Lonetree's behavior originated. It was something Beck himself had struggled with. When he did his own psychological analysis, extrapolating from Lonetree's admission to the NIS agents that he had been motivated in part by the American government's historical mistreatment of Indians, Beck had been willing to accept that maybe this was Lonetree's way of bringing the Native American cause to the forefront. But that was before he'd heard from June Dahl.

Mrs. Dahl, an elderly woman who had lost none of her sharpness, had read about her former student in the St. Paul papers and she had contacted the military authorities. When she was on the stand, Major Beck allowed her to tell the court the story she had told him.

In 1979 she had taught a course called "The 1920s and 1930s," and Clayton had been a class member. Periodically students were expected to turn in their notebooks, and when Clayton turned in his, she noticed a swastika drawn on the cover. Mentally she had raised her eyebrows, because they were not covering German history, but she didn't say anything; she simply returned the notebook. Until the next time the notebooks were turned in and she found the swastika had been embellished with other material she could not ignore. Incendiary slogans such as "The Holocaust is a lie," and "Jews are our misfortune," and "Hitler had the right idea" were scrawled like graffiti across the cover.

Mrs. Dahl said she had asked Clayton to stay after class, and when she tried to talk to him about the meaning of this, he had accused her of "believing all those Jew lies." The next time the notebook was turned in, it contained the names, addresses, and telephone numbers of members of the American Nazi Party. Never before or since, she said, had she seen such hatred in any of her students.

After initially protesting that what this witness had to say had nothing to do with the charges and was inflammatory, the defense tried to downplay Mrs. Dahl's concerns. This was the stuff of a teenage boy's fantasies. Clayton Lonetree did not have any idea what Nazism was about. How could he? It was a violent antiminority cult, and he was an Indian. Besides, Germany and the Soviet Union were enemies in World War II.

Major Beck thought it went deeper than that. The point that he tried to make had first been articulated for him during a conversation with the famous Soviet defector Yuri Nosenko. "You must realize, yes, the two countries fought against each other.

But the end result of Nazism and Communism is the same. The socialist state takes away all ownership of property. The fascists let you keep your property but take away all the rights that go with it. The end of both is complete control and power, and they accomplish it through repression and murder."

A light had switched on for Major Beck when he heard that. He felt that with full awareness both were repressive regimes, Lonetree had expressed a preference for the Soviet system as recently as 1986, and as far back as high school he had been infatuated with a fascist system that was equally repressive. What was the connection? Beck didn't know for sure, but by the time Mrs. Dahl left the witness stand, a nexus had been suggested: It was because they were both the mortal enemies of the United States.

When he shuffled the order of witnesses for the prosecution, Major Beck had decided that this was the right time for the jury to hear from an expert witness who was qualified to give testimony on Soviet intelligence recruiting practices. He had wanted someone without any CIA or State Department baggage, an American citizen who could express in layman's terms the modus operandi of Soviet intelligence agents. While reading the record of the espionage trial of John Walker, he had discovered that John Barron, a former naval intelligence officer and the author of several books about the KGB, had testified for the Justice Department. When he asked John Dion and John Martin about Barron, they spoke highly of him, calling him a great American, an excellent speaker, someone dedicated to the security of the United States. But they also said they were concerned about wearing out their welcome with Barron and did not wish to impose on him for a case that wasn't theirs. Beck, as persuasive as he was persistent, had characterized a meeting with Barron as essential to his education, so one had been arranged at the Justice Department.

Beck and Barron had conversed for about an hour when Martin and Dion were called from the room, and even though the major had been told that Barron was not the only expert witness on espionage matters, that others could be made available, Beck had heard enough to think that Barron would be the best.

"I sure appreciate your taking the time to talk with me today, Mr. Barron," he said with sincerity, "because your friends at Justice told me how busy you are and that I shouldn't bother you. But I knew how knowledgeable you were when it came to the KGB, and that you, of all people, know we aren't talking about an innocent love affair between a Soviet gal and an American Marine here."

When John Barron nodded, Beck continued. "It's such a shame that you aren't going to be available to testify, however, because we are talking about the first espionage trial in the history of the Marine Corps, and it would have been nice to have you part of that." Now he chuckled reflectively. "And I would have loved to have seen you match wits on the stand with William Kunstler. . . ."

John Barron eyed Major Beck for a long moment, seeming to appreciate the major's tactics at the same time he allowed them to pull on him. Finally he said, "Major, when these two get back, why don't we go out for lunch."

"What for?" Beck asked, barely restraining a smile.

At that point Martin and Dion returned to the room, just in time to hear John Barron say, "To prepare our strategy, of course."

As it unfolded under questioning by Major Beck, John Barron's testimony was riveting. He talked about the structure of the KGB, and the primary objectives of its intelligence operations, particularly as they were directed against the American Embassy in Moscow. After establishing that the KGB would consider the recruitment of a Marine security guard a major coup, Major Beck directed his questioning toward the KGB's use of sex to recruit Americans. Sexual entrapment, or the "tragic misrepresentations of affection," was a favorite ploy of the KGB, Barron said, because they found it so effective. The way it would normally proceed, a female KGB agent would use sex to initiate contact with an American, and then she would introduce the prospective recruit to a KGB officer, who would handle the case.

There was one other matter that Major Beck wanted this witness to settle.

"Mr. Barron, does the KGB pay money, in large or small

amounts, on more than one occasion, or several times, for extended periods of time, if they have received nothing of value?"

"In my experience, no. And I think there's a very logical and understandable reason for that. If we accept that they are employing money to condition and control, then they defeat their own purposes when they pay money for nothing, because they are thereby communicating to the individual that he need not do anything and he'll still get money."

Under cross-examination Mike Stuhff tried to suggest one or two hypotheticals that characterized Lonetree's involvement as an innocent mistake made by a naive young man who was love-addled and not very smart and wanted to singlehandedly bring in a Soviet spy, but John Barron dismissed them as implausible, and the entire effort succeeded only in setting up Major Beck for redirect.

"Taking the defense counsel's hypothetical, if you knew that this person, who he referred to as stupid or naive, had gone through Marine security guard school, and in that school signed documents, agreements of nondisclosure, which talked about the importance of nondisclosure and the fact that if you do disclose you're going to be violating the law, you're going to be jeopardizing national security . . . if this Marine security guard received courses of instruction at school wherein he was warned about foreign service nationals and what could happen and that he should be prepared . . . if this Marine had even read your books, Mr. Barron, wherein you outlined these very dangers . . . and yet in spite of all this, if this Marine went ahead and developed a relationship with a Soviet woman, and she introduced him to a case officer who worked for the KGB, and she brokered all of their meetings, attended those meetings, and after he left Moscow wrote letters to this Marine saying, 'Sasha is coming to see you'—this is the case officer's name—'please be nice to him, he wants us to be friends.' And then this Marine says at a later point, 'I didn't believe she was involved.' Do you think there's another possibility than stupid or naive? Is there a third possibility about this Marine saying he didn't believe that?"

"Well, I guess there is," Barron replied.

"And what is that possibility, in your opinion, Mr. Barron?"

John Barron seemed to have trouble finding his voice. He glanced at the jury, and it almost seemed as if a tear was forming. To himself Major Beck said, "Don't get too theatrical, please." But Barron came across as Mr. Sincerity when he answered, "That the Marine was being a traitor to his country."

In the recess that followed, John Dion from the Justice Department rushed up to Beck as though he wanted to slap high-fives. "You hit a home run with that redirect."

Beck shrugged. "When you're in a 300-foot ballpark and the defense moves you to the 290-foot mark and lobs a softball, you better hit a home run."

Meanwhile, a very different reaction was taking place at the defense table. Throughout most of the trial Clayton Lonetree appeared to be mentally absent. From time to time, in reaction to something that was said on the witness stand he would whisper to his defense counsel or jot a note on a yellow lined pad, disputing a statement. But it usually addressed some minor matter— the wrong color or an inverted sequence of events—and after a while he seemed to realize that he could not be an effective ally in his own behalf and almost to lose interest in the proceedings.

All that changed with John Barron's testimony. In some ways Barron had been his hero—Lonetree had read several of his books—and his testimony held Lonetree in rapt attention. As Barron described sexual seduction as a routine KGB activity, Lonetree leaned forward, as if to hear better. When Barron described KGB recruiting methods that precisely matched his own experiences, Lonetree was drop-jawed. Up until this point he had refused to accept that Violetta had seduced him for the purposes of the KGB. He had managed to hold on to the belief and even defended the hope that she had not been a witting part of his recruitment but was a victim of the KGB like himself.

But at a certain point in John Barron's testimony, when it was no longer possible for him to delude himself, Lonetree seemed to realize he had been used. Removing his wire-framed glasses, he stared up at the ceiling as though floating up there was a last brilliant, fragile image of Violetta that was suddenly shattered by the truth . . . and his head dropped to the table, and he covered his face with his arms, and he wept.

William Kunstler, who was sitting to his left, put his arm around Lonetree and offered him a glass of water, but Lonetree shook his head. "She didn't love me," he mumbled through his tears. "I thought she loved me."

It was time for the anonymous CIA witness. Identified only as John Doe even to the prosecution, in a cleared courtroom he provided the clinching piece of corroboration. He said that on December 27 he had shown up at the church in Vienna where Lonetree was scheduled to meet "George," and he remained there long enough to confirm that the Soviet agent whom Sergeant Lonetree had identified from photographs did indeed appear and seemed to be waiting for an appointment.

Although the judge had ruled during motions that this witness would not be identified and cross-examination would be restricted, Kunstler was unable to let the occasion pass without renewing his objections and at least attempting to sneak questions past the judge. He got away with inquiring about the conditions under which John Doe observed George: Was it day or night? Was the weather clear or was it raining? How close did you get to him? But he had no luck when he tried to challenge the qualifications of the witness that would allow him to make an ID based on an old photograph: Are you an expert? Have you done this before? How could you be sure it was the same person?

Corroboration aside, what most distressed Kunstler about John Doe was the impact of a deep-cover witness on the minds of the jurors. It created a cloak-and-dagger ambience. It couldn't help but lead them to think that if the government was going to this much trouble to protect this witness's identity, then Lonetree's crimes *were* extremely serious. Maybe more than they were being told. But given the constraints imposed on the defense, there was little he could do to counter the negative effect he was sure the CIA spook was having.

In rapid succession Major Beck called his final two witnesses.

In their opening statement the defense had brought up the fact that Aleksei Yefimov, a.k.a. "Uncle Sasha," had apparently for several years been an information source of a U.S. foreign service officer by the name of Shaun Byrnes. From this they had proposed a scenario in which Yefimov was in reality a double agent working for the CIA and Lonetree was a pawn used by the State Department to increase Yefimov's standing in the KGB. It sounded farfetched to Major Beck, but nevertheless he had Shaun Byrnes flown in from Moscow to testify.

Under direct examination Byrnes acknowledged meeting regularly with Yefimov, who represented himself as an official with the State Committee for Science and Technology, but said it was to discuss Soviet domestic political developments. Byrnes explained that such unofficial contacts between the two governments was an accepted way of life, and approved by the ambassador. He said he had not been aware of Yefimov's true profession, or of the fact that at the same time these meetings were taking place, in the role of "Uncle Sasha" Yefimov was recruiting Sergeant Lonetree. Only after Lonetree confessed and identified Yefimov from photos, Byrnes said, did he find out the truth, and then he was directed by Ambassador Hartman to confront Yefimov.

"What happened?" Major Beck asked.

"I asked him if he had known Sergeant Lonetree and if he had handled him. He looked me straight in the eye and told me he did not know Sergeant Lonetree, and had not ever known Sergeant Lonetree, and had not dealt with Sergeant Lonetree, and he asked me to pass that on to the ambassador and to Washington." Byrnes said he did not believe Yefimov was telling the truth, and several weeks later Ambassador Hartman instructed him to break off the contact.

The defense wasn't convinced. They thought the set of circumstances was too remarkable to be coincidental. One man's spy was another man's government-approved source? In cross-examination William Kunstler tried to illuminate this murky side of U.S. diplomatic relations with the Soviet Union, but other than eliciting the opinion that Byrnes thought Yefimov was "one of the sharpest Soviets I've ever dealt with," defense counsel was unable to make any headway with the scenario that the two were involved in covert intelligence activities.

Last in line was Gus Hathaway, chief of the counterintelligence staff of the CIA. From Hathaway's testimony Beck wanted the jury to hear why the U.S. government had intelligence officers overseas, and the contributions covert intelligence made to the national defense. He wanted him to talk about the time and money and resources, on both sides, that went into trying to identify the other's agents. He wanted Hathaway to remind the members that these were real people, most with families, and, when their cover was blown, what the consequences were—to them personally, to human intelligence assets within the Soviet Union, and to national security, which was why there were espionage laws protecting them. When Hathaway was done testifying, the prosecution rested its case.

Throughout the trial the defense team had conducted a running battle with Judge Roberts. Time and again civilian counsel had complained that by limiting the scope of their questions, especially regarding intelligence matters, the judge was handcuffing the defense. Nevertheless, the broad outline of a defense theory had emerged through Stuhff and Kunstler's cross-examination of prosecution witnesses. By the questions they asked and the objections they raised, it was clear that they were trying to establish that the accused's statements had been obtained through the use of coercion and unlawful inducement. They had tried to throw doubt on the charge that their client had sold his country's secrets by characterizing the information he passed as low level and already known by the Soviets. And they had done everything they could to impress upon the jury the idea that this was a case of a young man who was proud to be a Marine, who got caught up in a love affair, as so many men had over the centuries, but who, when he realized the situation he was in, being someone who had always wanted to be an American hero, had attempted to outwit the KGB. Which was a foolish mistake, the defense conceded, but he was no spy.

Now it was their turn to call witnesses who presumably would buttress their contentions, and expectations ran high. You needed a lot of evidence to sell a theory like that, and court observers were anxious to see how the defense intended to go about making its case. In the halls outside the courtroom people were whispering excitedly, "Now, we're going to find out what Kunstler has up his sleeve." Even Dave Beck was nervous, because in the military the defense did not have to declare its witnesses ahead of time, so he had been unable to prepare for what was coming. Having heard it alleged that Lonetree was a pawn in an intelligence scheme involving Uncle Sasha, he assumed the defense had a hole card it was going to play to back up that charge. And he certainly expected that Sergeant Lonetree would get up on the stand and present a version of his actions that supported what his defense attorneys had been saying. But for more than that he would have to wait.

When the defense submitted a list of five names that included two Marines friendly with Lonetree who would testify that he expressed pro-American sentiments in conversations with them, two expert witnesses who were going to testify about interrogation abuses and how they led to false confessions, and the former CIA employee and author Philip Agee, those books had publicly listed the names of hundreds of CIA agents, whom they expected to testify that it was easy for the Soviets to determine the identity of intelligence agents through a variety of methods, those in attendance were puzzled. Surely the defense had more than that going for them.

Rapidly it became clear they did not. When Judge Roberts denied permission to call all but the two Marine character witnesses, saying their testimony would be irrelevant to the charges against Sergeant Lonetree, Mike Stuhff made a motion for a mistrial on the grounds that the judge had "foreclosed our opportunity" to effectively present a defense before the jury. Roberts denied the motion with a rare public rebuke—"Counsel, you have with typical hyperbole expressed outrage at the rulings of the court [when] the notions of relevance you bring, quite frankly, take the breath way. . . . The court would not dream of reopening the case for the reasons stated"—and moments later the defense announced it would rest its case.

The silence in the courtroom was resounding. No one said anything, but everyone felt cheated, and the same thoughts ran through everyone's mind: *What? Wait a minute. I thought . . .*

Outside the courtroom civilian counsel explained themselves.

"We've had a rough set of rulings on what the judge considers proper and relevant to bring to this jury," Mike Stuhff told reporters. "He has very clearly restricted us from putting on a case. We think that he's way out of bounds and clearly not allowing us to tell Sergeant Lonetree's story."

William Kunstler went even further. "This judge, who is totally programmed, is determined to convict the defendant if he can. . . . He is a disgrace."

Asked why he did not let his client testify, Kunstler replied, "To ask him to make an emotional plea on behalf of himself subjects him to cross-examination. I don't think he's capable of handling that. If we put him on, I think Clayton would collapse under cross-examination."

Despite putting on no witnesses, Stuhff said they were not conceding defeat. "Even with the hanging of the ball and chain the judge put on us, I think we put on a pretty good case." When reporters asked him to elaborate, he said they scored numerous points for Lonetree during parts of the trial that were conducted behind closed doors.

Asked what verdict he expected his client to receive, Stuhff shrugged. "If indeed there is not an acquittal, the kind of record we have now is certainly the kind of record that any appellate lawyer would find many, many issues on which to base an appeal."

Closing summations were given on Friday, August 21, and Major Beck led off. "The issue in this case is quite simple," he said, "and from the evidence presented, the government contends the answer is equally clear. . . . Sgt. Clayton Lonetree violated his oath and the special trust and confidence that was placed in him, and sold out our national defense and intelligence interests to a nation which has since the early 1950s declared our country public enemy number one."

The defense, Beck said, "has come up with more theories, changed their theories more times, showing that all they have is a smoke screen, trying to hide the obvious fact of this accused's guilt. The accused was unwitting, they said at first. And then they said, Well, no, the accused was very witting, he was out on his own, he was trying to set up the KGB, he was going to haul them in. When it became obvious, the hollowness of that defense, then they said, No, no, no, Sasha was a double agent for the United States. You know, gentlemen, from the evidence presented, that all of those claims are preposterous. . . . There is no evidence before you [in support] because there's absolutely no basis in fact for such claims."

Major Beck liked to finish as strong as he started. "A message needs to be sent, a punishment needs to be made, that crimes like this will not be tolerated." After a lingering look at the defendant, he turned to the jury. "The defense would have you believe that Sgt. Clayton Lonetree is an innocent Walter Mitty type. He's not. While he wore the uniform of a United States Marine, he betrayed his country. He is a real-life Benedict Arnold."

William Kunstler delivered the closing statement for the defense, and after disputing the prosecution's claim that this was a simple case, he tried to show just how complex a case he considered it to be by going over the facts once again, only this time turning the testimony and the evidence in such a way as to present an interpretation of Lonetree's motivation that favored the defense. Lonetree was immature, Kunstler admitted. He was naive and stupid and a victim of his own fantasies. But he never intended to betray the United States. He was a scapegoat who was being tried to shield the Marine Corps from the embarrassment of a larger failure in its security guard system.

Straining for an equally powerful finish, Kunstler also looked from his client to the jury, before challenging them to be absolutely certain when they decided whether Sergeant Lonetree was guilty of espionage, because if they failed to render justice it would later haunt them. In conclusion he promised them that if they found Sergeant Lonetree guilty, "Then I tell you that some night, somewhere, sometime, you will wake up screaming."

After receiving instructions from the judge, the jury retired to deliberate. To convict Sergeant Lonetree two-thirds—six of the eight members on the panel—would have to agree on his guilt and vote for a conviction. Since it was Friday afternoon, it was expected that they would reach a decision sometime over the weekend, but three hours and forty-five minutes later they returned, and their decision was a unanimous one.

Standing ramrod straight at attention, Sergeant Lonetree listened to the verdict. Not only had all eight officers agreed on his guilt, they convicted him of every offense on the charge sheet.

Immediately after the verdict was announced, the counsels for the defense held a press conference in front of the television cameras outside the courthouse.

"As we've told you before, this judge did not let us have a fair trial," Mike Stuhff said. "We don't think this conviction will stand. We are going to appeal."

"Marine justice failed him," Kunstler told reporters. "Corps pride, Corps pressure had a lot to do with this verdict."

At that moment Lonetree appeared with his military guard escort walking toward the van that would take him back to the brig. The defense team and several supporters began to applaud. "Innocent," his mother, Sally Tsosie, shouted.

"How did Sergeant Lonetree take it?" a reporter asked.

"I put my arms around him and he was shaking," Kunstler replied, "but he took it like a Marine."

14

When Mike Stuhff announced in his opening statement that the defense intended to prove that Sergeant Lonetree had been acting as a do-it-yourself double agent, Major Henderson had been dumbfounded. They had discussed that approach to trial and he thought it had been rejected because there wasn't enough there. No supporting evidence, and Sergeant Lonetree never said he'd thought of himself as a double agent.

Henderson was not opposed in principle to throwing out red herrings as a defense strategy, particularly when you were saddled with a confession case. But if that was what civilian counsel had in mind, he felt the way they then went about presenting it was backwards. If you were going to try to sell a jury on a theory for which there were few if any facts, you didn't promise something in your opening statement you were not going to be able to prove. That was a killer. Not only did you give the prosecution a chance to bring in rebuttal witnesses, you'd also given them their closing: "Gentlemen of the jury, our opponent said he was going to produce X, and he didn't do that." What you were supposed to do was build your case through cross-examination, asking proper questions at the proper time of the proper people, laying the groundwork and getting evidence into the record so you had something legitimate to work with at closing, when you argued an interpretation of the facts that you hoped would confuse the jury enough to create reasonable doubt.

That wasn't the only problem Major Henderson had with the

defense put on by civilian counsel. Stuhff and Kunstler seemed unable to make up their minds what they wanted the jury to believe about Sgt. Clayton Lonetree. That he was someone who circumvented the rules in an effort to do something grand for his country? That he was a naive, hapless chump bamboozled by a KGB swallow? That he was a victim of CIA dirty tricks? That he was a scapegoat for the excesses and oversights of superiors? During the course of the trial they had sampled some of each explanation but had developed no one explanation in a way that would stand up to the prosecution's evidence.

The trial had been a frustrating ordeal for Major Henderson. Not only was he unaccustomed to being relegated to a backseat role, whenever he'd tried to make a contribution, he'd been slighted. Once, when he had detected an inconsistency in a witness's testimony on cross-examination, Henderson had written a note to Mike Stuhff suggesting a question he should ask, only to be given a backhanded wrist wave that said, *Leave me alone, I'm doing this my way.*

But that insult was not what brought Major Henderson to the decision that he could no longer sit idly by and grit his teeth. Nor was it the way civilian counsel continued to pursue legal issues he thought lacked promise, sniped at witnesses contemptuously, and were contentious with the judge—all of which he did think were destined to work against them. It was when he realized that civilian counsel appeared to have given up on the idea that the military justice system was capable of rendering a just and fair verdict, and to have stopped aiming their case to the jury and pointed it elsewhere. To the press, to whom they would make statements critical of military justice during recesses. And to an appellate court, where they seemed to think the errors of the current proceedings would be cured if they did not get an acquittal.

Major Henderson thought this was a major miscalculation. Whether civilian counsel liked it or not, the eight Marine officers in the jury box were going to decide the fate of their client. These were mature, educated, professional military people who took their responsibilities seriously. When the time came for them to deliberate, their desire would be to see justice done. If they felt an accused was wrongly charged and an injustice was taking place, that would mean a lot more to them than caving to the desires of a higher authority, which was what civilian counsel seemed so concerned about. To think they would do less demeaned them and insulted the process. For the jury not to follow their consciences would harm the system they were sworn to uphold.

And so to counter the negative impression civilian counsel was making before the jury, Major Henderson had made a decision to begin sending private messages their way. Ethically he was walking a fine line. As an officer of the court there were rules he had to obey and conduct that had to be observed. But there was nothing in the books to prevent him from getting up and leaving the courtroom at key times, indicating *he* did not consider a particular area of inquiry to be important. Nothing to stop him from signaling through body language his restlessness with a nit-picking cross-examination on the part of civilian counsel. And when he pulled out a pocketknife and began whittling at his fingernails, it was done to let the members know this was Bill Kunstler's show, and had little to do with him or their client.

What happened when final arguments were given had been the final straw for Major Henderson. At the start of the trial Mike Stuhff, in his role as lead counsel, had told Henderson that since he was the one most familiar with the military community, he would be giving the closing argument for the defense. Throughout the proceedings Stuhff had assured Major Henderson the closing was his, so Henderson had thought a lot about what he was going to say and how he was going to say it. Then, two days prior to closing, Mike Stuhff came up to him and said, "Dave, I'm sorry, but I'm going to let Bill do the closing."

"You're shitting me," Henderson said. "I don't believe it. He doesn't have the foggiest idea how to sell this case to a military jury. He hasn't even been here for the entire trial. How can you do this?"

Even as he asked the question, Henderson knew the answer. Throughout, Stuhff had deferred to William Kunstler. Whenever Henderson had voiced a different opinion, Stuhff had sided with

Kunstler. Stuhff seemed to assume that if it was important, then Kunstler would pick up on it.

Mike Stuhff shrugged. "He wants to do it. I've got to let him."

Henderson was livid. "What's more important? Your relationship with Bill Kunstler or your client?"

Kunstler's closing argument made Henderson cringe. At one point Kunstler deliberately brought in information that had been ruled inadmissible, so inflaming the judge that Roberts threatened to end the summation if Kunstler did it again.

In a military court-martial the jury also determined the sentence, and immediately after the guilty verdict was announced, Henderson cornered Mike Stuhff. "Okay, you guys have had your shot, and if you want my opinion, you've lost all credibility with the jury. I'm going to handle sentencing."

Stuhff seemed distracted by the defeat and agreed to let Major Henderson take over.

Lonetree had been convicted on Friday, the sentencing hearing was set for Monday, and on Saturday morning Henderson had Sgt. Clayton Lonetree brought from the brig to his office in the basement of Lejeune Hall to prepare him to testify. At this point it was a given that Lonetree was going to jail; the question was for how long.

In an attempt to minimize the time the jury decided Lonetree's crimes were worth, Henderson wanted to present his client as a remorseful figure. For several hours they ran through a gamut of questions—from the circumstances of his birth and the tragedy of growing up in a broken home, to his aspirations when he joined the Marine Corps, to his decision to come forward and confess. After they had spent several hours perfecting his answers, Henderson asked what he expected would be his final question. "Clayton, looking back at this now, after all these months, how do you feel?"

The obvious answer, the one he was expecting to hear, was, "I'm really sorry. I screwed up. I deserve to be punished for what I did."

What Lonetree said was, "I really don't think I did enough for the Russians."

Henderson frowned. What the hell did that mean? He didn't think he'd done enough to be punished severely? He wished he'd done more?

God only knew. But what that meant to Henderson was he couldn't put his client on the stand. Who knew what would come out of his mouth? He was unpredictable, uncontrollable. He'd murder himself in front of a jury.

In the military there was an option of allowing an accused to make an unsworn statement that could not be subjected to cross-examination. By necessity the range of his testimony would be restricted, but Henderson felt the risks of putting Lonetree on the stand were too great. Major Beck would carve him up. What Henderson wanted to accomplish now was simply to personalize Lonetree for the jury. The prosecution had made him out to be the worst thing to happen to this country since Benedict Arnold. Henderson wanted the members to hear his voice, get a better sense of him as a human being, and, he hoped, bring them to the same understanding that he had of Sgt. Clayton Lonetree: that he as not an Indian militant bent on taking revenge on America; he was a confused young man whose ideological inclinations, if they could be called that, were the emotional outcome of his personality, and the government had mixed up personal disorientation with principled betrayal.

When the sentencing hearing was called to order the following Monday, Major Henderson put on two witnesses. The first person he called to the stand was Lt. Comdr. Forrest Sherman, the brig psychologist who had met informally with Lonetree for months. He asked Sherman if, based on their conversations, he had formed any opinions concerning the reasons why Sergeant Lonetree had gotten into trouble. In reply, the psychologist talked about Lonetree as someone who came from "a very conflicted background with no sense of foundation," someone with a lot of unmet personal needs who couldn't feel good about himself unless others thought well of him, a bright young man who was nonetheless sophomoric and lacking in common sense. In summation, he described Clayton Lonetree as a "wise fool."

Major Henderson then told the court that he would be taking an unsworn statement from Sergeant Lonetree. This was the first time anyone outside the defense team or his family had heard from Sergeant Lonetree since his arrest, and his performance did little to satisfy those who were anxious to hear him talk about how and why he got involved with the Soviets. He spoke softly and haltingly. Much of what he said was mumbled and inaudible. Even the jury members strained to hear his words as he talked about his troubled childhood, his years in an orphanage, his overbearing father: "Every time I done anything, he criticized me. The only time he spoke to me, he was drunk."

Only at the end of the testimony did Major Henderson touch on issues pertaining to his crimes.

Q. Sergeant Lonetree, before you became an MSG, Marine security guard, did you ever think of becoming a spy?

A. No, sir.

Q. How would you describe the way you felt about Communism at that time?

A. I was a devoted anti-Communist. The reasons why, because of the Marine Corps, I felt they were—as an elite status that we have—they just seemed to have a—actually that is one of the reasons why I didn't like the Communists. I—Afghanistan, when it was invaded—just somewhat fanatical, anti-Red.

Q. Sergeant Lonetree, are you willing to accept the punishment this court awards?

A. Yes, sir.

Major Henderson had no further questions.

What was left were the closing arguments, and speaking for the prosecution, Maj. Frank Short made a powerful case for a sentence of life imprisonment.

"Since we started a Marine Corps, Marines with problems have served with honor, and very often have died with honor," he said. "But only one Marine has made the individual decision for which he must take the individual responsibility, the decision to betray his oath, his Corps, and his country. . . . Part of the job of this court is to set an example for the next two hundred and twelve years, so this won't happen again."

Short went on to ask the jury, "in assessing an appropriate sentence, to consider the victims in the case." By that he meant not simply the security of the United States as a free nation. "It's important for you to remember, also, even though you haven't seen them, you haven't heard from them, to remember the human victims. People who will pay for the rest of their lives the very personal price of having been identified, had their names and their addresses placed on a KGB target list."

Nearing the end, Short asked the jury, "Remember the dramatic picture Mr. Kunstler painted for you on closing argument for the defense? He warned of the horror that you would experience, of the possibility that some night you might, to use his words, 'wake up screaming.' Look at your list of those American patriots that the accused betrayed, and when you deliberate on your sentence, ask yourselves, How many people on that list will some night, somewhere, wake up screaming because of what he did?"

Judge Roberts had given the defense team permission to allow each of the attorneys representing Sergeant Lonetree the chance to speak, and over the weekend William Kunstler had typed out his final words. Major Henderson had received a copy, and when he read it he was dismayed. It was a bitter, vituperative statement that criticized the jury's verdict on the previous Friday as an example of "the self-protective myopia of the Marine Corps." Kunstler had written, "You must bear some of the stigma of this tragic proceeding," which he went on to describe as "an ugly and pathetic charade." And he chastised the members for their inability "to rise above the hysteria of the moment."

The morning of the hearing, just before the defense team went into the courtroom, Major Henderson took William Kunstler aside and said, "Bill, if you try and give that statement to the jury at sentencing, I'm warning you, I'm going to get up and I'm going to walk out of the room. I'm not going to ask the judge's permission, and I'm going to hope the judge yells at me and asks me where I'm going. Because then I'm going to tell him that I think what you're saying is a bunch of crap. It has nothing to do with our client, and I want this jury to know that I want nothing to do with it."

At first Kunstler tried to defend himself, but when Henderson wouldn't budge, he finally conceded. "Okay, I won't give it."

But that was before Major Short's closing, which so incensed Kunstler that he changed his mind. "I'm going ahead with this," he whispered to his colleagues, and with statement in hand he started to stand up. But he was stopped by the assistant military counsel to the defense, Capt. Andy Strotman, who grabbed Kunstler by the shoulder and slammed him rudely back in his seat.

"Don't you dare," the captain hissed through clenched teeth.

It was a considerably subdued William Kunstler who, after regaining his composure, rose a minute later and delivered a closing statement that, while not without its barbs, amounted to a rather mild appeal for "compassion, mercy, sensitivity, and justice."

When William Kunstler sat down, Major Henderson stood up. And he sort of ambled to the rear of the courtroom, where he paused, appearing to be deep in thought. Then he turned around, lifted his head, and when every eye in the jury box was focused on him, began to speak.

"Gentlemen, I'm gonna stand here in the back because I don't know enough about doing this to stand up in front like a lot of other people do."

There were titters in the courtroom as the major, in a folksy twang and with a touch of humor, proceeded to poke fun at some of the grand philosophizing that characterized the arguments of both prosecution and defense attorneys who had gone before him. It was a very different tone of voice than had been heard in the courtroom up until this point—relaxed, reasonable, and persuasive—and somehow it seemed less like it was coming from an advocate than from someone who was genuinely interested in fairness, in what truly the appropriate punishment was for these offenses—which was what the art of advocacy was all about.

There were two defendants in the courtroom, Major Henderson went on to say. There was the Clayton Lonetree who probably should never have been allowed to serve in the Marine security guard program in Moscow, but who was. There was the Clayton Lonetree who made some damn dumb mistakes, and who, no question, should be held responsible for his actions. But there was another individual in the room, and that was a sergeant in the Marine Corps. A sergeant who, "whether he was foolish or naive," in his own mind did set limits on his cooperation with Soviet agents. A sergeant who, told to fish or cut bait, said, Wait a minute, I can't do this any longer. And while honesty after the fact ought not to weigh in the verdict, Major Henderson stressed it was pertinent in the sentencing. The jury must remember, Henderson said, that this Marine sergeant did not go out and commit an infraction that would have been a sure ticket off the MSG program and back home, allowing his activities to pass undiscovered. "He could have walked, gentlemen, he could have walked scot-free." But he didn't. Instead he turned himself in, unconditionally.

"On the fourteenth of December 1986, Sergeant Lonetree didn't come in and say, If you'll make me a deal, I'll tell you what I know. He didn't come in and say, I need to have a lawyer. He came in without any promises and he put himself at the mercy of other people. Because he knew it was right. Clayton Lonetree had, once again, become Sergeant Lonetree. He put the rest of his life at the mercy of other people, and you gentlemen now are those other people."

In the end Henderson asked for a sentence of ten years, which he believed was what his client would have received had he been willing to plea-bargain.

After Judge Roberts delivered his instructions to the jury, the members retired to deliberate. Within three hours they had reached a decision. Sergeant Lonetree stood at attention and looked blankly at the jurors as the sentence was read. He was demoted to private. He was fined $5,000. He was ordered to forfeit all future pay and allowances and dishonorably discharged. And he was sentenced to thirty years in prison.

Lonetree had barely returned to his cell in the brig before a victory celebration commenced at a pub in Quantico Town, a civilian part of the Marine base. As members of the National Security Task Force lit up cigars and tossed back beers, Major Beck showed up and was greeted by a round of cheers and applause. He acknowledged the tribute, but it was a bittersweet occasion for him—he was physically and emotionally spent and in no mood for merrymaking—and after a single drink he excused himself.

Two news reporters were standing outside, peering in the windows, and when the major exited, one of them approached him. "Now that the trial's over, I'd like to compliment you on the fine job you did, Major Beck."

Beck nodded.

A swell of laughter from inside the pub turned their heads in the direction of the revelry.

"I see you guys are elated with the verdict."

Tight-lipped and solemn, Major Beck replied, "What's there to be elated about when a Marine is convicted of betraying his country?" and walked away.

In the days after the trial officially ended, the sentence was the subject of extensive reporting and editorializing. The majority of the conservative papers thought Lonetree had gotten off easy compared with other recent espionage defendants like John Walker, Jerry Whitworth, Jonathan Pollard, and Ronald Pelton. *The Washington Times* ran an article with the heading "Lonetree's 30 Years Scored as Too Light," in which a spokesman for the Washington Legal Foundation, a public-interest law firm that had lobbied for the death penalty in major espionage cases, denounced the sentence as an inadequate deterrent to others. "There is no better case that demonstrates why we need the death penalty in espionage cases that jeopardize the lives of American personnel or national security. . . . The Soviets would certainly know what to do with a traitor like Lonetree."

While no reputable papers went so far as to call the sentence a miscarriage of justice and Sergeant Lonetree a martyr, some of them, like *The Baltimore Sun,* did keep alive certain questions raised in the course of the court-martial: "What about the embassy security officer, who should have known these Marines were playing around with Soviet women? What about the administrative officer, the ambassador, the State Department's security office, the commander of the Marine detachment that trains embassy guards, the secretary of state? What, indeed, about the president himself, who was warned about this problem more than two years ago?"

Lonetree's civilian counsel condemned the sentence, of course, and said they had pledged to their client that appeals of what they called a "prejudiced" outcome, in which race had gotten in the way of justice, would be taken all the way to the Supreme Court, if necessary.

"They controlled the referee in round one," Mike Stuhff told *The New York Times,* "they" meaning the government. "And on appeal we're going to have a different set of referees for round two."

William Kunstler announced that he would seek to have the sentence set aside on the ground that prosecutors had "falsely and emotionally" portrayed Lonetree as the first Marine ever convicted of spying, when he was aware of at least four other cases of Marines having been convicted of espionage-related offenses. He maintained that this false impression had led the jury to an emotional decision of thirty years.

Meanwhile, in his office in the basement of Lejeune Hall, Major Henderson was dealing with more immediate concerns. Henderson took no satisfaction in having heard from the jury that they had been prepared to give Lonetree life before hearing his closing statement. He was doing what he could to get his client's sentence reduced even further. A host of counterintelligence agencies were anxious to debrief Sergeant Lonetree and obtain a full account of his recruitment by Soviet KGB agents and all his spying activities. Henderson, through discussion and negotiations, was trying to get as much time off as he could in trade for his client's cooperation.

He knew they did not have much leverage to bargain with, certainly nothing like they'd had before the trial, so it was not a matter of what it was worth to him but what it was worth to the government, which held all the cards. When it offered five years, which would take the sentence down to twenty-five years, Henderson was disappointed. He'd hoped for more. But he thought they should take it. When he spoke to Stuhff and Kunstler, however, they disagreed.

William Kunstler spoke for both civilian counsels when he wrote Major Henderson a letter to make his position perfectly clear. "I am totally against accepting such an offer for a number of reasons. First of all, it is so insignificant, insofar as time is concerned, as not to amount to anything. Secondly, I believe that it weakens our appellate position in that the acceptance of such a picayune offer is, in my opinion, tantamount to proclaiming that Clayton is so desperate that he will agree to anything because he does not trust the appellate process. Lastly, and perhaps most importantly, I think that further interrogation of Clayton will be used to try to get him falsely to incriminate others . . . so that NIS and the Pentagon brass, along with the State Department, can fabricate the Marine 'spy ring' at the Moscow Embassy and thus flesh out the original theories propounded last Spring. . . . I believe that the thirty years were imposed to force false admissions from our client, just as Judge Sirica imposed similar sentences in the Watergate affair. This case simply cannot be treated as any other court-martial. Its politics are far-reaching and pervasive. . . ."

Kunstler believed he had a better idea. In fact, at the very time he wrote that letter he was involved in negotiations with the producers of *60 Minutes,* the highly rated CBS newsmagazine, who were interested in opening their 1987 season with a sympathetic segment on Sgt. Clayton Lonetree. Diane Sawyer was slotted to conduct the interview, and Kunstler thought this would be an ideal forum for winning public support and exposing the weaknesses in the government's case.

Henderson thought that would be a big mistake—for the same reason he didn't put his client on the stand. It would be placing Lonetree in a public situation for which he was profoundly unfitted. No one knew what Clayton would say next, which could be disastrous. What if, on national television, he said something incriminating? Something that damaged his appellate hopes or could be used against him in a retrial?

The difference of opinion on the defense team was at an impasse when two men walked into Major Henderson's office and helped resolve matters.

Lt. Col. Jim Schwenk came storming in one day, slammed an order to testify on his desk, and said, "Dave, here it is. You can take this deal and get five years off. Or we're going to order him to debrief, and if he refuses, five more will be added on for disobedience. It's time to choose."

Henderson was sitting there pondering his next move when another man arrived: a Minneapolis attorney by the name of Lawrence Cohen, who said he had been retained by Spencer Lonetree, Clayton's father, to represent his son. Henderson looked at him askance. By this time he'd had his fill of civilian counsels. But before he could invite Cohen to kindly leave well enough alone, Henderson heard the man saying things like "Bill Kunstler is the last person who should have been representing a Marine in a court-martial. He should be fired."

As Henderson would later describe his reaction, "Bells went off. . . . At last someone was talking sense."

The dismissal of the two civilian attorneys who had been identified with Sgt. Clayton Lonetree from the start was public and messy. In a letter drafted for him by Cohen, Lonetree stated he had lost confidence in both Stuhff and Kunstler as far back as August and did not want "to continue to be represented by persons in whom I do not have faith." He instructed them not to talk with the media about his case any longer and informed him that his lead attorney from this moment on was Major Henderson.

Stuhff was outraged that a deal had been put together behind his back. There were solid appeals issues he wanted to pursue. He was also more than a little displeased at being booted off the case so unceremoniously after all the time, effort, and expense he had put into it. Kunstler, for his part, said he believed this was something initiated by the military, which was trying to drive a wedge between them and their client in an effort to get Lonetree to cooperate with authorities.

Meanwhile, a post-trial agreement was executed. In it, Lonetree agreed to submit to interrogations regarding the espionage activities under oath, followed by polygraph examinations. In return for his cooperation, five years would be subtracted from his sentence, and a grant of immunity against prosecution would apply to everything he revealed. Unless, that was, incriminating information was developed independent of the briefing that indicated he had withheld information, and then he would be charged and tried in another court-martial.

15

At six-thirty on the morning of October 12, Lt. Col. David Breme arrived at the Quantico brig to pick up his prisoner. Coincidentally, U.S. marshals were holding an Arab terrorist in the brig at this time, and as Breme would later describe the scene, "It looked like the Israelis had been brought in to guard him. There were more goddamn Uzis around than you see in a Steven Seagal movie."

After he was admitted to the sally port through an electronically operated door, Breme told the guard, "I'm here to pick up Lonetree."

Five minutes later the prisoner was delivered. "They brought him down this corridor that was lined with cinderblock walls and had a concrete floor covered with linoleum, so every sound was amplified with echoes. He had ankle irons on. He had hand irons on. He had this connecting chain between them so he could only take these mincing steps. You could hear the rattle and clank of him coming and suddenly there he was, looking like Marley's ghost, with these two apes—I mean two of the biggest brig guards I've ever seen—on either side of him. It was pathetic. He had a look on his face like you'd see in a dog pound. Like the faces in the pictures of the downed aviators at the Hanoi Hilton."

As a final precaution Lonetree was frisked, and then he was turned over to Breme and two MPs, who loaded him into a white Navy Dodge van and headed for a secret location in Washington, D.C., where his debriefing was scheduled for later that morning.

Lieutenant Colonel Breme had been handpicked to be the escort officer because of his reputation as the best shot on the Quantico base. He was armed with an Austrian 9mm seventeen-shot automatic pistol, which he carried in a shoulder holster under a sports jacket worn to conceal his weapon, and two loaded magazines filled a side pocket, so in total he was equipped with fifty-one rounds of ammunition. The nature of the threat had not been specified for him, and when he had asked his superior officer what he imagined they might encounter, Breme had been told, "You never know about these goddamn supposed diplomats in Washington. Half of them are communists."

Breme had hesitated before replying. "Sir, I'm afraid that's not who I'm concerned about. I don't think the KGB gives a shit about Lonetree one way or another. You know who I'm concerned about? I'm concerned about Billy Bob in a pickup truck who's an Amurican and has a Confederate-flag license plate and who might drive by and say, 'Goddamn, there's that sonofabitch Lonetree,' and open up with a shotgun. I'm more worried about a goofball like that than the Red Menace."

By nine o'clock they were pulling up to Building 159 in the Washington Navy Yard. It was a five-story brick structure that housed a multitude of different agencies, including a branch of the Library of Congress and the Government Printing Office, but a suite of rooms on the second floor had been dedicated as the debriefing center. In one of them an eight-by-ten sound-reduction module had been assembled that was furnished with two comfortable easy chairs—one for Lonetree, one for his interrogator—and a small table-desk inset with a polygraph instrument that was covered whenever it was not in use. An exhaust fan kept the air inside fresh, and a one-way mirror provided the view for a stationary video camera mounted on a tripod. At the same time the debrief was taped, it was going to be broadcast on TV monitors to an adjacent room where chairs had been set up for an audience of thirty.

Lanny McCullah had personally selected one of his premier interrogators for the debrief, an NIS agent by the name of John Skinner (not his real name). Short, bespectacled, soft-spoken, with a low-key personality that in some ways matched Lonetree's, Skinner was extensively trained in interview techniques. Along with an FBI agent he had debriefed John Walker. He was also one of the few NIS agents to have interviewed both KGB and GRU defectors for Soviet methodology in recruiting American military personnel.

Skinner had spent weeks preparing for the Lonetree debrief, reviewing the Lonetree case files and collecting questions from interested agencies. But perhaps most helpful to him had been a report on Lonetree put together by a CIA psychologist. After considering the biographical data accumulated on Lonetree, listening to the tapes of his confession, and reviewing the results of the mental examination ordered by the prosecution, the Agency man had logged such observations as, "Although Lonetree, in his own mind, thinks he is logical, rational and given to theorizing, he displays an unconventional thought process which is rich in fantasy, possibly bordering on the mystical, all of which he uses as an escape from an often unpleasant everyday life. . . . [He] sometimes experiences a distrust of his senses, not really being sure of what he sees and hears or its meaning. Sometimes, reality is blurred for him. All this said, Lonetree displays a definable moral/value system. Morally he is clear relative to the dos and don'ts of society. However he is less firm of the 'whys' of actions."

Regarding his inner workings, it was written that Lonetree "projects self-doubt, low self-esteem, an amorphous identification, a lack of direction and an absence of a clear, guiding philosophy." At the same time he was "self-centered, almost narcissistic, and prone to withdrawal and suspiciousness. In his own little world, Lonetree thinks of himself as a 'special' but often misunderstood person."

Regarding the outside world, "Lonetree feels rejected and alienated. . . . He is sensitive to criticism, is somewhat suspicious, and distrusts people and their motives. . . . It is clear that one of the worst things that can happen to a person like Lonetree is to be criticized or embarrassed in public. Comments directed

to Lonetree, even casual ones, if interpreted negatively, are probably never forgotten."

The psychologist also provided insights into mannerisms and
thinking patterns of Indians that could easily be misunderstood
by a non-Indian in an interrogation setting. Specifically he referred to the way Indians, under questioning, tended to avoid eye
contact—looking down, up, to the side—and to be mute for long
periods of time before responding to a question. An investigator
who didn't know better might think that the subject was making
things up, but that wasn't necessarily true. Indians, for the most
part, did not react quickly. They needed time to go through their
way of thinking, which was to connect a particular to the larger
scheme of things before responding. Speed them up and you'd
mix them up, he said, which was what happened with Agent
Brannon in London.

Finally the CIA shrink stressed the importance of establishing
a rapport with Lonetree before interrogating him. He suggested
that to build a bond of trust Skinner should do things like share
facts about his own personal life. Engage Lonetree by openly referring to other cases he might find interesting. And since Lonetree was a reader, discuss similar tastes in books. Above all
Skinner should not appear to pass judgment on anything that
Lonetree said.

As it turned out, the rapport-building process took a lot more
time and was far more difficult than Skinner anticipated, because
when he sat down with Lonetree to get acquainted, it became
immediately clear that he was dealing with a profoundly divided
man. It was as if Lonetree were someone standing on a bridge
with the United States on one side and the Soviet Union on the
other side, and with his loyalties torn, he didn't know whom to
trust or where his safety lay. As Skinner would come to understand, this division was as much a reflection of the subversive
effect his civilian attorneys had had on him as it was an indication of how deeply Clayton Lonetree had been recruited by the
Soviets.

While Lonetree was in Moscow, the KGB agent Aleksei Yefimov, dressed in sheep's clothing as Uncle Sasha, had skillfully and successfully managed to brainwash him into believing that the CIA was the locus of evil in the world, and that the United States had been taken over by capitalist warmongers. Philosophically, Lonetree had been brought to a place where he no longer saw the Soviets as the bad guys. He believed Yefimov when he was told that the CIA was determined to overthrow the Soviet government and harm the Russian people, and that the CIA was responsible for the Cold War; he believed that the sole purpose of the KGB was to protect the Soviet people against the CIA. In an amazingly short period of time Yefimov had been able to dominate Lonetree's thought processes and convince him that everything he was doing for the Soviets was right and honorable.

Eventually Lonetree had been able to shake off that indoctrination, and guilt-ridden, he had finally approached the CIA, the very people he had been warned about. But still he had been ambivalent, choosing what he thought was the lesser of two evils.

Ironically, his experience since his confession had brought him full circle. He had returned to a place of distrust toward the American government because Stuhff and Kunstler had told him the authorities were out to get him. In the process of mounting their defense, his civilian attorneys had reinforced the very notions propagated by Uncle Sasha: that the American intelligence community was involved in conspiracies against "the people" and that Indians were the convenient scapegoats for policies that profited the powerful. Stuhff and Kunstler had apparently even convinced Lonetree that the government could not be counted on to honor its side of the bargain, and the promise of five years off his sentence for cooperating was just a trick to get him to talk.

So Skinner took his time, trying to relax Lonetree and build a basis for trust. He talked about himself and his childhood in Vermont near the Canadian border. He told Lonetree of his own Indian heritage—his father was half Algonquin. He talked about his tastes in literature—he preferred nonfiction and had been reading espionage books since the age of ten. He said his two dreams in life were to play professional baseball or go into law enforcement, and guess which one didn't pan out. He talked, he listened, and he answered honestly the questions Lonetree asked of him. And when he felt they were on firm ground, Skinner said, "Clayton, I'm not here to confirm the government's case, or to prove a theory. My sole job is to help you tell the truth. I won't let you take a polygraph until I am convinced that you are telling me the truth. And even then, we will only use it for confirmation. Because I want the truth without the machine."

With those words, Clayton took the hand extended to him and came over to the American side.

Skinner wanted Lonetree to tell his story chronologically, beginning with his arrival in Moscow, because the atmosphere in the embassy and Lonetree's response to it constituted the background for his eventual recruitment. Very little new information was derived in this area. Hostile intelligence agents assessing potential targets for recruitment looked for outsiders who felt misunderstood and underappreciated and who were willing to violate the rules. Lonetree had been placed, as much as he had put himself, square in their crosshairs.

After John Barron's testimony, Lonetree no longer seemed to believe that his love affair with Violetta had been driven by real feelings on her part, and there were times during the debrief when he would start calling her names—"You bitch!"—as if she were present in the room. He seemed to realize now that the evolution of their friendship had been progressive steps in a sophisticated recruitment operation designed to emotionally involve him at the same time he more thoroughly compromised himself, so that by the time she introduced him to Uncle Sasha he would feel that he was caught in a chain of events he could not break.

When they began to talk about Uncle Sasha, it became immediately clear to Skinner why Lonetree had failed questions on the polygraph in London. He'd failed because he was minimizing his involvement with the Soviets and withholding information. What he actually divulged was more extensive and more specific than he had acknowledged either to the CIA or to NIS.

Painstakingly, Skinner helped Lonetree reconstruct each meeting with Uncle Sasha, of which there were seven in Moscow and eight in Vienna, almost twice as many as he had previously admitted to. They went over everything from where and when each meeting took place, to what was asked and what was said.

As expected, Yefimov had primarily been interested in identifying CIA agents and determining the location and features of CIA spaces within the embassy. "How did you know who the CIA agents were?" Skinner asked, since all of them operated under diplomatic cover. Lonetree replied that the Marines were briefed by someone from the Agency on how to handle defectors who came in, so that was one way. He could also tell them by the hours they kept and the access certain people had to floors and spaces that were off-limits to others. And they were generally recognizable by the fact that in all weather they wore trenchcoats.

As improbable as that description may have sounded, it so happened that at this point in the debriefing there were two CIA agents in attendance, and sure enough, both were wearing trenchcoats. The next day it rained like a monsoon in Washington, and the only two people who showed up not wearing trenchcoats were the CIA guys.

It was easier to identify CIA agents in Vienna than in Moscow, Lonetree said, where he admitted to turning over to Yefimov photos of CIA personnel and writing their local addresses, obtained from a restricted address book, on the back. He estimated that he identified eighty percent of the CIA staff in Vienna, and said he had seen this as part of a larger effort to neutralize the threat the CIA posed to world peace.

As the debrief went on, Lonetree admitted to providing Yefimov with other sensitive material. After he was tasked to acquire floor plans of different floors in the embassies in both Moscow and Vienna, he sat down and annotated them with amplifying information that made them valuable intelligence documents. He provided information on the location and control of security cameras, alarms, and MSG responses to intruder-alarm activations, as well as assessment data on different Marines he believed might be homosexuals, alcoholics, or drug users. He identified a walk-in—a Soviet who on his own had visited the embassy in Vienna and offered his services to American intelligence.

And yet as cooperative as Lonetree had been, he had had his own standard of what he refused to do, and there were certain requests he had denied. When Yefimov encouraged him to consider applying for a Marine counterintelligence program, Lonetree balked. On several occasions he had had second thoughts at the last minute and refused to pass material he had been tasked to collect. And when Yefimov tried to talk him into defecting—promising him the opportunity of living with Violetta with a car, in a nice flat, possibly a dacha—although tempted, he turned them down.

What a political coup that would have been, Skinner reflected. An American Indian Marine in full uniform standing up in front of the cameras and going public about the brutal treatment of Indian people in America and the sinister activities of the CIA would have had tremendous propaganda value, particularly when combined with another incident in a similar time frame—the redefection of the KGB agent Col. Vitaly Yurchenko, who claimed he had been abducted by the CIA and then escaped.

As professionally as this operation seemed to have been run, there were puzzling aspects to it for Skinner. It might have been a ploy, but the KGB did not seem to have a good understanding of the kind of information a Marine security guard would possess. On several occasions Sasha asked Lonetree philosophical questions about U.S. strategic plans. Why ask him? No Marine would have the slightest knowledge about those issues. The ambassador might not even be privy to that information.

Furthermore, the KGB seemed to have miscalculated catastrophically in their handling of Lonetree in Vienna. Their first mistake was they misjudged Lonetree's primary motives for working with them. He was in love with Violetta and he wanted friendship with Uncle Sasha. Money was not what interested him, and by not giving him continued access to Violetta, and putting things on a business footing, they were dooming the relationship.

Their biggest error, however, was when they attempted to pass him to Yuri Lysov, a.k.a. George, the senior KGB officer stationed in Vienna. At their one meeting, Lysov had set a more demanding, operational tone. He let Lonetree know that from here on out he would be expected to behave in a more efficient, productive manner. This scared Lonetree. Even as he agreed to make plans to return surreptitiously to the Soviet Union, he was fearful about his future. If the Soviets had played their cards right and delayed his turnover to another case officer, chances were Lonetree would never have turned himself in.

Of course, all of this was based on Clayton Lonetree's memory of what he was asked, what he said, and what he did, which was not totally reliable, because some of his meetings with Uncle Sasha were occasions for heavy drinking. At one of their sessions, he reported, a strange thing had happened—after only one or two drinks, Lonetree felt ill and spent several hours in a daze. Vaguely he remembered a third party entering the apartment. His description of the incident sounded to Skinner as if he'd been drugged, which highlighted the fact that Lonetree was only able to testify to what he remembered.

In this instance hypnosis was tried as a method of enhancing his memory, but Lonetree was unable to fully enter a hypnotic state.

The question of reliability as it pertained to Lonetree's statements was given further uncertainty by his idiosyncratic behavior during the course of the debriefing. "It was like he was operating in a different ether," one of the intelligence officers observing him would comment. "Skinner would ask him a question about where he met Uncle Sasha, and it seemed to send Lonetree into some kind of trance. We were getting a profile of him on the camera and for what seemed like eons all he did was stare at the wall. Now remember, this is an acoustic room and there's not a lot to look at on the walls. But he kept on staring until those of us watching are thinking, What the hell is with this guy? Some thought he was just being evasive. Others said No, that's the way Indians are, he's just roaming with the buffalo. . . . Then, when he finally answered, it was weird stuff. A total non sequitur: 'You know, there are some very fine restaurants in Vienna.'"

Having had the benefit of the CIA psychologist's report, Skinner brought a more encompassing understanding to Lonetree's tics. But even he was getting anxious to put Lonetree on the polygraph so the truth could be determined.

Prior to the first polygraph examination, Skinner led Lonetree through a series of questions that focused on the key concerns: Before Cpl. Arnold Bracy recanted, he told investigators Lonetree had said he was letting Soviets into the embassy after working hours. Bracy said he'd seen Lonetree escorting a Soviet through the embassy. Bracy alleged Lonetree had solicited his assistance in resetting alarms after penetration had occurred in secure spaces. How much of that was true? Did Lonetree provide the Soviets with unauthorized access to the embassy? Did he allow a Soviet entry team to come in and install listening devices? Did he turn over classified documents? Did he plant bugs? To his knowledge, were any other Marines involved in these activities?

When Skinner asked him these questions, Lonetree denied virtually everything. But again, the odd character of his denial was disconcerting. There were a couple of times when it seemed Skinner had him on the verge of admitting to letting the Soviets in and collaborating with Bracy. When Skinner asked him, "Isn't it true that . . ." instead of saying, "Hell, no," or "That's bullshit," he'd sit there and his Adam's apple would bob up and down and a tear would form in the corner of his eye and he'd look at the floor and then at the ceiling. On one occasion two minutes and twenty-two seconds lapsed between a question and Lonetree's response. .

This was not what most people would do if they were accused of something as serious as espionage. They would immediately deny it and move on to the next question. When Lonetree got like this, the intelligence officers observing him couldn't help themselves; they would coach him. "Come on, Lonetree, come on. Say it. Say it."

Then Lonetree would gulp, and what he would say was, "Oh, no, we didn't do that."

When it was the polygrapher's turn to go over the prepared list

of questions, it was impossible for the intelligence types gathered
in the adjoining room to know what the instrument was registering while the exam was going on. All they knew was that Lonetree answered "No" to every single question. When at last the
exam was completed and the polygrapher walked out with the
charts in his hand, John Skinner and Angelic White were waiting
for him in the hallway.

"Well?"

"He's clean."

"You're kidding."

"Nope. He's clean."

The full debriefing of Sgt. Clayton Lonetree would last for almost three months, during which time he would be given eight
different polygraph examinations. Lonetree would continue to
answer "No," and the results of the polygraph examination
would continue to be NDI: no deception indicated.

SECRETS

16

The Marine Spy Scandal was no longer page-one news by the time Sergeant Lonetree's debriefing was finished, but the results were newsmaking nonetheless. No specifics, no details were given. The public was never told what questions were asked, nor Lonetree's responses. "Sources familiar with the interrogation" were simply quoted as saying it was official now, the security disaster everyone feared apparently had never taken place. Sergeant Lonetree did have prohibited contacts with Soviet agents and did pass sensitive material to them, but there was no evidence of a spy ring in the Marine guard detachment in Moscow, and Soviet agents had not been allowed to roam through sensitive portions of the American Embassy.

At Eighth and I, and Quantico, it was like the end of a war. At long last it could be said that Sergeant Lonetree was the one and only Marine guilty of espionage, and the degree of damage he'd done was less than had been thought.

No knowledgeable counterintelligence person was prepared to say that Lonetree's admissions were insignificant, however. The KGB, like any intelligence agency, was never satisfied with just one source of information. They were always checking the word of one informant against another, because historically they were suspicious of whatever they were told. When Lonetree confirmed the identities of intelligence agents, that meant the Soviets put them under twenty-four-hour surveillance and followed their every move to determine who their Soviet contacts were. This, in turn, conceivably could have led to the loss of human assets inside the Soviet Union, as well as setting up the now-known CIA agents for possible recruitment efforts within the Soviet Union; and when they were transferred to their next posts in Africa or Asia or wherever, the KGB residency there would be notified and once again the agent would be followed to determine his contacts, or targeted for an operation.

These were important issues in the intelligence business. They could compromise an operation or national security just as certainly as penetrating the code room and placing an electronic listening device on the communications equipment could. But they weren't perceived as major in the press, where an outcry took place over the pitiful payoff. A demand arose that before this episode was dismissed, the witch hunt should be unpacked. A lot of innocent folks had had their careers blighted. The reputation of the Marine Corps had been tarnished. Millions of dollars had been spent removing, shipping, and replacing equipment. Relations between the superpowers had been severely strained. It wasn't good enough to say an unfortunate but understandable overreaction had taken place. Errors had to be explained. Responsibility for this ludicrously overblown mess had to be assigned.

Because the investigation of the affair had been entrusted to the Naval Investigative Service, the consensus was that the NIS had badly bungled the case. Even before the charges against Arnold Bracy were dropped, the press had changed from a mode of reporting the event to critical scrutiny of the investigation. Under such banner headlines as "Marine Scandal Puts Probers Under Cloud," it had been written that the NIS had made an important decision early on to focus on damage assessment, and in its rush to determine the extent of the spying it had failed to adequately collect physical evidence for prosecution. After Bracy, the question on everyone's mind was summarized in a *Time* magazine article: "There was sufficient detail . . . to see a classic espionage pattern, but did the accused embassy guards sketch that pattern, or was it provided by aggressive, overzealous agents of the NIS?"

The search for an answer was initiated by Reps. Daniel Mica and Olympia Snowe, who requested a formal inquiry into the NIS investigation by the General Accounting Office, the official Congressional investigative agency. But to the dismay of those hoping to pin excesses and exaggerations of the Marine Spy Scandal on the NIS, the GAO report concluded that while the Bracy confession remained an unexplained hole at its center, the Naval Investigative Service had conducted a "logical, thorough, and professional" inquiry.

Despite the exoneration, disappointment ran deep at the NIS. When Lonetree cleared the polygraph, Lanny McCullah, who had worked tirelessly for months on the case and had been absolutely convinced that Lonetree would confirm at least a portion of Bracy's statement, was so devastated he didn't show up for work for three days. When he resumed his duties as director of Bobsled, McCullah put on a philosophical face, maintaining that just because the NIS effort had not resulted in more people being convicted or brought to trial, that didn't denigrate the performance of the Bobsled task force.

"Should we have looked for wider recruitment and deeper penetration?" he would say. "We'd have been remiss not to. Should we be criticized because we didn't find anything? That's not fair. Maybe it seemed we spun this all up, but how do you look at that without spinning it up?"

In this regard he felt the blame for what went wrong ought to be shared by the Congressional committees who had been insatiable in their demand for briefings and updates, and had taken NIS's investigative leads and prematurely released them as facts; the impacted organizations who had taken NIS's raw intelligence data and, if it made them look bad, used it for damage-control instead of damage-assessment purposes; and the press, who had relied on unverifiable leaks from anonymous sources with political agendas and hyped the worst-case scenarios, creating public expectations that were greater than what NIS could ultimately prove.

This had been one of those frustrating investigations where something looked red today and then two months later another piece of information would come along and suddenly what you had was a different color. As it turned out, it was also a case in which outside circumstances functioned like a light source that projected a larger and more ominous shadow than the actual object. But espionage was a world in which shadows often had substance, and Lanny McCullah was convinced that any reasonable person, having access to the same information he had, would have made the same decisions. He had not concocted the idea that a KGB worldwide MSG recruitment campaign was going on—that notion had come from a Soviet defector. He had not come up with the theory that the American Embassy had been penetrated—no one was even thinking like that until Arnold Bracy raised their suspicions.

Throughout the investigation McCullah had talked confidently about an inevitable "big break" he knew would come with the next witness interview or the discovery of a planted eavesdropping device. But the closest he'd come to something like that turned out, in the end, to demonstrate the impossible situation NIS had found itself in.

By early June, notwithstanding press reports of an embassy riddled with Soviet "bugs," he had yet to receive official notification of the results of technical sweeps of the embassy and the inspection of dismantled embassy communications equipment. Given the difficulty he'd encountered obtaining any information from the CIA or State Department that might prove embarrassing to either agency, he reasoned that if a planted device was found, that information might not be released to NIS, because to do so, while providing the needed corroborating evidence, would invite additional outside scrutiny and significant embarrassment to both agencies.

While discussing the dilemma with his deputy Bud Aldridge, McCullah hit on another strategy. They could sit back and wait for a report that might never arrive, or they could become proactive and maybe by pushing the right buttons generate sufficient pressure to force a candid and truthful response. It was decided that McCullah would arrange a meeting at FBI headquarters with their director of counterintelligence, Buck Revell, and the

CIA director of counterintelligence, Gus Hathaway, to discuss Bobsled and Moscow, leaving the specific agenda intentionally unspecific.

At that meeting, after presenting the group with a status report, McCullah surprised everyone with an exfiltration proposal. He named three candidates—Galya, Violetta, and Uncle Sasha—and suggested the CIA contact them and offer them a million dollars to defect from the Soviet Union and testify in the United States, after which they would be placed in the FBI's defector program.

McCullah realized the proposal was a wild shot that the CIA would probably turn down because its exfiltration procedures and routes for defectors were closely guarded and reserved for the most critical situations. He suggested it anyway to project his displeasure at what he perceived to be a lack of assistance from both the FBI and the CIA, and to put them on the defensive before he moved on to the main issue: the lack of information being provided regarding the technical inspection of the embassy and its communications equipment. Not one word had been received by NIS in that regard, he said in a voice that made no effort to conceal his annoyance, yet the media was reporting unnamed FBI and other government sources of having knowledge of bugs. If it was true, if there was evidence the embassy had been penetrated, he wanted to know before Lonetree's court-martial.

The discussion obviously got the FBI's attention, because they advised they would take the lead and make an inquiry into the matter. Several days later a package arrived at Bobsled headquarters that contained an explanatory letter and a photograph of the code machine used by the State Department and the CIA in Moscow to take messages and scramble them into electronic signals that could only be deciphered in Washington and Langley. Attached to the cable leading into the machine was an anomaly that had been discovered by technical personnel. No one knew what it was, but it didn't belong there. There were safeguards built into this particular piece of equipment that supposedly made it tamperproof, and if it had been tampered with—if, for instance, a repair had been done—there should be an audit trail.

But there were no records to indicate any work had been done on it. Its location suggested that it might be a device to decode encrypted electronic messages and that it may have been installed by Soviet technicians.

McCullah and Aldridge were less than thrilled. An anomaly was exactly that: something that could not be explained. It might be significant, it might not. Had technicians from the KGB'S Technical Support Group penetrated the embassy's most sensitive and guarded inner sanctum long enough to make or install a subverting modification? Or had an overworked embassy technician simply made a repair and in haste forgotten to make an annotation in the equipment log? Was it the elusive "smoking gun," or just another lapse in security procedures?

There was a degree of cautious excitement at Bobsled. McCullah knew this was not an exploitable piece of courtroom evidence, but finally, after all the disappointments and bad press, he felt they were on the verge of that "big break."

But information on the anomaly was followed by several weeks of silence. So just before the Lonetree court-martial, inquiries were initiated to obtain the results of the examination and a conclusive opinion. The response was deceptively simple: McCullah was told it was an unexplainable, benign anomaly, without purpose or audit trail, perhaps a manufacturer's defect or the result of sloppy paperwork.

A frustrated Lanny McCullah was left without confirmation or denial, and the realization that if, in the process of examining the equipment, hard evidence of penetration had been discovered, chances were the NIS never would have known it. The information would have been kept in-house. The priority would have been to determine the manner in which it had been penetrated and to initiate countermeasures, not to notify NIS and say, "Yeah, you guys were right. Now you can silence your critics." Better to keep the Soviets guessing and the public in the dark.

Looking objectively at what the NIS had accomplished, McCullah thought they'd done an outstanding job under extremely difficult circumstances. Marines who admitted to violations that potentially made them national-security risks had been removed from their positions. Others who appeared to be in the early states of recruitment were rescued from continuing with activities where they might have inflicted damage. The identification of problems within the Marine security guard program had precipitated changes in procedure and policy within the Marine Corps and State Department.

But success had a thousand fathers while failure was an orphan, and the Naval Investigative Service was left looking like a bastard son, because when all was said and done, after interviewing 564 Marines and more than 1,300 other people, administering 264 polygraph examinations and opening 143 investigations into possible espionage on security-related infractions by Marines, it had scored a single successful prosecution: Clayton Lonetree.

The Marine Corps draws heavily on traditions, and every battalion has its heroes. Those who have come before, who distinguished themselves in combat, are continually held up as examples to emulate. Stroll down the corridor of any Marine facility and you will find rooms named for soldiers who lost their lives in the line of duty, and memorial plaques dedicated to individuals who stood fast before machine-gun fire and exploding mortar rounds. Recruits are told that when they read about the exploits of other Marines, they could be looking at their own future. The ghost of Sergeant Tuberville, killed when Communist terrorists attacked a U.S. mission with hand grenades during an embassy softball game in Phnom Penh, is believed to patrol the halls at the Marine security guard battalion, looking over the students' shoulders. . . .

In a somewhat similar fashion, after the Marine Spy Scandal, Clayton Lonetree was never far from the minds of the Marine Corps. His memory was invoked in the upper echelons of leadership: When the commandant delivered a speech about the importance of integrity in the Corps, invariably he made reference to the worst example in its history, Pvt. Clayton Lonetree. Drill instructors in boot camp, indoctrinating troops with the notion of *Semper fidelis,* referred to the one who was not. At MSG school, where Marines were taught how to guard the secrets of the

United States, they also heard about the Marine who turned over the keys to the kingdom. For the Marine Corps, Lonetree, like Quisling, became a shorthand term for "traitor."

The demoted and disgraced Clayton Lonetree, whose journey to infamy ended at the U.S. Disciplinary Barracks at Fort Leavenworth, Kansas, in January of 1988, did not dispute any of this. He seemed to know very well that a Marine did not slap America with a Russian hand in the Cold War and expect to simply walk away. He was stunned by the thirty-year sentence. Those who visited him at Quantico before his transfer described him as looking like someone who had been spun in circles and had yet to focus. But when he did speak, the anger he expressed was at his own foolishness, the exquisite little psych job he had performed while convincing himself the truth of things was what he wanted it to be.

In fact, once he got over the initial emotional shock of a thirty-year sentence, Lonetree seemed almost to embrace the judgment. During a farewell conversation with his military attorney, he remarked, "I got myself into this, Major. I've got nobody to blame but myself, and nobody could have gotten me out of it."

Afterward, Major Henderson found himself thinking about civilian counsel and how different things would have turned out if they had not come aboard. The nation would have been spared a trauma, the government would have saved millions of dollars, and his client would have received a significantly reduced sentence.

Personally, Henderson held William Kunstler responsible. In retrospect he would believe that the cause behind the case was more important to Kunstler than the fate of his client. He knew what Kunstler would have said about that, because Henderson had heard him say it. "Going along with the military never works. You become a tool of the government's lie. Only when you fight do you have a chance to win." But Kunstler's role in discouraging a pretrial agreement in the face of overwhelming evidence, his cavalier disregard for the facts in favor of a pat conspiratorial interpretation of the case, and his willingness to fight to the last ounce of his client's blood made Henderson wonder if, in that part of his mind where he saw himself as serving a higher social purpose, William Kunstler wasn't capable of rationalizing the conviction of certain clients as a victory of sorts—because it provided him with a chance to dramatize claims of racism and injustice. And he needed to lose from time to time in order to prove his point that the system was corrupt.

When he asked himself why Lonetree had gone along with Kunstler, Henderson felt that from the start his client had known damn good and well that he was going to be convicted for his crimes, but when told by civilian counsel that they could get him off, it had been a natural thing to let them try. If that had happened, however—if Lonetree had managed to slip through the justice system on a technicality—Henderson believed that, emotionally and intellectually, Lonetree would not have been satisfied. Because Henderson believed that for the scenario begun when Lonetree came forward to be complete in his mind, he needed to be found guilty. And he needed to be given a substantial sentence so he could stand tall while taking his punishment.

That said wonderful things to Henderson about his client's character. That indicated a mature acceptance of responsibility for the consequences of his actions.

In the years that immediately followed the court-martial, Major Henderson's impression would remain intact. Lonetree never complained that justice had not been served. Though rejected by the Marine Corps, he continued to align himself in his mind with behavior expected of a Marine. It was almost as if he thought that if he honored the image he had singlehandedly tarnished, redemption was possible for him.

There remained one disturbing area of doubt for Clayton Lonetree. To his family and lawyers he would swear that he had been stripped of his illusions about Violetta. He would say that he had been stupid to think her feelings for him were genuine, there was nothing more to be said, he didn't want to talk about her. When he had no choice—when, for example, he was asked about her by members of the Navy Clemency and Parole Board considering further reductions in his sentence—he could not even bring himself to speak her name. She was "that person." If he ever saw that person again, he said, he hoped she would be standing at the end of a breadline.

But from time to time there would be a lapse and he would ask—just out of curiosity, he assured his attorneys—if she had ever tried to get in touch with him.

So of course it was that person I set my sights on when I flew to Moscow in the spring of 1993 to get the Soviet side of this story.

17

When the publicity surrounding the Marine Spy Scandal shone her way, Violetta dropped out of sight, and as far as I knew no one in the West had heard from her since. I had gotten her last address from NIS investigators, and I was counting on the fact that the housing shortage in Russia prevented Muscovites from moving around much.

The exact nature of Violetta's relationship to the KGB was open to question: She could have been doing her duty for her country, or she might have been involuntarily coerced into cooperating. But I knew enough about the way the system operated to suspect that when I did locate her, her ability to talk freely about her involvement in this affair was probably going to be limited. The Soviets had always been strict keepers of secrets, the immutable principle of the Soviet agent being: Keep your silence to the end. And in spite of the recent liberalization of Russian laws, it was still illegal to disclose "state secrets."

In the absence of hard information, and feeling the need for a vision that would give me the confidence to dive headfirst into unknown circumstances, I had invented a scenario in which Violetta's exposure in the press had caused her to lose value in the eyes of the KGB, and she had been shunted into some internal low-level secretarial position where she was resentful and bitter about her fate. Since she had always been told that humanism was the end product of Soviet socialism, she had now become cynical about the whole game of espionage and begun to empathize with the American Marine she had betrayed. It made her want to strike out and expose the hypocrisy and cruelty of the system, but she didn't know how until the fall of Communism, the end of the Cold War, and, now, the arrival of a Western writer anxious to hear her story. It would be the chance she was waiting for, an opportunity to break with the past, tell her truth, redefine herself, and in the process answer questions that haunted a young man who was sitting in prison for having fallen in love with her.

There was a major problem with that scenario, I knew. Redemption through publicity in the mass media was an American phenomenon. It had no tradition in Russia, where newspapers and books historically were organs of propaganda for the state, and public confessions of sins were an important part of ideological propaganda. People in Russia remembered the show trials of the thirties, when innocent people were tortured until they admitted they were "enemies of the State," and their confessions were published in the newspapers so everyone could see that Stalin's conspiracy fears were justified. As recently as the sixties and seventies, when the "dissident movement" began, the newspapers would print so-called retractions signed by people who had been given a choice—labor camps, or a statement to sign that said the struggle for human rights was instigated by the West, and now they were convinced of the advantages of Soviet society. That was the tradition, and applying that history to Violetta, to expect a woman who had cooperated with the KGB in the Soviet era to bare herself to the world about what she did and why and how she felt about her choices now—well, it was a lot to ask.

I had decided not to write a letter or make a phone call and to just show up. A word of advice I'd received was that Russian people respected resourcefulness. If you went to the trouble to locate and confront them in person, I'd been told, they would be so impressed it would be hard for them to turn you down.

Accompanied by a fearless young Russian woman as my interpreter and toting a bag full of knickknacks—cosmetics and Kleenex, two items I'd been told were in short supply—we

boarded the metro to Tekstilshiki, exited at an underground station, and surfaced along a busy boulevard lined with the metal
kiosks that have become the symbol of the new commercialism
in the new Moscow. They were stocked with liquor, beer, chocolate bars, and a brand of cigarettes I had to smile at. Between the
expected Camels and Marlboros was a pack of Hollywoods, and
the small print assured the smoker it was an "All-American
blend."

With little trouble we found the small, prefabricated, rather
characterless apartment complex, and having agreed it would be
best for her to go ahead and smooth the path for me, my interpreter disappeared in a dark entryway while I took a seat on a
bench in the tree-filled courtyard.

Several kids rode by on bikes; a woman strolled by pushing a
baby carriage. I looked up once and saw someone peering at me
from behind drapes. The ten minutes she was gone seemed like
twenty, and when she came walking out, I tried but was unable
to read her expression. "I'm talking with the mother," she said,
"but she's afraid to talk with you. I will give her what you've
brought."

I held out my bag of gifts, and watched her until she disappeared. I had no idea what was going on, and was even more
confused when she came back out and gestured rather abruptly,
"Let's go."

We were halfway back to the metro stop before she explained.
My theory was correct: Violetta still lived there, along with her
mother and her sister. But only the mother was home, and she
was absolutely paranoid. Told that an American writer who
wanted to talk to her was waiting outside, she had gotten extremely upset, and only some fast talking had kept her from
slamming the door.

"So how was it left?" I asked.

"I gave her your presents, and I wrote your phone number
down and mine and said we hoped to hear from her."

The call never came. A week went by, then a second week, and
finally I could wait no longer; I had to make something happen.
Another tip I'd been given about dealing with Russians was that

they respected perseverance. I should expect to hear no, but that wasn't necessarily the last word. So at ten o'clock one evening I decided to make a personal appeal.

It was getting dark by the time I arrived at the apartment building, and the lights were out in the second-story apartment where Violetta and her family lived. Once again I took a seat on a bench outside and waited. It was shortly after midnight when I heard footsteps and watched a woman enter the building. Unable to speak Russian, and without a description to go by, I had no way of knowing whether it was Violetta, her mother or sister—or even a neighbor, until a light went on in the flat. Within seconds I was ringing the buzzer to apartment number six.

There was silence, and then a woman's voice spoke from behind the door. No doubt she was inquiring who was there, so in fumbling Russian I recited three phrases I'd memorized from a Berlitz tape: "Good evening. How are you? Do you speak English?"

A safety chain rattled, and the door opened a crack, enough for me to see that I was addressing a plump woman in her late fifties with two gold front teeth and oversized eyeglasses. She said something, but I had reached the limits of my Russian vocabulary. I assumed that I was being asked to identify myself, so I did, in English. To which she spoke again in Russian, and once more I answered in English. And we went back and forth like this several times before we both gave up. She looked bewildered, and I did not know what to say next.

Suddenly I had a thought. In an elaborate pantomime, I pretended to make a phone call, and when an imaginary Natasha answered, I handed over the imaginary receiver. It worked. After a moment's hesitation she opened the door to me.

Sitting in a 1950s vintage kitchen, I called my interpreter, who mediated a conversation with Violetta's mother over the phone. The gist was that yes, my package had been received. She was sorry for not responding, but if I would meet her tomorrow afternoon at her place of work, she would explain.

The following day Natasha and I met at a central location and walked together to an ornately columned, eighteenth-century building that housed the Artists Union. Violetta's mother, whose name was Genrietta Khokha, and her second daughter, Svetlana, an eye-catchingly pretty seventeen-year-old with short-cropped hair, were waiting inside. Noticeably absent was Violetta, but her presence hovered over the conversation, as we all knew that without her we would not be sitting here talking.

After a round of introductions and small talk during which I learned that Genrietta was a retired teacher of geometry at an oil-and-gas institute who now designed leather goods, she invited us to join her in her studio. Leaving a high-ceilinged, pillared ballroom, we walked up a flight of stairs, down a series of corridors, through what looked like the dressing room of a theater troupe, and into an attic area, where we followed a walkway of boards across the old rafters before arriving at a safe and private room where chairs were arranged around a table on which a cake and a bottle of Coke were waiting. And there, with very little preamble or prompting, Genrietta announced her willingness to answer what questions I might have.

I couldn't believe my luck. Perhaps the timing was right, I thought. It almost seemed providential.

But relatively soon Genrietta disclosed the real reason she was confiding in me. "It will be hard for Violetta to talk with you because she has been unable to break off her connections with the KGB. She is still under their control," she said. "But I will talk to you on her behalf because I am no longer afraid of them. And because"—there was a catch in her throat, and tears welled in her eyes before she finished—"because the KGB stole my daughter from me."

18

For her own protection Genrietta had been told very little about
her family history, because after the Revolution and the Civil
War, when the Communists idealized the peasantry and the
working class, families of aristocratic or Jewish origin, families
with "foreign connections" or intelligentsia status, were labeled
"class enemies" and a threat to socialism in the U.S.S.R. and
would hide their heritage out of fear of oppression and purges.
She did know that both her parents were Ukrainian. She also
knew that as a young man her father had served in a Russian cavalry unit as a "recorder of events," and that the atrocities he wit-
nessed during Stalin's forced famine in the thirties so disturbed
him, he found a way to be transferred to Moscow, where he was
employed as an accountant in a military plant. And she knew
that he had brought his young wife, Zoya, with him, and they
had named their firstborn Genrietta after the heroine in an English novel her mother was reading at the time she was born.

Genrietta's childhood memories were dominated by the Great
Patriotic War, which had a devastating effect on her family. With
the advance of German troops, the plant where her father
worked was evacuated to the Ural Mountains, but he remained
behind to defend Moscow. By this time German planes were
dropping bombs on the city—Genrietta could distinguish the
enemy planes by the sound of their engines—and the Moscow
suburbs were a front-line town. She was expecting at any mo-

ment to see tanks painted with swastikas rumbling down Moscow streets.

Genrietta vividly recalls the day her father left the house for the last time. Authorities were evacuating all women and children from the city, but her father's parting words were that no matter what happened, they should stay in Moscow. If they left, he said, they would be sent to Siberia, and when the war was over they would not be allowed to return. With that he said goodbye, and like millions of other Russian soldiers, he never returned.

Education had always been important to Zoya, who found work in the postwar period as a librarian, and she successfully passed on the love of learning to her daughter, who at an early age decided to become a teacher. Teachers earned relatively good pay and enjoyed social prestige; and education was recognized as a major force in building the new Russia.

As a student Genrietta was serious and erudite, interested in science as well as the arts. But student activities also provided social occasions, and it was at a university event that she met Sein, who would become her first husband. Looking back now, she found it hard to understand how she could think of him as marriage material. He was the son of a railway worker from an ordinary Russian family, and their temperaments were very different. She was spiritual and progressive in her thinking; he was materialistic, and destined to be the manager of a classified military-defense plant and a district party leader. But he was handsome, clever, and well mannered, and one thing led to another and the next was marriage.

Within a relatively short time, Genrietta realized she'd made a mistake, and their relationship was breaking up when she found she was carrying his child. This was an unplanned, unwanted turn of events, and she gave serious consideration to having an abortion, a common form of birth control in the Soviet Union. She was still in school, she had ambitions, and she knew by now if she had a baby she would be facing single parenthood. But her mother was living with her, so that would be a help, and she just couldn't bring herself to terminate the life that was growing inside her.

Once she had made that decision, she knew it was the right one, and she found joy in the preparations, embroidering baby diapers by hand. Her daughter was born on October 27, 1960, and she named her Violetta because she thought it was a beautiful name and it rhymed with her own. At the time she was unaware that Violetta was also the name of the expensive courtesan in the opera *La Traviata,* with whom a young man fell in love to tragic results.

In many ways Genrietta was a woman ahead of her time. She had feminist notions—she didn't believe men should decide important issues without taking into consideration the woman's point of view—and she was determined not to let motherhood deter her plans for a career in academia. With the help of Zoya, who babysat Violetta when she was an infant and walked her to and from school when she was older, and Violetta's father, from whom she was divorced but who would occasionally visit his daughter in the evenings and help her with her studies, the parenting chores were shared in a way that allowed Genrietta to pursue her professional aspirations.

And when she did arrive home, she would do her best to make up for her absence by taking evening walks with Violetta and reading to her until bedtime. Genrietta believed that Violetta's interest in foreign languages originated with the myths and legends from countries around the world that she read to her daughter at a young age. Hearing stories about magicians and giants, beautiful damsels in distress and rescuing heroes was a lot more interesting to a young girl than what was taught in Soviet schools, where lessons infused with Communist ideology were drilled into the students repetitiously from the day their formal education began. And Violetta exhibited an amazing memory. When she played with her dolls, she would pretend she was reading to them and could repeat the stories her mother had read to her almost word for word.

When Genrietta, who believed that the educational process should take into consideration the God-given nature of the individual, noticed that Violetta was responding with great curiosity to learn more about foreign countries, she encouraged her. At a shop in Moscow that sold international educational materials she purchased a game made up of disks on which different images were painted, and the players were supposed to spin an arrow and name in English the figure or animal it pointed to. Then she bought a record player and a variety of children's musical records on which the Russian name for something was followed by the English name, all sung to a catchy melody.

Genrietta liked the idea that she and her daughter were on a parallel learning track. She had visions of raising a "Renaissance woman," and that impulse led her to introduce Violetta to a variety of activities. She took her daughter to classical-music concerts, arranged for her to receive piano lessons, and interested her in collecting stamps of painting masterpieces. Winter skiing forays into the forests were complemented with skating ventures at a public rink, where Violetta showed such instinctive coordination that Genrietta enrolled her in classes with a professional. During Genrietta's summer vacations the two of them would travel to vacation spots around the U.S.S.R., where they would swim and hike and climb mountains. Wherever they went, people were struck by Violetta—she had ash-brown hair and radiant blue eyes that turned green as she grew older before settling on hazel—and that attention would sometimes lead to invitations and opportunities that turned their trips into adventures.

As Violetta began to develop a personality of her own, her mother noticed several distinct features over which she felt she had no influence, however. Violetta had a mind of her own and could be headstrong. Even as a toddler she wanted to make her own choices. Once Genrietta took her to Children's World to pick out a party dress, and when she selected a dark-cherry one with white polka dots that her daughter didn't like, Violetta started to scream so loudly the store manager ran over as if to rescue her from abuse.

Violetta was also a very private child, withdrawn almost, and wary of making new friends. Rather than running around in the courtyard and playing with the neighborhood kids, she would sit by herself in their flat and wait for her mother to come home and take her to the theater, or to put flowers on the tomb of the unknown soldier near the Kremlin in memory of her grandfather.

If there was one particular area of concern Genrietta had about her daughter as she grew up, it was her attitude toward men. It wasn't that Violetta exhibited anything abnormal as an adolescent, other than that it always seemed to work out that the boys who were smitten with her she found annoying. When she was a first-year schoolgirl, the runt of her class became ridiculously infatuated with her and told his mother if he could not sit at the same desk with Violetta, he would refuse to attend school. When the teacher sat them beside each other, Violetta did everything she could to drive him away. She deliberately spilled ink on his notebook. Once she pushed him so hard he fell to the floor. When nothing else worked, she complained to her mother and said *she* would not go back to school until he stopped pestering her.

Then, when she was twelve years old and in the sixth form, another young boy had such a crush on her he would climb the tree outside her window just to watch her.

What worried Genrietta was that Violetta was growing up without a male presence. She had no regular father and no brother, and she was living in a household occupied by three generations of women.

And then along came Vladimir.

Genrietta and Violetta were at the skating rink one day when this handsome young man approached them and struck up a conversation. His name was Vladimir, and he said he recognized them from the neighborhood, where he had seen the two of them taking walks. They asked him to skate with them, and that was the beginning.

Though he was hardly the ideal match—he was thirty-one, whereas Genrietta had just turned forty, and he was employed as an electrician, which was socially beneath her position as head instructor of descriptive geometry at one of Moscow's top technical institutes—it was exciting for Genrietta to be pursued by a virile younger man. Almost as important, he was an absolute dream around Violetta. His knowledge of physics and math enabled him to be of great help to her with her homework, he was a genius with electricity, rigging games for her so they lit up when she played with them, and the two of them loved to skate and ski together. Indeed, as an intimacy ripened between them, Violetta would rush home from school just to be with him. And if he was late, she would look petulantly at her watch and say, "Mom, why isn't Vlad here yet? He was supposed to be here fifteen minutes ago."

The complications that Vladimir would introduce into the household would not be fully appreciated, or understood, until years afterward. Unbeknownst to Genrietta, Violetta, who was fifteen years old at the time, developed a romantic attachment of her own to Vladimir. She even fancied the notion the two of them might end up together. And when Vladimir and Genrietta announced their intention to marry, she was shattered with jealousy.

At this point in the telling of her story Genrietta paused, as if to catch her breath. And in that brief interlude I tried to imagine the family dynamics, the lines of tension this marriage must have drawn between mother and daughter. What it must have been like for Violetta—at an age when girls idealize romantic love, when she was beginning to feel the first stirrings of passion—to lie awake at night in their small two-room apartment and listen to the sounds of her mother making love with the man she wished were lying beside her.

As it turned out, Genrietta was not just taking a breather; she was debating how much to tell me. When she decided, she added a macabre postscript. Several years before Vlad entered her life, while she was teaching at the technical institute, a young student had developed a neurotic obsession with her. He had been a sensitive young man, uniquely talented at painting and music, but high-strung and intense. She hadn't realized he was also emotionally unbalanced until the day she received a love letter from him, imploring her to marry him. She was astonished, but she didn't want to hurt him, so she answered him with gentle play-fulness. "When I was young, I all the time felt a great love to-ward my teachers as well," she recalled telling him. "It will pass."

But this one was not to be discouraged. He thought that per-haps she was rejecting him because she felt it would be unethical for a teacher to have an affair with one of her students, and he offered to transfer elsewhere if that would make their relation-ship more proper. Once again she treated his overtures lightly. "I am not the right person for you," she insisted. "Someday you will find a woman your age, someone more like you, who will make you very happy. Who knows, maybe you will even marry my daughter Violetta, and I will be your mother-in-law."

It was simply unthinkable that anything could come of his at-traction for her, and when at last she convinced him of this, he became distraught, delirious. After a final appeal he went on a cognac-drinking binge, and after passing out he never regained consciousness. In the note he left behind, he let it be known that without Genrietta he could no longer bear living on this earth.

The story didn't end there. His spirit continued to haunt Gen-rietta. Sitting by herself in her flat, she was unable to shake the feeling he was standing in the hall outside and at any minute the door would swing open and he would stride into the room. At night she was afraid to go into the bathroom because she thought his spirit was in there waiting to pounce on her. Once, walking alone down an empty street, she thought she heard his footsteps following her, so she quickened her pace, and just when she knew his hands were about to reach out and grab her by the throat, she wheeled around to defend herself, but there was no one there.

The point Genrietta wanted to make was that she had missed what was going on with her daughter and Vladimir because of something internal that was preoccupying her. "Vladimir, you see, was the same age as the love-struck student. Physically they even resembled each other. The coincidence was too much to ig-nore. When he proposed I simply could not take a chance on cre-ating another human tragedy."

Silence filled Genrietta Khokha's dimly lit loft-studio. In a whispered voice she said very few people were aware of what I had just heard. Even Violetta was unaware of this history.

She went on to say it was an awful feeling to know that you were responsible for inflicting an unforgivable injury on someone to whom you intended no harm, and how when that happened you damaged your own life. She was speaking for herself, but I somehow sensed she was letting me know that this was a feeling her daughter had come to know as well.

The opening line of *Anna Karenina*—"Happy families are all alike; every unhappy family is unhappy in its own way"—kept coming to mind as the tale of Violetta's teenage years unfolded. Her mother's marriage to Vladimir was an emotional trauma that became a turning point with the birth of a baby girl, Svetlana. Not only did Violetta resent the attention bestowed on her new half sister, her grandmother, Zoya, emerged as a destructive force in family relations. The old woman was getting senile, and fearing that her own position in the household was being usurped, she did everything in her power to turn her granddaughter against Genrietta.

"Your mother has traded both of us for this man," she whispered to Violetta. "Watch out now or she'll turn you into a babysitter."

Zoya even went so far as to confide to Violetta, "I am the person you have to thank for being on earth, because I'm the one who stopped your mother from having an abortion. She never wanted you."

After that, the domestic atmosphere became very strained. Violetta felt betrayed—by her mother, and by the man she'd fallen in love with. Now that a younger sister had come along, she felt replaced and no longer part of the family. At home there were constant scenes and quarrels. She was rude with her stepfather and hostile toward her sister, and she treated her mother with cold-hearted contempt. Genrietta saw what was happening, knew she was losing her daughter, and did not know what to do about it.

As with all Soviet children, growing up Violetta had joined Communist youth organizations. She had attended the Octoberites club as a little girl, where she was taught to play games through which ran themes of Communist ideology. When she was nine she received the red kerchief of the Young Pioneers, which she wore proudly around her neck as a badge of honor. And at the age of fourteen she had become a member of Komsomol, a political organization that prepared Soviet youth to become party members, though by this time a lot of the idealism had been lost and joining was almost an automatic act.

But Violetta was not particularly interested in politics. She would sit without protest through relentless ideological indoctrinations that shaped virtually every class, but more often than not her mind would drift to more pleasant topics. In this regard she asserted her independence in the same way a lot of Soviet girls did—by escaping from the required readings about class struggle and social conflicts in the West into romance literature. Her fondness for Pushkin was extreme—she kept a special notebook in which she wrote his poems in her own handwriting, and she knew his biography by heart. She read everything that was translated of Alexandre Dumas—her favorites were the adventure stories *The Three Musketeers* and *The Count of Monte Cristo,* where the hero and heroine, after an exciting adventure, arrive at a happy ending. Margaret Mitchell's *Gone With the Wind* topped the list of American titles she read and liked.

As she neared the end of her high school years, Violetta began to think seriously about her future. It was a logical choice for her to set her sights on entering the prestigious Maurice Thorez Institute of Foreign Languages. A degree from the institute would mean a better job than clerical or secretarial work, and it contained the exotic promise of nice clothes, good food, and even travel opportunities. But gaining admission was no easy task. There was a lot of competition to get in. Only the students with the top grades from the best schools were accepted. Unless your family had political clout, that was. Although the institute had a good academic reputation, the admissions process was known to be corrupt. If you did not make a passing grade on the entrance examination but your parents were well off or well connected, an exception was made.

Although her mother could be classified as part of the intelligentsia, Genrietta had no political connections, the schools Violetta had attended catered primarily to children of the working class, her teachers were average, and her language skills were mediocre. So she had very little chance of getting into the Institute of Foreign Languages by the normal route, but she was an ambitious girl, willing to do whatever it took to forge a career for herself.

There were two departments at the Institute of Foreign Languages: the Pedagogical Department, where teachers of foreign languages were trained, and the Interpreters Department. Women, who traditionally were involved in education, made up the bulk of the pedagogical student body, whereas the majority of those studying to become interpreters were males. There were also day classes and evening classes, the former for the full-time students, the latter for those looking to upgrade their skills. It was through a combination of personal charm and resolution that Violetta managed to land a laboratory-assistant position in the administrative offices of the Pedagogical Department, where she would also be permitted to attend evening classes.

That first year she made passing grades in all of her classes. But when she was given permission to become a day student at the Pedagogical Department and, not only that, allowed to audit interpreters' classes in the evening, the arrangement had little to do with her performance in the classroom.

The term *stukach* is derived from the verb "to knock." In Russian it refers to a person who knocks on the door of his boss and informs on fellow workers or students. It translates into English as "snitch."

The way it usually worked, an assistant to the dean at the institute would call into the office a student whose grades were poor and would promise a passing grade on the next examination, or give an assurance that there would be no expulsion. There were a number of variants, but they all added up to the same offer: The student would be allowed to continue with his or her studies if he or she was willing to cooperate with the administration in addressing some of its security concerns.

"Our instructors are very concerned about the moral character of those whom we are training to interact with Westerners, or to serve overseas," the school official would say. "Do they drink excessively? Do they have a weakness for women? Do they exchange rubles for hard currency? Are they critical of the Soviet system in private? Are they secret admirers of Western lifestyles? Do they have contacts with Westerners they do not report? These are things we need to know, because these are the things that will make them vulnerable to blackmail if they are given overseas assignments. So please understand, it is our intention to help our students, and by helping us identify problem areas, you will be helping them, too."

In Violetta's case, in trade for accelerated educational opportunities she agreed to play the role of the bright and attractive student who had been given permission to audit interpreters' classes, and after ingratiating herself into the confidence of her fellow students who were preparing to work as interpreters in the West, she would report on their activities and conversations. Her responsibilities were not characterized as spying; it was more a matter of advising the instructors on their students' politics, personal habits, tastes, and weaknesses.

For Violetta, this was a strictly pragmatic choice. It would have been impossible for a woman of her background to advance to higher levels in society on merit alone. That was the nature of Soviet society: If you wanted to better yourself and improve your lot, and your parents weren't wealthy or influential party members, you had no choice but to seek favors. In this instance that meant cooperate with the system. It wasn't a matter of morality, but expediency. And it wasn't as if she were alone in playing the game. Many of the students she would be informing on had gotten where they were because of privileges.

Over the next three years Violetta established herself as disciplined and competent in all the assignments that were put before her. She was not a particularly popular student. Ever since her mother's second marriage she had adopted a guarded stance toward people, and as a fellow student would describe her, "Violetta was a person without half-tones: She either loved or hated, and if she loved someone she would do anything for them, but if she hated she could be cruel. Others, similarly, either loved her or hated her." But at the institute she would find several close friends with whom she would bond for life, and she would accomplish the goal she'd set for herself, graduating from the Pedagogical Department in 1982.

It was during the fourth and final year at the institute that the "servants of intelligence" began trolling the waters in search of recruitable prospects. After observing and appraising Violetta, they decided she would make an excellent candidate for future projects. She was maturing into a beautiful woman, she had a strong desire to promote her career, and she had a proven ability to perform "Judas functions." They rewarded her with the invitation to take a two-year postgraduate course at the Ministry of Foreign Affairs that would prepare her for a position in a foreign embassy, and she accepted.

Once again, it was not a difficult choice for her to make, in part because of the personality of the people who approached her—contrary to popular impressions of KGB officers as scheming and base men, those she met were sophisticated, charming graduates of the institute—and in part because of Violetta's outlook. She'd gotten a taste of the privileged life, and she knew that if she continued to cooperate, all kinds of paths could open to her that would provide her with a measure of liberty and gaiety absent from normal Soviet life.

Although the KGB did have "charm schools" where young women were taught seduction techniques, the purpose of the course that Violetta attended at the Foreign Ministry was to polish social skills. This meant raising her general level of cultural awareness so she would be able to conduct conversations on different topics and on different levels with well-educated foreigners. She was also taught the behavior, manners, and etiquette appropriate to a diplomatic setting. While the effective application of cosmetics was one of the lessons, the teachers stressed that too much makeup would create suspicions, and there were ways to be sexy at deeper levels. Western men in particular tended to be drawn toward "soulful" relationships with women who projected interesting inner qualities; women who asked intelligent questions, were willing to listen, and showed an interest in them as people. As for engaging in sexual activity, she was never explicitly told that would be a requirement, but it was implicit that there were circumstances under which that was the direction a relationship might go.

There was no specific training on intelligence issues—nothing more specific than things like the value of not showing how well she understood the English language at first—but there was no misunderstanding either: She was being groomed to become a more efficient informer.

Throughout this training Violetta continued to work part-time in the administrative offices of the institute and to teach English on a freelance basis. She also served as an interpreter at different international congresses that were held in Moscow, and in the spring of 1985 she was recommended for employment at the Administration for Service to the Diplomatic Corps. Known by the initials UPDK, and pronounced Ooh-Pay-De-Kah, it was the Soviet agency that provided a Russian workforce to every foreign embassy.

19

At this time in the Soviet Union the tentacles of the KGB reached into just about every organization, but its interest in UPDK was greater than most others because of the contact the members of UPDK had with foreigners. While a certain percentage of the UPDK staff at every embassy was professionally trained by the KGB, the majority owed their position to family connections. Every Russian who worked for UPDK was screened for "political correctness," however, and all were required to meet with a supervisor on a weekly basis and report their observations. Everyone also knew that the time could come when he or she would be called upon to serve the security services in an active capacity.

When Violetta was informed in May 1985 that she was being recommended for a position in the American Embassy, she had mixed feelings. It made her nervous, because throughout her life it had been stamped into her head that America was the enemy and the American Embassy was staffed with professional spies. Indeed, at that very time she, like millions of Russians, had been transfixed by a popular espionage thriller series on Soviet television that pitted the KGB against the CIA. A James Bond–style adventure that starred some of the Soviet Union's top movie actors, the program focused on a fictitious African republic with a pro-Moscow government that appealed to Soviet help to quell a CIA-backed coup plot, and the action included bloody assassinations, clandestine agents shadowing U.S. diplomats in Moscow, and codes transmitted by U.S. spy centers via shortwave receivers. Like many Soviet films, this one had a clear message: The United States was plotting not only against the Soviet Union, but also against nations friendly to it—and foreigners were not to be trusted.

On the other hand the embassy position was an exciting opportunity to meet and interact with Westerners; the salary was more lucrative than at any of the other foreign embassies; and she was told that Russian employees were even given a uniform allowance. A pittance by Western standards—$300 a year—but the right to flip through Neiman Marcus, Macy's, and Sears catalogues and order things that were impossible to get in the Soviet Union was a big perquisite.

As it turned out, Violetta's first position was not in the embassy proper but as a temporary replacement in Spaso House, the residence of the American ambassador to the Soviet Union, Arthur Hartman. She acted as sort of the house executive, sitting at a desk, answering the phone, and communicating with the domestic staff, but worked there barely a month before she was relieved of her duties because of a conflict with Donna Hartman, the ambassador's wife, who found her sulky and uninterested in her work, and rated her performance as unsatisfactory.

Within a matter of weeks she was hired to fill a long-standing vacancy in the customs section of the American Embassy as a file clerk. She almost didn't get the job because of what had happened at Spaso House, but UPDK advised the embassy that she was the only person available, her English was fine, and her clerical skills good enough. In her interview with the American General Services officer she projected a desire to prove herself worthy of a second chance.

Over the course of the summer of 1985 Violetta became "a stylish presence" at the embassy, in the words of one foreign-service employee. Her father, now a party boss, had reentered her life, and as if to make up for the years he'd been away, he bought her new outfits, so her attire was fashionably up-to-date. Dressed to kill, tall at about five feet nine inches, with shoulder-length brown hair and striking hazel eyes, she became the center of attention among male staff members at the embassy.

Much later, when NIS investigators would interview embassy employees, they would be given a tawdry portrait of Violetta that would support the impression she was on the make. "While an employee at the General Services office, she visibly spent much time doing her fingernails, reading trashy English novels, and displaying a brazen lack of interest in her job," they would be told. "She made overt eye and facial expressions indicative of a sexual approach . . . and her frequent attempts to physically lure American personnel became an office joke. Coworkers referred to her as 'the dangle.'" Some even assessed her as an individual who attempted to make herself attractive to either sex.

It's hard to know what to make of these observations, because the way Violetta told it to her mother, numerous Marines made passes at her while she worked at the embassy, but she wasn't interested. At least one political officer became a nuisance, calling her at home and inviting her to dinner and embassy functions, until finally she told her mother to refuse his calls. And when she first noticed Clayton Lonetree following her home from work, she was convinced he was a CIA agent, which was what she told the KGB when she called to report on him.

By the time Violetta made her call, Sgt. Clayton Lonetree was already under KGB observation. The Second Chief Directorate of the KGB was the Soviet counterpart to the FBI, its specialty internal counterintelligence, and to fulfill its charter it was divided into twelve departments. Because America was perceived as the primary enemy, the First Department directed its interest and activities toward the American Embassy and its personnel. On staff at the First Department was a chief; several deputies; about fifty staff officers, recruiters, and agent handlers; and several hundred professional surveillants who did nothing but follow people who came out of the American Embassy. These were the people who first noticed Lonetree, and they had filed several reports on his bizarre activities. He left the compound by himself in violation of the rules they knew were laid down for Marine guards. He rode the metro miles beyond the travel limits they knew were specified.

Those who worked in surveillance were a laconic bunch, and when their shift was complete, they would regularly go out for coffee or vodka and grumble about what had been written in the daily newspaper. These days the conversation invariably returned to the American Marine and what he was up to. They couldn't figure it out. The guy was breaking every rule in the Marine book, he was doing it all the time, and nothing was happening to him.

Within the First Department, whose headquarters were a half mile from the embassy in an unassuming five-story building, analysts considering the Marine guard's behavior were asking the same questions, and came up with a theory. It was a commonly held belief at this time that the CIA group in the American Embassy was the most reckless and adventurous of all the intelligence offices attached to any of the embassies in Moscow. This was perceived to be a direct reflection of the personality of the CIA's current director, William Casey, under whose leadership the CIA had been willing to take more than the usual number of risks to recruit human sources. They speculated the Marine might be some sort of crude bait in yet another provocative CIA scheme.

But after Violetta's call the picture became slightly clearer: Perhaps it was nothing more than the matter of a Marine falling for a Russian beauty, and a lapse in security vigilance at the embassy.

The individual who initially handled the case was a recent graduate of KGB school, a young man who went by the name of "Slava" but whose real name was Vladimir Pavlovich Gerashchenko. Slava worked in a department of the KGB that took the reports from the Russian workers in foreign embassies, specifically the branch that concerned itself with the American Embassy. He was relatively inexperienced but he was also a go-getter, anxious to move up in rank. He knew that a big concern within Soviet counterintelligence throughout the eighties had been that it had very few agents in the embassies of the main capitalist states in the U.S.S.R., and that its inside work was carried out mainly by Soviet citizens employed by the embassies.

Therefore the idea of recruiting someone from the "stronghold
of the spies," as the American Embassy was known, could lead to
a rapid promotion, even if it was just a guard. As the Russian
proverb said, "When there is no fish, a shrimp will do."

After interviewing Violetta in his cubicle at headquarters,
Slava reported the results to his superior, who in turn sent the report up the chain of command, where it arrived finally on the
desk of Gen. Rem Krasil'nikov, head of the First Department. A
slim, white-haired man in his late fifties with sparkling brown
eyes, Krasil'nikov had earned his position by being a very good
operational officer. He was reputed to have successfully recruited
American agents, including several from the CIA, in Lebanon in
the early seventies. Normally a report like this would have captured his full attention, but at that very moment the general was
dealing with bigger issues. His officers had recently arrested a
Soviet expert in stealth technology by the name of Adolf Tolka-
chev, caught in the act of passing secret documents to U.S. intelligence agent Paul Stombaugh, who was posing as a second
secretary at the U.S. Embassy; and Krasil'nikov was then investigating a hot tip that a double agent was working in his department. So he did not take a special interest in Slava's report. His
response was "Stay on top of it. See what you can get out of it.
Keep me informed."

Even though his boss may have been nonchalant, Slava was
thrilled and called Violetta back in. She seemed nervous to him
and said she wanted to tell the Marine to leave her alone, but
Slava told her just to keep on doing what she was doing and see
what happened. Outdoor surveillance would keep an eye on the
Marine so she would be safe, and she should contact him immediately if she was actually approached.

Slava knew that the best recruitment scenarios were the simplest and closest to life. He also knew the critical step in any recruitment was the initial contact, and it would be best to let the
Marine make the first move.

In the meantime an order went out to expand the "recruitment
dossier" on Sgt. Clayton Lonetree. A file of this sort was kept on
virtually every person at the American Embassy—from the small-

est child to the ambassador—as a matter of course. It included all the paperwork required by Soviet customs before entry into the Soviet Union was allowed; special applications embassy employees were required to submit; and the résumés and biographies of everyone were factually checked by researchers working in the Soviet residency in the States. In this file details that were relevant to the development of an individual recruitment plan were noted, and in those cases where a diplomat was suspected of being an intelligence agent, or a weak link was identified, a special investigation was undertaken.

The dossier on Lonetree was fat by the time Violetta reported that he had approached her on the metro. At this point she was not technically an agent, so she was given a standard statement to sign that read: "I, Violetta Seina, agree to voluntarily cooperate with the organs of the Soviet Committee for State Security, for the sake of combating enemies of the Soviet Union and for the purpose of strengthening state security. . . ." It ended that she was not to divulge to anyone that she was working for the security services, and she understood the full consequences if she were to break faith with them. She was then put through a series of brief but intensive training sessions with sophisticated teachers from the intelligence schools, who instructed her on how she should conduct herself in this matter.

Although technically this was a "sexual recruitment" and in internal KGB reports it would be referred to in this way, it was not a contrived sexual entrapment in the traditional sense. Gone were the days when the KGB relied on blackmail to recruit a foreign agent. In fact, in KGB school the anecdote was told about the Soviet "swallow" who lured a diplomatic official into bed so photographs could be taken of him in a compromising position; and when he was presented with the pictures and told they would be shown to his wife unless he agreed to collaborate with the KGB, the fellow had held the photos up to the light for a better look, complimented their high quality, and said he didn't mind at all their being shown to his wife because they would prove how virile he was.

Experience had shown that blackmail subjected a person to

great psychological pressures that backfired more often than not. The recruit would become resentful and angry toward those who were blackmailing him and would begin to look for a way out of his predicament. The modus operandi these days called for cultivation through emotional attachment. Gradually and subtly drawing the subject in through friendship, and then intimacy, so that when he agreed to become an agent he would be motivated by positive feelings.

Violetta was instructed not to rush things but to let each step evolve naturally. She could agree to meet with the Marine, but she should act with the discretion and caution he would expect of a Russian citizen who was breaking the law by seeing him. She should take steps to avoid the attention of authorities so he would become convinced that she was engaging in authentically clandestine contacts, and she should encourage him to behave circumspectly within the embassy so as not to draw attention to their relationship.

She was also told to write down the details of every conversation she had with Lonetree the day she had them or immediately the next morning, so she wouldn't forget anything. Included was to be all he said that related to his background, his family, his friends, and his vulnerabilities as he verbalized them. This information would be entered into his dossier for the purpose of analysis and checked against the information that had come in from America.

For a nonprofessional Violetta played her part superbly, bringing the relationship along systematically, and over the next few months the development of Sergeant Lonetree proceeded by the book. The only people in the KGB who had reason to complain were the outdoor surveillance people who were assigned to follow Lonetree whenever he left the embassy, including the night details when they stood outside Violetta's apartment in the freezing cold, cursing their jobs and "the American who lost himself in a Russian cunt."

20

According to the KGB textbooks, the time for a professionally trained handler to enter the picture is that moment when the person realizes that if he tries to take a step backward it will hurt him more than if he continues to go forward. When he is caught and knows no amount of thrashing will throw the hook, in other words. Usually it took months and even years to reach this point, but in Lonetree's case there was a scheduling consideration. He had already extended his Moscow tour of duty once and was supposed to be transferred to Vienna in March 1986. For this reason, sanction for the consolidation of his recruitment was given in December of 1985, and it was signed by Viktor Mikhailovich Chebrikov, chairman of the KGB since 1982, who had taken a personal interest in the case.

The selection of Aleksei Yefimov to act as Lonetree's handler reveals a lot of what was happening internally to the KGB at this time. In his mid-thirties, Yefimov was one of the new generation of KGB officers. He had joined the KGB through his own initiative, enlisting as a border guard; and when he proved to be smart and dedicated, his superiors recommended him for the Higher KGB school. Upon completion of his studies he was assigned to the department that oversaw Russians who had frequent contacts with foreign tourists and press people, and after attaining the rank of captain he had been promoted to the position of deputy chief of the branch that supervised UPDK workers at the American Embassy.

Although it was a step up, new pressures came with the job. The department was run with an iron hand by an old Stalinist wolf, Col. Aleksei Barovikov, a gruff, narrow-minded man who thought the new generation of KGB officers had it too easy. It was the department's responsibility to collect information about the internal order of the American Embassy and American personnel, and the UPDK workers reported to his staff what they saw, whom they talked to, what they talked about, who paid attention to them—things like that. But nothing was absolute, and not everyone was reporting what they should. Some gave partial reports and kept things to themselves, such as favors Americans had done them and the extent of personal friendships. There had been a time when Russians would not have dared think of withholding information, but fear of the KGB was on the wane and these days you could never be sure who was telling the truth or who was playing tricks.

When Violetta had been escorted into his office and told him of her strange situation, Yefimov's first thought had been, Why is she telling me this? She could have simply discouraged the Marine, and that would have been the end of it. That she didn't, made him think she was personally drawn to intrigues and that maybe she was one of those pretty, nervy girls who wanted to work at a foreign embassy for the fun of "fucking around" with a Westerner, and who entertained the outside hope that she might possibly marry a foreigner and leave the country. Yefimov had become a cynic by this time. Russians who worked at the American Embassy knew the score, and he'd come to the conclusion that most of them accepted the conditions because they had some kind of personal goal in mind. Rather than their being exploited by the security services, which was the popular myth, he thought it was often the other way around.

Over the course of the next few months, as Violetta developed a deepening relationship with Lonetree, Yefimov was kept informed of its progress but was not involved in a direct way. Instead he was occupied with his own American Embassy contacts. In his position he had been authorized to meet regularly with specific State Department officials for informal exchanges of ideas and information, and since 1983 he had actively maintained a relationship with several diplomats, answering their questions about new members of the Politburo while making his own inquiries into American attitudes toward the Strategic Defense Initiative.

This made it all the more startling to him when Colonel Barovikov called him in and told him that the decision had been made "to use this situation for our purposes," and that he, Yefimov, had been chosen to consummate the recruitment of the Marine guard.

Yefimov reminded the colonel that he had very little experience in intelligence gathering and operative work, and suggested that surely there were more seasoned counterintelligence agents who were trained for spywork. His superior said there was no one qualified who was available, and besides, to bring in an agent from elsewhere would only complicate things.

Yefimov made no further protest because he understood the situation. This operation already included several employees of the First Department, dozens from the Surveillance Department, and a number from the Twelfth, which handled secret technical observations, such as wiretaps and videotapes. To ask for a counterintelligence expert would mean more people, more bosses, another layer of bureaucracy. Barovikov's desire to keep control of the operation rather than seek assistance was typical of a system that was based on rewards. If this operation was a success, credit for recruiting a foreign agent would have to be shared, and the colonel wanted to keep as much for himself as he could.

Before this, the closest Yefimov had come to being involved in the recruitment of an American was when a woman from the American Embassy driving her car along the Rublonsky Highway ran over a Russian citizen, and instead of leaving waited for the traffic police to show up. It was an opportune time to initiate a recruitment effort, but when they ran a check and found she was a legitimate diplomat, they decided she would probably report on their efforts, and they decided not to bother. So this was going to be his maiden effort, and to prepare him, counterintelligence specialists came over and reviewed the character of the target and the details of the situation with him, and discussed the strategy and tactics of this kind of operation. He was briefed on the "Uncle Sasha" charade. He was counseled that his interest in Lonetree should appear to be motivated by friendship and goodwill. He was reminded to appeal to Lonetree's vanity, and let him know he was not alone, others had done what he was doing.

Finally, he was told that even though Lonetree's awareness of his compromising activities with Violetta, together with his interest in continuing his relationship with her, should assure his compliance, it would be a good idea to develop with him an ideological justification for what he was doing before actually tasking him with questions and assignments. "The string to his soul," Yefimov was told, would be to connect his minority status as an Indian and the plight of his people at the hands of racist, capitalist America with the Soviet Union's ideological struggle against imperialism and desire for a society based on justice and equality.

It was a lot to keep in mind, and at this stage of the operation Yefimov's feelings were complicated by ambivalence. Half of him was excited by the challenge of recruiting a foreign agent, and having only read about recruitments accomplished "with the help of a skirt," he was curious to find out for himself how influential women could be. At the same time he was unsure that the outcome would be worth the effort. It had been his understanding that counterintelligence tended not to bother with the recruitment of military people, because even though they were more vulnerable, they had more structure and oversight than civilians and were required to account for their time almost up to the minute. That made it more difficult to maintain ongoing relations with them.

He was nervous too because it was a case with political ramifications. Bosses with high ambitions and great expectations would be looking over his shoulder and assessing his every move. If for some reason the operation went bad, if the Marine did not produce what the bosses expected, Yefimov knew that he could be held personally accountable—which was also the Soviet way.

Yefimov's first impressions of Lonetree were strictly professional. Purposely he did not allow himself to have any personal
feelings. He had been fully briefed on the Marine's background
and was aware that he was dealing with "a very sad and unhappy
man"; but his understanding of Lonetree did not go so far as to
include compassion, because that would have been inappropriate, and he knew that he was recruiting Lonetree on the basis of
his shortcomings.

It became rapidly clear to him that subterfuge was not a requirement. Lonetree appeared to immediately figure out who he
was, and wasn't, and since he knew very well who Lonetree was,
the game of hide-and-seek was unnecessary. For this reason Yefimov also decided not to dwell for too long on the cliché of Indians in conflict with the white man. He knew his bosses were
hoping for confirmation of the Leninist interpretation of American society that maintained disaffected minorities were anxious
to overthrow the yokes of their capitalist oppressors, and in the
reports he filed he told them what they wanted to hear. But these
were exaggerations. To stress this theme, he felt, would confuse
Lonetree and had the potential to jeopardize the case. The key to
Lonetree's cooperation, he realized, was not his grudge against
Western society but his obsession with Violetta.

In his meetings with counterintelligence Yefimov had been instructed to ask questions that would enable them to identify
American intelligence officers working behind the facade of the
embassy under the guise of diplomats. CI generally had a pretty
good idea who the CIA agents were, but there were always a few
people they had difficulty identifying, and Lonetree was in a position to help them confirm their suspicions.

Then there were the other areas CI wanted him to cover, such
as updating and detailing renovated spaces inside the embassy;
information about the security systems (where they were located
and how they functioned); and data on embassy personnel (the
location of their work spaces, the hours they kept, their personal
habits and characteristics) that would expand the KGB's recruitment dossiers.

Ideally an agent inside an embassy could also do things like procure secret documents, but in this regard Yefimov had been instructed it would be a mistake to task the Marine beyond his means. Each employee in the embassy had his own circle of issues he dealt with, and if Lonetree suddenly started asking questions about matters that were none of his business, or attempted to acquire documents not normally available to him, it could raise suspicions that would give him away.

Something a Marine guard could do, however, particularly when patrolling the embassy by himself at night, was install listening devices, and Yefimov did hope that he would be able to get Lonetree to follow the example of the guard recruited at the British Embassy years ago. After describing an important meeting room in the embassy, he was asked to bring a lightbulb from the chandelier to his handler. KGB technicians reconstructed it, planting a microphone inside, and the bulb was returned to the guard, who replaced it. The ruse worked perfectly. Not until the British began to realize that information was somehow being leaked, and the walls and ceiling and floor were torn apart, was the bug in the lightbulb discovered. But when Yefimov asked Lonetree if he would be willing to do something similar, he balked at the suggestion, and rather than pressure him, Yefimov had backed off.

It would be up to others to analyze and decide on the ultimate worth of the information supplied by Lonetree, but from what Yefimov could tell, a greater satisfaction was derived from the fact that the security services had an American agent in their control than from any particular piece of information Lonetree delivered. This was true on the lower levels of the KGB, where at this stage of the Cold War there had been so many defections to the West that the recruitment of an American was perceived as giving "the finger" to the CIA, as well as among KGB higher-ups, who regarded Lonetree as a major ideological coup. KGB Chairman Chebrikov was receiving daily reports on the progress of the operation, and would brag at various intelligence and political functions how "under the toughest working conditions," a security guard at the American Embassy was doing KGB work.

Much to Yefimov's dismay, certain members of the Central Committee of the Communist Party of the Soviet Union (CPSU) were also aware of the case, and had decided to become involved. This was a time of economic and military uncertainty within the Central Committee, and a growing number of people were concerned about the future of Communism and looking for confirmation that the Western democracies were in an even greater state of decay. What better proof could there be, some of these apparatchiks decided, than for a Marine, an esteemed member of the enemy's military elite, to become a Russian agent? And so they made requests that came to Yefimov in the form of orders to ask Lonetree questions about matters that no Marine guard would have knowledge of, or that were beyond his intellectual ability to answer.

Yefimov was not in a position to argue, and dutifully he asked Lonetree if he agreed with Marx that objective future historical developments were on the side of Communism, and what his thoughts were about President Reagan's position on medium-range missiles in Europe. But privately he fumed at the interference of these nonprofessionals in the operation. And when the word came down that he should ask Lonetree if he would be willing to seek political asylum, Yefimov almost rebelled. He knew what they were thinking—that Lonetree would make for a great propaganda exhibition, paraded before the cameras, and then given a consultant's position at one of the intelligence schools. But he knew too that this was dilettantism. In any respectable intelligence operation, political asylum was a last recourse, offered only to foreign agents who found themselves on the border of catastrophe. Certainly he recognized the political benefits of defection, but he also knew that what this would be saying to the other side was that Lonetree's propaganda value was worth more than his spying activities.

This was what Yefimov had been afraid of: that interference from bosses, who wanted more from Lonetree than he could logically produce, would create tensions that would complicate the operation. And when Lonetree was transferred to Vienna, things proceeded downhill at an accelerating rate for more bureaucratic reasons.

Just as an interservice rivalry existed between the CIA and the FBI in the United States, a similar competition thrived in the Soviet Union between the Second Chief Directorate, whose responsibilities were internal security and who conducted counterintelligence operations, and the First Chief Directorate, whose activities took place on foreign soil and were oriented toward intelligence gathering. The First thought the personnel in the Second were unsophisticated and possessed limited creativity, while the Second thought those in the First were overconfident and untrustworthy, as proved by the larger number of traitors from their ranks.

When Lonetree was still in Moscow, top officials in Intelligence had heard that Counterintelligence had successfully recruited an American Marine, and Intelligence made inquiries, believing the information he was providing might be of use to them. But the Second had been protective of their agent and refused to reply. Even after Lonetree left town and was stationed in a foreign city, they had been reluctant to pass him along to the other service because a lot of effort and money had been expended, his recruitment looked good on their reports, and they knew that once he was in the hands of Intelligence, the very top bosses would forget who had recruited him.

While this internal bickering was going on, Yefimov had been flying into and out of Vienna and continuing to handle the agent. But he could see that Lonetree was becoming increasingly discontent with his role. He was missing meetings. He was not responding to requests. He was drinking heavily, a sure sign of stress. And Yefimov felt he understood the nature of the problem: Lonetree was a fish on a hook, but the worm was gone. Letters from and pictures of Violetta weren't enough.

In a report he filed, he suggested that Violetta be allowed to accompany him on the next trip. Give the two lovebirds a few days together, he recommended. As it was, Lonetree had nothing with which to combat his feelings of guilt for his spying activities.

But the bosses had refused to sanction a visit, because by this time they were afraid that Violetta herself was unreliable. It all went back to an insulting remark made to her by someone in the department about the fact that she was sleeping with the Marine. Operationally her sleeping with Lonetree had been a legitimate step; the comment had been more a reflection of a chauvinistic attitude among certain agents who suspected that Russian women enjoyed having affairs with Western men. Violetta had taken offense and threatened to quit. A tense situation had resulted and the operation hung in the balance before she was calmed down, but her fierce reaction made her superiors suspect that she had crossed over a line and gotten personally involved. Which angered them, because she had known the rules of the game before she got involved, she had agreed to play the game, and she should not have let herself forget that it was just a game.

It also reminded them that a person who was willing to engage in duplicity and deception with a target might be willing to do the same with an organ of the state.

In October 1986, Chairman Chebrikov put an end to the dispute when he formalized the transfer of Lonetree from Counterintelligence to Intelligence. Yefimov was instructed to prepare Lonetree for the transition. But even as he did this, Yefimov suspected that the outcome was inevitable. Lonetree, in Yefimov's mind, was a *nechiporenko*. Literally the word translated as "condemned agent," though in this case it meant someone whose value was used up and whom sooner or later they could expect to lose.

He had no idea what plans Intelligence had for Lonetree. Had he been asked for his advice, he would have said use him as a "sleeper"—leave him alone, let him go on with his life, hope that he would be elevated to a career in a sensitive intelligence position, and if so, recontact him at a later date.

He didn't know that KGB agents operating out of the Soviet Embassy in Vienna had detected CIA personnel lurking around his meetings with Lonetree, suggesting that American counterintelligence people were aware of the Marine's espionage activities. Nor did he know that rather than continuing to task

Lonetree for information from inside the embassy in Vienna, Intelligence had other uses in mind. Such as converting him to a chip in a double-agent operation run at the CIA, in which a Soviet intelligence agent would bona-fide himself by providing exclusive details about a leak inside an American embassy. Or exposing Lonetree in a way that would provide protective cover to a more important source of inside information.

21

As a rule the KGB paid very little attention to the motivation of its agents, provided it had a handle on them. Its main concern was to establish control, and it didn't really care whether anybody liked it or not. The security services knew, for instance, that UPDK workers were generally so grateful for their jobs that fear of losing their employment status was not just an adequate driving force, it was insurance of loyalty.

For the most part they would be right. One of the things that people not closely acquainted with Soviet life tend to have difficulty understanding is on what an elemental level people in the U.S.S.R. lived, and how extraneous the considerations of motivation were to most people. In this case, however, it was a fundamental miscalculation.

After Violetta had reported that someone was waiting for her when she left the embassy, keeping his distance but following and watching her, and was told they would keep a watchful eye on the situation, she was still anxious about the whole development. Why she had been singled out? she wondered. Were there forces within the embassy that were interested in her for some special reason?

Even before Lonetree approached her, she began to investigate him, asking questions of her coworkers and taking note of his behavior. It didn't take long for her to conclude it was highly unlikely that he was a Western intelligence agent pretending to be a security guard, though she also determined that he was not a typical Marine. She was put off by the antics and attitudes of most Marines. They reminded her of German shepherds who barked loudly and strained at their collars. This one, however, was more like the shy pup with hurt eyes who hung back. He did not appear to share his fellow Marines' appreciation for rowdy parties in the Marine House, and seemed to have few if any friends in the detachment. By the time he worked up the nerve to actually approach her, she felt she had nothing to fear from him.

She had been instructed to pay him attention but to be careful not to appear as if she was provoking a relationship, which posed no difficulties because her curiosity was genuine. Prior to this she'd had very little direct contact with Westerners, so strictly from a language point of view the chance to converse with someone whose native tongue was English was new and different and interesting. It helped their communications that he did not use big words or express complicated thoughts, but he did impress her with his knowledge about a range of subjects. She'd found this to be true about Westerners in general: They drew from a broader base of information than Russians, which made for stimulating and informative discussions.

The one topic they all seemed to be sorely misinformed about, however, was Soviet society. Every American she'd met, including Clayton, seemed to think communists were no different from fascists. It must be the anti-Soviet ideological propaganda in America that makes them think so, she decided.

"Befriend him. Encourage him to talk about himself. Get to know him," she'd been told. In other words allow a personal relationship to flourish. So she followed her official guidance, not for a minute suspecting that they would have anything in common. But over the next few weeks, as they discussed American movies and books and food, his impressions of Russia, his likes and dislikes, she was agreeably surprised to find they hit it off quite well. Even more surprising, because Russians on the whole were very circumspect when talking about their inner feelings with strangers, he very quickly took her into his confidence.

Until he told her he was a Native American, she hadn't put his swarthy face and dark hair and eyes together with her picture of an Indian. From official discussions she had heard that America was built on the bloodshed of Indians, there was hatred between the races, and the human rights of Indians continued to be violated, but she had given very little thought to the subject. Hearing him talk with pride about his heritage, and yet admit to feeling at times like "a second-class citizen" in his country, struck a sympathetic chord; and although she'd been advised to stay away from political discussions, she was just being honest when she said in her country ethnic orientation didn't matter, and talked about the great communist ideology where all men were equal and no man was oppressed.

It was when he opened the floodgate of feelings from his unhappy childhood that she had a reaction for which she was unprepared. When she heard about the lack of love and attention he'd received from his parents, how he'd spent lonely years in an orphanage, and how he'd joined the Marines to get away, the pity she felt for this person was profound.

One story he told her touched her in a special way. Attempting to explain why he had difficulty making friends, he said as a small boy he'd had poor eyesight but no one had tested him for glasses; and because his vision prevented him from keeping up with the other kids he had stopped playing games, turned inward, and become a withdrawn person.

It was heartbreaking. He struck her as someone who had stored up his thoughts and feelings for years and years, just waiting for someone to come along and ask him about himself. But more than that, she identified with his feelings. Her parents had also fought frequently and separated when she was young. She too felt unwanted and alienated from her family. Like him she had come to believe she could count on no one but herself. And the core of loneliness at the center of his being reminded her of an empty place within her own soul.

Violetta knew this was precisely the kind of background information that her superiors wanted her to collect—poignant personal details that exposed the target's weaknesses and vulnerabilities—and dutifully she fulfilled her reporting requirements. But because she knew that the resentments and longings he was sharing with her were being considered by others for their value in his recruitment as a spy, an unexpected discomfort began to worm its way into her consciousness.

Approval had been given for her to show Clayton where she lived, and after one of the conversational walks she brought him home. Genrietta had a fit.

"Why are you bringing this American spy into our home?" she demanded to know. "You shouldn't do this. I don't like it. You are compromising your family."

She retreated to her room and refused to come out. She was furious with Violetta. Under their system, if one member behaved inappropriately it could have implications and consequences for the rest of the family. It could even cause problems for their neighbors.

But Violetta had been nonplussed. "Give him a chance and get to know him better," she told her mother. "Then you will change your attitude and feel toward him as you do toward my other friends."

It turned out that she was right. Prior to bringing him home again, Violetta explained that she was just being friendly to him because he did not get along with the rest of the Marines at the embassy, he was lonely and interested in meeting Russian people, and she felt sorry for him. Genrietta was still wary of the whole idea, but she knew Violetta did not make friends with just anyone, and if Violetta insisted he was worthwhile, then maybe she was being unfair.

It was Genrietta's idea to invite Clayton to the house to celebrate a winter holiday, and the occasion was a breakthrough for her. He didn't speak Russian and she knew just a few words of English, but Violetta translated, and from the conversation they had around the dinner table, Genrietta could tell how much it meant to him to be included in a family affair. She could see that he was a shy and reserved young man, quite an ordinary person, really, with no strangeness or sharp edges to him. In fact, he was polite, appreciative, and sincere, and his presence added a pleasant element that made the celebration memorable. Genrietta also saw, from his eyes and the way they lingered on Violetta, that this American Marine was hopelessly infatuated with her daughter.

What happened next was a result of the risks inherent in operations that depend on human emotions.

The theory behind this kind of recruitment was that Violetta, in addition to gathering personal information on Lonetree, was supposed to create the impression they were conspirators engaged in something that those around them knew nothing about. This involved not just walks and talks, but coded exchanges—a glance here, a touch there—which built up personal memories that implied intimacy and created confidence and brought a sense of specialness to the relationship. The idea was to get the target to believe that he and the recruiter were forming their own world in which it was the two of them together on the inside, and everybody else was on the outside.

But in order for Violetta to play her part realistically, she had to be given certain freedoms. Just as Lonetree broke the rules when he would sneak away from the embassy to see her, she had to be given a license that allowed it to appear that she too was moving beyond the normal limits allowed a Soviet citizen. This entailed a freedom of movement, freedom of expression . . . the freedom to act, in other words, as if she were a free spirit.

The result was something almost magical. Violetta had been granted a range of liberties previously unknown to her for the purposes of exploring the interior life of a Western man. At the same time she had been told to encourage his affections by enjoying herself and giving him the impression that she was falling in love with him. But what she wasn't given was adequate preparation for the emotional consequences of this behavior. Which is to say, when you fiddle with emotions as primal as love and whatever generates that between two people, you simply cannot predict or control what is going to happen.

More rapidly than she ever would have imagined, her fondness for Clayton deepened. A large part of their relationship was playful: When she tried to give him Russian language lessons, he had great difficulty getting the accents right, and said SAMovar instead of saMOvar, baBUSHka instead of BAbushka; and she corrected him with increasing sternness until she realized he was doing it wrong just to get a rise out of her. And when she nick-named him "Yozhik"—Russian for "hedgehog"—and he pre-tended to be offended, she assured him it wasn't only a reference to the spiky hairstyle of the Marines in Moscow, it was also a term of endearment peasant farmers used for favorite children. But at other times, as when they leafed through her photo album and both reminisced about what it had been like growing up, just as she was a source of happiness to him, she felt him filling a void in her life.

It had not been her intention for their friendship to take a sex-ual turn. Even when they walked hand in hand and kissed good-bye at the metro, it was because she had begun to care a great deal about him, and she did not necessarily consider it a prelude to greater intimacy. When she had first seen him, she had not thought of him as physically attractive—he was slightly built, ap-proximately her own height, and not the handsome or heroic type. But his stoicism, his sensitivity, his gentleness had a certain appeal; his romantic interest in her created a heightened aware-ness of herself as a sensual being; and sleeping with him some-how seemed like a way of compensating for the duplicity she was engaged in.

It was after they made love that he began to talk about mar-riage. They discussed two scenarios: he could stay in Russia and become a citizen—he did not want to seek asylum because he would be doing this for her, not for political reasons—or she could come to America and marry him there. It was an impossi-ble dream, she knew. The KGB was not going to allow her to leave the country with him. But they were living in the moment, and she enjoyed the reveries his words conjured up for her. It was a joyful escape from the depressing reality to leaf through maga-zines and pick out the car they would drive and the kind of house they would live in and talk about the life they would have to-gether if she went to America as his bride.

When the time came to introduce him to "Uncle Sasha," the fact that Violetta was keeping a secret from Clayton seemed not as important now as the bigger secret she was keeping from the

KGB. This was no longer just an act. The romantic rhythms of love on the sneak had won her over.

She could see that it wasn't easy for Clayton to answer Sasha's questions and go along with his requests, and on her own she had second thoughts about the entire affair and considered putting an end to it, or at least being perfectly honest with Clayton about her complicity. Several times she started to say something, then stopped, unable to get the truth out. Because by then another dynamic had taken over. She realized that he was not deceived about their relationship: he was fully aware of its outlaw status and its other, "official" level. And his willingness to participate, in spite of the imminent danger to himself, was his way of showing her how much he loved her. He was doing this to prove his feelings for her were true.

At least that was the way she viewed the situation, which was why she decided to let things play out on their own, and to allow fate to decide how it would end.

By the time Clayton left for Vienna, Violetta, in her mother's words, had been "conquered" by Clayton's love. They met to say goodbye to each other, and then Clayton left for the airport and Violetta rushed home because he promised he would call and say goodbye one more time. Watching her sit by the telephone waiting for it to ring, Genrietta thought she had never seen a girl so desperately in love.

His final words before leaving Russia were "Whatever happens, I will come back for you."

Violetta waited a "whole week" before she sat down at the table in her room, set out her favorite picture of Clayton wearing blue jeans and a faded workshirt and standing in Red Square with the domes of St. Basil's Cathedral as a backdrop, and wrote him a letter. In it she told him she knew it was silly but each day when she returned home from her job at the Irish Embassy, a small part of her would be disappointed not to find him waiting for her. No matter where she was or what she was doing, she wrote, he was never far from her thoughts. "I can't get rid of the memories and I don't want to."

Before leaving, he had talked about going to Vienna as an adventure, and in her letter she said she envied him and wished she could be there with him, sharing "new impressions, new places, new people," instead of sitting in her room, alone, "staring at your picture and thinking how much I love you."

Several days later he surprised her with a phone call. He was having trouble adjusting to Vienna, he said, and missed Moscow, missed her. They were words she wanted to hear, but as she wrote him afterward, it worried her to think of him feeling depressed. "I want so much to be in Vienna, next to you and share all your troubles so that you don't feel alone there."

After that she wrote him every few weeks, telling him about the ballets she attended at the Bolshoi Theater; a vacation she took with a girlfriend to the Caucasus, where they stretched out on the beach, swam in the sea, climbed mountains; and how much she anticipated the day when he would return. "I think that all the things that parted us—distance and circumstance— are temporary and we will be together again. . . . Now I am absolutely sure that I can't feel happy, completely happy, without you by my side."

The letters that he wrote her were filled with daily details of his life, made less boring by sharing them with her—a detachment inspection by the company commander, a required attendance at a diplomatic function. But they would almost always end with his reassuring her that his love for her continued to grow stronger by the day, and that he was looking forward to coming back to Moscow and visiting her, he hoped by the end of the year.

Throughout this period Violetta was never able to forget completely the "official" side to their relationship, because she had been instructed to encourage Clayton's ongoing cooperation in her letters. Which she did, reminding him that Uncle Sasha's blessings were important to their future plans. But even as she played her part, there was a difference now, because at the same time she was doing her duty she was staying true to her inner feelings. She wanted them to be together and knew this was the only way it could happen.

Their clandestine relationship had been going on for over a year, and as time had passed and nothing bad had happened, Violetta had begun to believe that maybe fate watched over young lovers. The year 1986 was drawing to a close, and she was waiting to hear precisely his plans for returning when she learned that he had been arrested.

She was frantic. There were no letters from him to explain what had happened, Uncle Sasha claimed ignorance, one or two small articles appeared in the Soviet press but they added little to her understanding, and the next thing she knew, her name had surfaced in the Western press as the woman at the center of the sex-for-secrets spy scandal and Western reporters had tracked her to the Irish Embassy and were requesting interviews.

Violetta left work one day, did not return the next, and put her life on hold, awaiting the outcome of Clayton's trial. She rarely left home and tuned in daily to the Voice of America and Radio Free Europe on the radio, listening for news about Clayton's case. What she heard made her despair. She had not given a great deal of thought to the specific worth of the information Clayton had passed to Uncle Sasha, and in particular she hadn't thought about his actions in terms of punishable criminal offenses. But she thought there was something clearly exaggerated and not quite real about the charge that he had seriously damaged the national security of the United States.

The evening she received a phone call telling her that a military court had found Clayton guilty of espionage and sentenced him to thirty years in prison, she was devastated. Until then she had held out the hope that some miracle would happen that would scale down the dimensions of this tragedy.

For the first time she became really scared. If what they had done together had brought such a terrible fate to him, that started her thinking that perhaps something equally awful was meant for her. Would the KGB blame her for the failure of the operation? she wondered.

She was crying softly when she called her mother into her room and broke the news that Clayton had been sentenced to prison. And then, in a voice so low Genrietta could barely hear her, Violetta said, "Mama, if something bad happens to me, I want you to promise that you will do something for me."

Genrietta protested, "Veta, don't talk like that."

"Please, Mama. Promise me."

Tears welling, Genrietta asked her daughter what it was she wanted her to do.

"I want you to bury me in the dress that Clayton gave me."

Genrietta knew what dress she was talking about. Clayton had given it and a bottle of perfume to Violetta as a gift. It was a black-and-white-checked dress, made of wool with a white collar, and it hung in Violetta's wardrobe beside the two white dress shirts he had also given her. Although she had yet to wear it out, she would put it on for special family occasions because, she said, it made her feel closer to Clayton.

"If that is your wish," Genrietta replied.

In the days that followed, Violetta entered a depression that seemed bottomless. She was unable to sleep, so she stayed up all night smoking cigarettes and drinking wine and listening to foreign broadcasts on the radio on the chance they would have something new to report about Clayton. Finally, as the dawn lightened her window, she would fall asleep, only to rise late in the day, fix herself something to eat, and return to her room. She was silent, sullen, and unresponsive, and on the rare occasions she shared her feelings, she would frequently speak about death.

"I'm not afraid to die," she said on one occasion. "To me it's one and the same as life."

When she talked like this, Genrietta was at a loss. She wanted desperately to help her daughter through this difficult period, but Violetta could not be comforted. Genrietta now believed that if harm came to Violetta, it would not be instigated by the KGB but by Violetta herself. On those occasions when her depression seemed dangerous, Genrietta would call her friends and they would take turns coming over and keeping a suicide watch through a particularly hard night.

It pained Genrietta to see her daughter let herself go like this, ignore her appearance, and indulge in unhealthy habits, and around the house she tried to maintain an upbeat attitude, hoping it would brighten Violetta's mood. But nothing seemed to work. A doctor said she was suffering from a nervous breakdown, but when the days turned into weeks, the weeks added up to months, and still Violetta remained in her room, reading, watching TV, listening to the radio, smoking, and drinking herself into a stupor, it was apparent that this was more than an illness: Violetta seemed almost to have given up on life itself.

It wasn't until she had a late-night breakthrough conversation with her daughter that Genrietta understood what was going on. As Violetta explained it, even though she believed that anyone in her place would have made the same decisions she had, and even though Clayton had understood the implications and risks inherent in their relationship, she knew that he'd done what he had to keep their relationship going, and she felt such regret and guilt and personal responsibility for his misfortunes that she had to find a way to stay faithful to him. She did not believe there was anything she could do to help him get out of prison, so she had sworn before his memory that as long as he was in prison, she would never marry, she would never have a child, and she would confine herself to her room because it was the closest she could come to sharing a cell with him.

A year passed, then another, and Violetta honored her vows, bearing the burden of her grief in lonely privacy like someone under a decree of eternal damnation. Outwardly the circumstances of her life continued to resemble Clayton's in an uncanny way, as her self-imposed sentence of solitary confinement remained inviolate. Inwardly, she had no way of knowing how he was feeling—for all she knew he was bitter and thought of her as his betrayer, not his beloved. But every day she looked at the picture of him standing in Red Square and recalled his parting words, "Whatever happens, I will come back for you." And when the day did come that he was a free man again, whether he returned to her or not, she knew in her heart that she would be able to say, "I too have served time in prison, I have made peace with myself, and my soul is clean before you."

FROM RUSSIA WITH LOVE

22

Clayton Lonetree's legal appeals were handled by a Washington, D.C., attorney who had been part of the military team that investigated the 1968 My Lai massacre, which led to the conviction of Lt. William Calley, Jr., for participation in the murder of 102 unarmed Vietnamese civilians. Lee Calligaro, a congenial, chain-smoking, forty-five-year-old, had become Lonetree's attorney when Lawrence Cohen, a longtime acquaintance of his, phased out his involvement to become a judge in St. Paul. Although his specialty was in the health-care field, he took the case because he had a background in military law and he liked to have at least one pro bono case going on at a time. Before he'd even read the trial transcript, based solely on his reading of the news accounts, he had concluded that the court-martial had been conducted in such a way as to exaggerate public fears, which, in turn, had led to an unfair and excessive sentence.

Calligaro took a decidedly less contentious approach than that adopted by Lonetree's former civilian attorneys, who had repeatedly criticized the military justice system before, during, and after the court-martial. Believing that the military was basically fair and well suited to correcting mistakes, and working closely with a bright appellate military defense counsel, Lt. Comdr. Lou Saccoccio, who was a graduate of Harvard Law School, he prepared a brief that argued that a number of serious legal errors had been committed in the court-martial. But there were three areas in particular that they felt held the greatest promise for a retrial, reversal, or reduction in sentence.

The first was the one that Stuhff and Kunstler had banked so heavily on: that Lonetree had been promised confidentiality in connection with the statements he gave to the CIA, and therefore those statements should not have been used against him at trial. The second was that Lonetree's Sixth Amendment rights were violated when his attorneys were denied the right to fully cross-examine the pseudonymous witness, John Doe. And the third was that Lonetree had been ineffectively represented by his civilian counsel, who ignored plea-bargaining overtures so they could continue the case as a forum for publicity to further their own political agendas.

The appeal was filed in mid-1989 with the U.S. Navy–Marine Corps Court of Military Review (CMR), which was made up of nine military officers, Marine Corps colonels and Navy captains, people who for the most part had spent twenty years as lawyers. Delays piled up, so it was a year before the CMR rendered its decision, which was a virtual strikeout for the appellate team. The CMR judges wrote that when Lonetree approached the CIA in Vienna he "knowingly stepped outside of his military chain of command," the Agency's debriefings had been conducted for its own damage-assessment purposes and were entirely independent of the military's criminal investigation, and "the two sets of investigators were at all times fulfilling their own unique duties and that neither side became the agent of the other."

As for the legality of the "hooded witness," the CMR ruled that "mindful of the dangers inherent in ongoing undercover work in a foreign country," and recognizing "a compelling government interest to protect the identity of the undercover agent and the intelligence resources and methodologies used by that agent which could lead to his exposure," the military judge had not erred in setting limits on the defense team's right to cross-examine John Doe. Going one step further, it said that John Doe was only a "corroboration witness," and after conducting its own review of John Doe's background as contained in a top-secret affidavit, the court said it would not have been "a fertile area for cross-examination" and "would not have negated the guilt of the appellant which was overwhelmingly proven at trial."

In the argument Calligaro made for "ineffective assistance of counsel," he argued that the schism between the civilian counsel and the military defense lawyers went beyond a difference of opinion as to trial tactics and strategy, whether a pretrial agreement should be negotiated, and what was an acceptable amount of confinement. Calligaro asserted that Stuhff and Kunstler not only failed to adequately explore the possibilities of a pretrial agreement, negotiate with the government in good faith, and present a potential agreement to Lonetree for his consideration, they deliberately sabotaged his relationship with Major Henderson by maligning his motives and loyalties, and oversold to Lonetree the idea that the outcome of a court-martial would be favorable to him.

The Court of Military Review rejected the argument, but in a revealing footnote to its decision conceded that part of its consideration was the "unfortunate effect it may have in future cases." In short, the CMR did not want to set a precedent that would allow for a situation where the government could prosecute a perfectly good case, only to have it reversed on appeal because of a defense counsel's incompetence.

The U.S. Court of Military Appeals (COMA) was the court of last resort in the military justice system. It was a five-judge court, and the judges were all people with civilian rather than military backgrounds. So that they would bring a completely civilian perspective to the review process, they were not even permitted to be retired military officers.

As it turned out, that didn't make any difference when it came to COMA's evaluation of most of the defense's arguments. They upheld the decisions of the CMR in every instance—save one. They concluded that Stuhff and Kunstler's failure to seek a plea agreement potentially deprived their client of his constitutional right to competent counsel.

In a majority ruling the COMA judges wrote, "Lonetree offers us colorable claims . . . that civilian counsel offered him bizarre and untenable advice, consistently attempting to instill in him a distrust of his military counsel and consistently inducing him away from a plea bargain assuring him substantial leniency in the face of overwhelming evidence of his guilt." They recommended one of two remedies: a hearing by a lower court to determine if civilian counsel's level of advocacy fell "measurably below the performance ordinarily expected of fallible lawyers," or a rehearing on the sentence to determine if Lonetree had been punished more severely than he deserved because of the conduct of William Kunstler and Michael Stuhff.

The language of the appeals-court decision was remarkable for its colorful bluntness. Courts rarely embarrass lawyers with the use of words such as "bizarre." Asked by the *New York Times* to comment, William Kunstler said that as a matter of principle he would not dispute the claims of ineffective counsel. "If they can win their case by proving any dereliction on my part, it would be all for the good and I cheer them on." Mike Stuhff was less charitable. In a letter he fired off to Lee Calligaro, he branded the complaint against his representation of Lonetree as a "cynical, dishonest and harebrained scheme" and demanded "you retract all the allegations of your brief."

That didn't happen. Instead, a rehearing on sentencing was held at Quantico on October 29, 1993, to consider whether Lonetree had been misled by his civilian lawyers, resulting in an excessive sentence. If such a determination was made, he was to be immediately resentenced.

Although the hearing was held in the same building and the very courtroom where the court-martial took place more than six years earlier, this proceeding bore little relation to what went on before. It was conducted before a military judge, Lt. Col. David Anderson, not a jury. There were no armed guards patrolling the grounds and no passes required for admission, removing the impression national security was at stake. In place of a media horde a mere three reporters showed up to cover the event, along with Lonetree's parents. And in complete contrast to William Kunstler's abrasive and combative style, Lee Calligaro epitomized reasonableness and sincerity.

"We are not here to decide questions of guilt or innocence; we are here to determine an adequate and sufficient sentence," Calligaro announced in his opening remarks. And toward that end he had flown in two key witnesses to testify: Maj. David Henderson, who had since retired from the military and was now working for the U.S. Attorney's Office, and Clayton Lonetree.

Lonetree went first. He had put on weight since his court-martial, his hair was longer, and the dark frame of his glasses lent a bookish aspect to his appearance. Entering Lejeune Hall, he had worn an E-1, or private's, uniform, but for the hearing he was allowed to wear his sergeant's uniform with the ribbons and stripes. After taking a seat on the witness stand, he was led through a highlighted recitation of the sequence of events that had resulted in his espionage activities in Moscow and Vienna. But while drawing out this information Calligaro tried his best to achieve a balance: He did not want to bring the offenses back to life too vividly, but he did want the court to see that Lonetree accepted full responsibility for his actions, was able to bring understanding to his "absence of judgment," and was genuinely remorseful.

The second phase of Lonetree's testimony left the distant past for the recent past, turning to the six and a half years he'd spent in the military barracks at Fort Leavenworth and the occupational skills he had developed in the print shop and woodshop during that time, the fact that he was pursuing his associate of arts degree, and the list of books he'd read by authors such as Stephen Crane, Herman Melville, and Jack London.

In his performance on the witness stand Clayton Lonetree continued to project the image of an introverted and reserved person, taking a customary moment to reflect on the questions before answering in a soft-spoken voice. And yet, clearly, he was a different person. The impression he made was that the enormity of his court-martial and sentence had hit him in a way that forced him to realize this was as low as it goes; and his intelligence was such that, finding himself in a situation where he could do one of two things—grow and mature, or despair—he appeared to have chosen the former, utilizing the enormous amount of time he had for introspection, and taking advantage of the opportunities around him. His records from Fort Leavenworth and the evaluations of the staff psychologist supported that notion. Calligaro read just a few excerpts, the ones that described Lonetree as a "model inmate," someone in whom there was "surprisingly no bitterness or blaming of others or blaming the system," someone "with a great degree of insight into how he was manipulated," someone with "no orientation to the continuance of such behavior," who had been "successfully rehabilitated and serves no current risk for future acts against the United States Government or other criminal behavior."

When it was Major Henderson's turn to testify, he put the Lonetree court-martial in context, describing in compelling detail the frenzied atmosphere of the time, when this case had been portrayed as the spy scandal of the century, and the impact those sensational allegations had to have had on the members of the jury who issued a thirty-year sentence. Henderson characterized his former client as a lightning rod for circumstances beyond what the facts of his offenses warranted, and maintained that when all was said and done, Sgt. Clayton Lonetree's actions had had minimal impact on national security. In support of his opinion Henderson referred to a letter the defense had received from the commandant of the Marine Corps, Gen. Al Gray, within two years of the court-martial, wherein it was written, "Our review of post trial damage assessments satisfies us that [Lonetree's] misconduct did not equate to the seriousness of other recent national security cases, and that his sentence is disproportionate to that of other convicted service members or employees of the Department of Defense. . . ."

Finally, Calligaro addressed the question of where he expected Lonetree to go from here, and along those lines he played a trump card. His main client in the health-care field had recently signed a contract with the Navajo Nation to establish a substance-abuse program on the Reservation, and they had offered Clayton a counseling position. Obviously he was not going to provide clinical treatment and therapy himself, but he could be a buddy to those in the system. Someone who could put himself in the other guy's shoes because he had made mistakes, and he knew what it took to overcome adversity. It would be employment that would permit him to turn some of the very problems that got him into trouble around to help others, make a positive contribution to society, and regain his self-esteem.

In his closing, Calligaro mentioned the Court of Military Appeals' ruling on ineffective assistance of counsel, but purposely he did not dwell on it. His thoughts on the effective role of an advocate within the military system were that the judge was well aware of the ruling, the issue before them was appropriate sentence, and he had decided it would be more productive to focus on Lonetree and the progress he had made. But he did introduce an affidavit from former prosecutor Dave Beck that said, "Sgt. Lonetree deserved to be punished and a tough message had to be sent in sentencing. But the service of justice needs to be monitored . . . and in Sgt. Lonetree's case the purpose of punishment has been served." And referring to the fact that Lonetree, without asking anything in return, was cooperating with a study conducted by the FBI's Behavioral Science Unit, which was trying to develop a psychological profile of individuals who had committed espionage, Calligaro reminded the court that his client had done everything you could expect of someone who had made a mistake, recognized it, and tried to make it right.

"Clayton doesn't ask for forgiveness. He knows what it means to be a Marine. Those who serve with pride, honor, and faithfulness often take for granted what Clayton Lonetree knows in his heart: what it is like to lose that dignity, that uniform. He has said that the worst part of this whole thing is that he will never again wear the Marine uniform. If ever someone knows what that means, and regrets it, it is Clayton Lonetree."

As the courtroom emptied, leaving the judge alone to deliberate, the appellate defense team allowed itself to hope that Lieutenant Colonel Anderson would see his way to remedying what had happened the first time around. Calligaro had specifically requested a sentence of time served, in which case Lonetree would be a free man in a matter of days.

Fifty-five minutes later the judge indicated he had arrived at a decision.

In his closing argument the Marine prosecutor, Maj. Ronald Rogers, had said, "Your honor, your job today would be far easier, I believe, if the accused were sitting here in the courtroom in a red outfit carrying a devil's pitchfork. But he's not. He's a man of flesh and blood, just like the rest of us. But he's wearing a Marine Corps uniform, sir. And to those of us who wear this uniform, who believe in the Corps and believe in our country, who believe in the sanctity of the commitments we make on a daily basis—that he used his office as a Marine to come into contact and gain information which he passed to the Soviet Union; that he used his office as a base of knowledge to compromise intelligence agents—covert intelligence agents—who truly represented the point men in America's efforts in the Cold War; that he did those things wearing this uniform is unforgivable.

"To label this conduct a mistake is blasphemy. Your honor, the accused has earned substantial punishment. It is the government's recommendation that the punishment you award almost approach the maximum."

Judge Anderson was apparently persuaded. He reduced Clayton Lonetree's sentence, but only by five years, from twenty-five to twenty.

The appellate defense team was stunned. Sally Tsosie began to wail. Spencer Lonetree was enraged. The only person who seemed to take the decision calmly was Lonetree himself. After thanking his appellate attorneys for doing their best, he turned his sergeant's uniform back in and submitted his wrists to be handcuffed by a Marine guard, who would escort him from Lejeune Hall to the van outside that would take him to the brig.

In the lobby, just inside the exit door, something stopped Lonetree. It so happened that I was standing beside him at that moment, and I could see that he had just spotted perhaps a dozen cameramen and photographers waiting outside for a photo opportunity.

On TV we have all seen criminal suspects with their jackets draped over their heads, ducking the cameras as they are led from a law-enforcement facility to a waiting vehicle. But that was not Clayton Lonetree's style. Unable to lift his hands because they were chained to a leather belt, he asked his guard to adjust his fore-and-aft cap to a slightly smarter angle. Once that small measure of dignity was achieved, he nodded he was ready and marched forward into the flashing media lights.

23

When the KGB talks openly about a case, it is usually one in which their "intelligence" has prevailed over another service's and their officers can be portrayed in a heroic light. As he sits in a Moscow restaurant drinking beer and reminiscing, this is not the spin that Uncle Sasha gives to *Tyulpan*—the code name for the Lonetree operation—which is Russian for "tulip," a fast-growing flower cultivated from a bulb.

Dressed informally in jeans and a sweater, a receding hairline losing the battle of baldness, Aleksei Yefimov is neither a charismatic nor a chameleonic personality, but straightforward and friendly. His appearance is typical of Russian men in their mid-forties: If you met him once, you might not recognize him if you were to pass him on the street again. What is distinctive is his voice—it is deep and resonant, like a disc jockey's—and his attention to detail. In his hands an article of clothing casually thrown on that morning becomes a character revelation.

Although Aleksei Yefimov could not be called a reformer, like many of the people who were working on the frontier of intelligence during the Cold War, now that Russia is no longer a communist state and the former enemy is an ally, he has ambivalent feelings about his past. At one time he believed in the State and the system, and even though he understands the reasons for the decline and fall of the Soviet empire, it disturbs him. He thinks Gorbachev ought to be prosecuted, and Yeltsin deserves little better.

While he is not ashamed of his involvement in this case, now that the service his organization provided for the country is discredited, reviled, and in some cases even labeled criminal, he is embarrassed to talk much about it. It's not that he thinks the twenty-odd years of his life involved in spywork were wasted on meaningless activities, it's just that he's more comfortable talking about his performance as a professional, from which he does take personal satisfaction.

Yefimov scoffs at the idea that the relationship he developed with Clayton Lonetree was special in a familial way. "That is definitely an exaggeration," he says. "It is what you Americans would call 'bullshit.'" He acknowledges that there is an odd, almost paternalistic feeling that develops when you recruit an agent, particularly one who is considerably younger than you are. And he would express a certain sympathy for Lonetree as a victim of his "complexes" and "noncynical attitude towards women." But as for personal feelings, according to Yefimov he cared a lot more about the impact of this operation on his own career than what it meant to Clayton Lonetree's future.

Yefimov says he was not totally surprised when Lonetree turned himself in. He had a feeling it would go that way when he realized that Lonetree's motivation for cooperating with the KGB could not be transferred from his emotional attachment to Violetta to his ideological admiration for the Soviet system. In his view it was a shortsighted miscalculation by his bosses that cost them Lonetree. They considered Violetta nothing more than an "approaching instrument," and once she brought them Lonetree, in their eyes she became expendable. This led to future problems, because the only real chance they had of keeping the agent under control was if he thought it would win him Violetta.

It was a testament to Lonetree's lack of guile, says Yefimov, that rather than bargaining for more access to Violetta, he experienced a "moral or nervous breakdown," gave a "simple confession to his countrymen," and "agreed to be punished."

For Yefimov this meant reams of paperwork. Filling out dozens of forms. Writing up explanations for why the agent was lost. There were no claims lodged against him from bosses, but neither were there the major promotions he was hoping for. During the course of the operation his work had been highly complimented, and from time to time he had received "incentives"; but his rewards were relatively minor because ultimately the operation not only failed to achieve its potential, in the eyes of some bosses it was a debacle.

An internal assessment of what had gone wrong questioned the very wisdom of recruiting Lonetree, pointing out that the personality defects that made him susceptible in the first place—his lack of reliability and "businesslike properties"—complicated his effectiveness in the end. He was an agent who contained the seeds of his own destruction, it was written.

In the final analysis it would be the unexpected repercussions that flowed from the exposure of their efforts to recruit Lonetree that would account for why this operation was judged as a calamity for the Soviet security services. Because the KGB did not just lose an agent when Lonetree turned himself in. After his confession, the United States took dramatic security measures that hardened virtually every American embassy as a target. The KGB liked to use military analogies to describe its operations, and in this case they likened the recruitment of Sgt. Clayton Lonetree to a trigger that was pulled without regard to the blast at the other end—which blew up in their face.

Today Aleksei Yefimov still works for the intelligence services, but in an internal position. Just as he had feared—it was another of the reservations he'd had about being the point man on the operation—Lonetree identified him to the CIA, and it spelled the end of his involvement with the American Embassy. He has not been directly connected with recruitment and operative work since the Lonetree case.

When he reflects on his "moment in history," the area Yefimov seems most uncomfortable talking about is what happened to Violetta. He developed a fondness for her as they worked together, and over the course of the operation he realized that she had been inadequately prepared for her role. It would have been better if they had used someone who possessed a detachment that would have allowed her to act in a loving way and would not have subjected her to raw emotions that would pull her in different directions.

"I feel very sorry that this girl ended up so poorly," he says. "I thought she would come out of this experience in a better fashion than she did."

Asked to elaborate, he returns to his belief that the women who worked at the foreign embassies had personal reasons for taking those positions. But then, using another of the military analogies favored by his organization, he expresses a sincere regret that Violetta "found herself in the path of a big tank, and thought she could sneak underneath. But it didn't work out that way, and she got run over."

24

When Genrietta Khokha cracked the book on her family history, which included long chapters on Violetta's life story, I understood her motivation to be a resentment toward the KGB for "stealing" her daughter. Over the course of more than a dozen interviews, during which a genuine friendship evolved, I realized there was a subtext for her. In her own way Genrietta feels responsible for what happened to Violetta. Had Violetta not become estranged from her family, had her home life been more satisfying, then perhaps she would not have become involved with the "servants of intelligence." Or so Genrietta thinks.

When this story broke in the press and Violetta was identified as the woman who "seduced" a Marine into spying and then betrayed him, Genrietta was so upset at the characterization of her daughter as a whore for the State that she considered marching into the American Embassy, asking for the ambassador, and telling him it was not her daughter's fault. Blame the KGB, an evil organization that brought an entire population to its knees, that created generations of people who were "neither the lords of their deeds, nor their will." Much tougher people than her daughter had been unable to stand up to the system, and to single out a young woman was unfair.

She never followed through with her plan—after she told Violetta what she was thinking, two men who represented themselves as Soviet diplomats showed up at the house and calmed her down—but she did continue to entertain the notion of challenging her daughter's slanderers to a duel, with pistols, as they did in the nineteenth century when the honor of an innocent woman was sullied.

Genrietta's efforts to create a more understanding and forgiving context for Violetta's behavior would find support from social psychologists who teach that, a lot more than we rugged individualist Americans like to admit, people are reflections of the culture in which they are enmeshed, and before we judge them too harshly we must consider the society and times in which they live. When one takes into consideration the perverse pressures the Soviet system put on its people, the absolute control the secret police had over the average person's life, the manipulation of opportunities and privileges by the ruling elite, and the duplicity and deception that were woven into the social fabric—where leaders lied to citizens, citizens lied to one another—it is hard not to be sympathetic toward Violetta. When she says she was a victim of circumstances and anybody in her place would have made the same choices, only those who have been in her situation and chose otherwise are truly qualified to take issue.

To one of her friends Violetta said she imagined her life as a kind of literature—a drama turned to tragedy. When I heard that, it made sense that she would view her life with the sort of shape and charge found in the romantic fiction she so loved to read as a student. In some ways hers was even a conventional love story: The lovers meet, impediments are placed in their path, they surmount them or seem to until at last they have to face what appears to be an obstacle that threatens to keep them apart forever.

After learning that she sentenced herself to a misfortune comparable to Lonetree's, when I thought about her self-imposed punishment and penance, I found myself thinking of Violetta in the tradition of the great Russian tragic heroines, women ennobled and purified by suffering, women brought closer to God by their grief. . . .

But before drifting too far into melodrama, I was yanked back to earth by a Russian contemporary of Violetta's, a woman her age who also attended the Institute of Foreign Languages, who also was approached by the "servants of intelligence," but who declined to cooperate with them.

"The people who were open to the charms of the KGB, who allowed themselves to be recruited, were people lacking in moral character," she insisted. "If you chose the path of covert collaboration, it meant you agreed to do dirty things. You would sit and drink vodka with your friends and ask them about their feelings, their family. And if they criticized society or told you a political anecdote or made the slightest comment that was unfavorable, they could never go to the West. Their careers would be ruined, and they would never know why. You cannot forget the lives that were affected by her. Thanks to those 'bloody bitches' we all lived in fear and distrusted everyone around us."

Evoking a Faustian motif—the willingness to sell one's soul to the devil in return for worldly gains—this woman condemned Violetta for committing herself to a life of treachery, not out of an idealistic protest against the enemies of socialism, but out of self-interest and for material advancement, which was worse.

"She knew the rules. She knew her relationship with Lonetree could have no future. Soviet citizens who collaborated with the KGB received benefits, but permission to go abroad with someone they recruited was not one of them. And yet she lied to him and got him to believe that somehow, if he continued to cooperate with 'Uncle Sasha,' their difficulties would be overcome."

And yet, even as this woman called people who engaged in such duplicity despicable, she acknowledged that "Violetta is a product of the Soviet socialist system. She is a typical '*Homo sovieticus*.' And this is what distinguishes her radically from the heroines of Russian literature. The worst thing that seventy years of socialism did for my country and the national consciousness of the Russian people was to destroy the moral basis of human existence. . . . I see Violetta more like an anti-heroine. A kind of socialist perversion of the marvelous Russian women characters created by classic Russian literature. Because in spite of the trials and suffering endured by Violetta, I do not believe that she has cleansed her soul. I do not believe that she has repented her sins.

Because if she were truly remorseful, she would have broken off all her connections to the KGB, and she has not done that."

After several years, Violetta gradually emerged from her seclusion to lead a somewhat normal life. With the end of Communism had come an infusion of Western companies that set up branch offices in Moscow and were in need of people with bilingual skills. She has worked for several joint-venture firms as both interpreter and administrator, facilitating the complicated business of doing business in the new Russia.

From time to time she is contacted by Slava, who brings her flowers and takes her out to a restaurant for lunch. And although she has made it clear there are limits to what she will do, she has found there continue to be employment advantages to maintaining her connections with the security services. She changed her last name from Seina to Kosareva in an effort to separate herself from her past, as well as to make it more difficult for journalists to find her. The freedom of the press that came with democratization in Russia unleashed reporters to write about the "dark truths" of Soviet history, and both the Western and the Russian media have pursued this story, albeit without success. Out of concern that an open discussion would encroach on state secrets, the Federal Counterintelligence Service, the successor to the KGB's Second Directorate, refused to give her permission to talk to reporters. Which was fine with Violetta, who has always been a private and guarded person, and who felt she had nothing to gain from going public, and that nothing she could say would help Clayton Lonetree.

"There have been times when kings were criticized in the press, and presidents have been taken to task, just as I have been," she said to her mother one day. "But they lived through it, and in time it passed. I have no desire to argue with anybody, nor to prove anything to anybody. I don't want to do anything that keeps this story alive. I just want to forget it."

In the years that followed, Violetta would collect her share of male admirers, some serious enough to propose marriage to her, but always she refused. There had been no contact with Lonetree since his arrest, and for all she knew his resentment toward her was too deep and bitter for forgiveness. She was also realistic enough to know that they both had changed over the years, and there was no way of knowing how compatible they would be now. Nevertheless, she intended to stay true to her promise to wait for him. Only he could release her from her vows—by sending for her, coming back to her, or telling her he wanted nothing more to do with her.

25

When Clayton Lonetree returned to the DB, as the inmates referred to the disciplinary barracks, he was not overly disappointed. Twenty years was less than twenty-five, was the way he thought about it.

Although there were things Clayton Lonetree did not like about prison life, overall he had adjusted quite well to his situation. He didn't like mowing lawns in the summer heat and shoveling snow on freezing winter days, and he didn't have much good to say about litter detail: picking up cigarette butts and gum wrappers. But that being the extent of so-called hard labor, he wasn't about to complain. And on the positive side he had a clique of friends. He enjoyed taking academic classes and exercising regularly. He had a radio he listened to late at night, he could watch sports on television, and he had all the time in the world for the activity he enjoyed most: reading a good book. He had even come to appreciate the view from his two-man room: fields and hills and the 1850-vintage buildings that had stood since the facility was first constructed as an outpost in Indian Country.

All in all, it wasn't bad duty. And increasingly he had come to recognize that it even had its advantages: These were the kinds of comforts some people would like to escape to.

There was another plus for Clayton Lonetree where he was: As a prisoner, he enjoyed a peculiar sort of celebrity status. Across the country there were people who saw in his plight an example of the ongoing persecution of Indians by the American government. He had received dozens of letters from them since his incarceration. Some were straightforward letters of support, encouraging him to keep his spirits up and to remember Billy Mills, the Oglala Sioux who ran in the Olympics in the fifties and against all odds won a gold medal. Some included money, five- and ten-dollar bills, toward a Clayton Lonetree Defense Fund. He heard from activists and housewives, students and professors, many offering to write protest letters to congressmen or the press. One of his biggest fans was an elderly woman living in a retirement home in Salt Lake City who wrote long letters to him recalling her youth in the Netherlands during World War II when she had sheltered Jews from the Nazis. In her opinion sentencing Clayton Lonetree to prison for his misdeeds was a harbinger of the coming of death camps to America.

To his credit, though it offered an easy and tempting out, Clayton Lonetree was not comfortable being perceived as a victim or a martyr. He hated it when people expressed pity for him as a poor Indian boy, troubled by a deprived upbringing, abused by a feckless father, and stuck in an orphanage by an uncaring mother, and this was why he became a spy. You heard no whining or special pleading from him on that account. Nor had he said or done anything to reinforce the notion that he had been wrongfully prosecuted for offenses he did not commit. He did feel his punishment exceeded his crimes, which in his mind were still relatively minor; and if he was accused of something he did not do, he would be the first to speak up. But the image he wanted to project now was of someone who had done wrong, was man enough to admit it, and was willing to stand up and take his punishment, so when the day came that he did walk out of prison, he could hold his head up and say he had paid his debt to society and was entitled to put the past behind him.

And yet, paradoxically, at the same time Clayton Lonetree rejected the pity factor, underneath he also thrived on it. While he recognized there were people who invested his issue with something other than what was there for him—maybe it was white guilt, or they were seeking reflected glory from his stature as a media figure, or they had a personal grudge against the government, he didn't know—the interest, the benevolence, even though it came from strangers and was often off base, countered the shame he felt for disgracing the Corps, his family, himself. And in its own strange way it kept him going.

The reason was perfectly understandable. Prison was a lonely experience, and prisoners were desperate for attention. They were surrounded by people they would prefer not to associate with and did not trust. Almost anyone who reached out a friendly hand from outside the prison walls was welcomed.

And if it happened to be women who were fawning over you, as was frequently the case with Clayton Lonetree, whether or not you agreed with their motives was often beside the point.

There exists a whole class of women who develop romantic obsessions with high-profile prisoners, especially those who appear to be victims of injustice, and among their numbers are a group of women, mostly white, who develop improbably erotic fixations on Native American male prisoners. While his court-martial was still in progress, there were women swooning over Sgt. Clayton Lonetree as a contemporary Native American warrior being crucified by the American military. Before he was even sentenced, he was receiving proposals of marriage; and after he was sent to Fort Leavenworth, the love letters kept coming. Some were from obviously disturbed women—one woman stalked his family in an effort to get close to him—but some bright and, by their pictures, quite attractive women of genuine merit also wrote him.

A young woman from Iowa with a history of crusading for the freedom of Native American "political prisoners" became a special one. Glory, as she liked to be called, started out writing to Lonetree as a pen pal. Then a friendship flourished, and soon they were exchanging several letters a week and talking on the phone almost as often.

Glory brought out the wistfully poetic side of Clayton Lonetree, which he expressed quite poignantly in writing. "Last night I heard the geese approaching through my barred window. Immediately I dropped what I was doing and searched the dark sky, hoping to catch a glimpse of at least one. . . . I saw none so I could only guess and speculate on the numbers in formation flying overhead. I am sure they were both beautiful and handsome . . . and then their quaint distinctive sound faded away."

He offered his dreams to her for analysis. "In this one dream I had a year ago . . . I was in this cellar and the windows had bars from top to bottom. There was another person in the cellar with me and I am sure this person is someone I haven't met yet. I can't remember the person's sex, but he/she was a friend. While we were talking a hummingbird flew in through the window and was trying to communicate with me. I would describe the situation as adorably cute. Yet, on the other hand, strange. Every time I touched the walls with my hand the little bird would fly and touch the spot that I had touched, as if it were worshipping it. Finally my friend said, 'It loves you and wants to have your children.' I was captivated and charmed. Immediately the little hummingbird flew out and in and started making a nest in the cellar. . . . I finally woke up feeling happy."

He rhapsodized over his love of literature. "My sweet, don't be alarmed about my seeming lack of attention. Other than you I have another friend of equal importance that has sustained me during these times. They are my books, most written by men long ago before we were conceived. If you were not here I swear I would be engrossed in them. They have helped me become wiser. As one author said, 'It's as if the authors were talking with you from a distant past.' In today's devotions it mentions how the apostle Paul while sitting in a prison cell imposed by the Romans had asked his friend to bring him parchments (books). I thought it was neat. They help keep your mind alert and some can even be heartwarming. They are a part of my life."

Glory was part of Lonetree's thinking as he looked toward the future, and they began to talk about moving to Arizona together when he got out of prison, where she would continue her education while he worked for the tribe as a counselor. There was a tremendous appeal to stepping straight into a family situation with someone who knew his past and was willing to accept him under these conditions. But there was also an aura of unreality to the relationship, and when Lonetree's legal status changed again, so did his plans with Glory.

Every convening authority who refers charges to a court-martial takes some sort of action subsequent to a trial. He can either approve the sentence of the judge, or disapprove the sentence and reduce it. The convening authority at Quantico, Gen. C. Krulac, was still considering a decision on Lonetree's sentencing rehearing when the Aldrich Ames case broke.

A fifty-two-year-old CIA counterintelligence agent, Aldrich Hazen Ames was arrested by the FBI in February of 1994 on charges he had been a Soviet mole since 1985; and during his debriefing sessions he admitted to things that added yet another twist to the Marine Spy Scandal. Ames said that after he had passed information to the KGB that allowed them to identify intelligence sources working for the CIA in the Soviet Union, a number of those assets had been rounded up and executed. Concerned that the CIA would suspect a traitor in its midst, Ames had complained to his handler, a Russian named Vladimir, who apologized for the rash response and told him that the KGB intended to implement a variety of diversionary campaigns to lead the CIA to think the problem lay elsewhere. Among the ploys Vladimir mentioned was creating the impression that there had been a breach in the security of the communications systems in the American Embassy in Moscow and that somehow the KGB had been able to obtain access to CIA operational records maintained there. Within two months Clayton Lonetree turned himself in, and within a matter of months the Marine Spy Scandal became a national sensation, leading Ames to conclude that this crisis was in part a deception manufactured by Soviet intelligence to throw CIA mole hunters off the scent.

These admissions clarified several unresolved issues for the intelligence community. Now the way Lonetree had been handled in Vienna could be understood in a larger context. He had come to the attention of the First Chief Directorate at a fortuitous time. Lonetree was of decreasing value, indeed headed toward self-destruction, but the KGB had one final use for him; as a human shield to protect Aldrich Ames.

The KGB knew that if Lonetree was "exposed," the CIA, in the process of conducting a damage assessment, would be forced to consider him responsible for its losses. But the KGB needed it to happen in such a way that it did not give their real intentions away. This was why they wanted him to return to the Soviet Union: not for training or to see Violetta, but because once he was under their complete control they could announce that he had defected, leading inevitably to an assessment of his prior activities, which would take investigators to the American Embassy. And if Lonetree had balked and refused to return, his new handler would have continued to push him harder and harder, driving him to suicide or surrender, which would have served their purposes equally well.

At the same time this added a new perspective on the Lonetree case for intelligence officials, it also raised questions. Had the entire Marine Spy Scandal been an elaborate KGB scheme to shield Aldrich Ames? Had Lonetree been blamed for disclosures that actually came from Ames?

Lonetree's appellate attorneys immediately requested a meeting with the general, and their pitch was basically this. All along, the Marine Spy Scandal had been characterized as a major espionage case that caused considerable damage to national security. The agency that claimed it was impacted the most was the CIA. The CIA said its agents were compromised. It said it had to bring equipment back and redo codes, and the cost of its damage assessment ran into the millions. Now we find out that a lot of what the CIA blamed on Lonetree was caused by one of its own people. Now we really know what a major espionage case looked like. The Marine Corps took the hit back in 1987; by further reducing Lonetree's sentence, it would put the word out that the Corps now realized it had been disproportionately blamed for problems that belonged to the CIA, and that it was setting things right.

After listening to the appellate attorneys and reviewing the records of trial, General Krulac decided the facts of the Ames case did not excuse Clayton Lonetree from the standpoint of criminality. His conduct was unacceptable and should have been tried and punished. As for whether Clayton Lonetree had been wrongfully accused of crimes actually committed by Aldrich Ames, certainly the difference in their positions made them agents of different orientation and different value, and the evidence suggested that Lonetree had not been initially recruited for this purpose but rather that this was one more use for him subsequent to his recruitment. If that was the case, if the KGB had been using Lonetree as a decoy and through his complicity with Soviet agents at that critical point in time it had allowed Aldrich Ames to carry on his spying, the role Lonetree unwittingly played might well have been the most harmful thing he'd done.

But as a matter of extenuation and mitigation these significant new developments did undercut some of the CIA's claims, and justified in General Krulac's mind a further reduction of Lonetree's sentence to fifteen years. Factoring in the credit the military justice system extended for good behavior, this meant that Clayton Lonetree would be released from prison in the spring of 1996.

Now that the future was no longer beyond the horizon but within view, Clayton Lonetree began to reassess his plans and dreams. In this light his relationship with Glory began to pale, and his letters decreased until, with an apology and an awkward offer of friendship, they stopped altogether. The offer of a position working with young Navajos trying to overcome substance-abuse problems remained on the table, but he wasn't so sure anymore that was what he wanted to do. Everyone around him had ideas about what was best, but he didn't want others deciding for him; he wanted to keep his options open for the time being and decide for himself.

Caught between an uncertain future and the weight of a past he was anxious to leave behind, Clayton Lonetree pondered his alternatives. He had to go back a long ways to remember when he'd last been on his own. The seven years at Fort Leavenworth had been preceded by a year at the brig in Quantico, two and a half years on embassy duty, four years in the Marine Corps, four years in a household run by his father like a boot camp, and before that five years in an orphanage. He didn't think of himself as being institutionalized, but he did realize that life was going to be very different for him once his time was no longer regulated.

One of the most unsettling considerations he faced was how to deal with his parents. United in their crusade for his freedom, they were typically divided over what was best for him, and his mother was counting on him to come to Arizona once he was free, while his father had plans for him in Minnesota.

What he really wanted was to walk out of prison and step into a situation that offered him, as much as a fresh start on a new life, a different ending to his story. Clayton Lonetree's favorite book from the Bible was the story of Job, who had been robbed by Satan of every sign of God's favor, losing family and property and experiencing personal adversity. Lonetree could relate: He felt as though he'd gone through a similar ordeal. And just as Job had persevered, believing that everything that happened to him was part of a higher purpose, so had he maintained faith that the trouble and suffering he'd endured was not merely a sinner's punishment, but would end up serving as a trial that culminated in spiritual gain and perhaps vindication before his peers.

"Once I'd acquired the taste, it was like going back to the apple tree every summer," Lonetree wrote me in a letter responding to a query about the significance of the Book of Job to him. "The content is just as sweet as the first time I absorbed it, satisfying the taste buds of the heart and mind every time."

When a journalist researching his story in Russia returned with a letter from Violetta in 1993, in which she wrote that she still loved him and was waiting for him, he did not immediately recognize it as the opportunity he was waiting for. His astonishment was too great. The overture was completely unexpected. After it had been pointed out by experts at the court-martial how gullible he'd been to think that Violetta ever really cared for him, he'd done his best to cross her out of his mind.

He didn't know what to think. He knew what his lawyers would say, because they had drilled him in preparation for his second hearing before the Navy Clemency and Parole Board, and told him he should expect to be asked, "How do we know the next sexy pretty thing that crosses your path isn't going to lead you down another primrose path?" They intended to argue that proof of their client's rehabilitation was his insight into the various ways he'd been manipulated. They anticipated that he would respond that he understood now what had gotten him into this mess, and was immune to further foolish temptations.

But what if she was telling the truth? What if he'd been right about her all along?

For better or worse, Violetta was the great love of his life. They were inextricably linked in history. He had no idea what would happen if they were reunited, but he did know there was only one way to find out.

AFTERWORD

On January 19, 1995, the CBS newsmagazine *Eye to Eye, with Connie Chung* devoted a segment of its broadcast to the Clayton Lonetree story. Lonetree did not appear in person on the program—military policy denied the press access to prisoners in the disciplinary barracks except under extraordinary circumstances—and in his absence the star of the show was Violetta. "The KGB's most famous seductress," according to the CBS correspondent.

Using Spencer Lonetree as a go-between, CBS had approached Violetta with the incentive that cooperation could increase the chance of an even earlier release for Clayton, and she had made an appeal to her contacts at the reconstructed KGB, which, as it turned out, was currently embarked on a public-relations campaign to improve its image. After a discussion of the parameters of what she could talk about, she had been given permission to participate in the program.

Violetta was filmed strolling across Red Square, riding the same metro line on which Lonetree first approached her, applying cosmetics in front of the vanity in her apartment, and sitting at the kitchen table answering questions. She admitted that she had delivered her lover into the hands of the KGB, but said she had done it only because "I was put under conditions such that there was no choice for me. I absolutely had to do it."

Asked "Do you feel guilty about what you and Clayton started years ago?," she nodded vigorously. "Yes, absolutely. He fell in love with me. As a result, he's in prison."

The program was sympathetically scripted to suggest that

when Clayton Lonetree decided to engage in do-it-yourself double-agentry, he had been under the influence of the spy thrillers he liked to read. "He was convinced he could use his romance with Violetta and the KGB to obtain information to help his own country," viewers were told.

It was a program rich in redemptive purpose. Like a Greek chorus bearing witness to a tragedy, two former U.S. ambassadors to the Soviet Union, Arthur Hartman and Jack Matlock, were interviewed and they agreed that the security breaches attributed to Lonetree had been exaggerated, and his sentence had been excessive. It was an assessment shared by Aldrich Ames, whose letter to *Eye to Eye* stating, "There is no doubt in my mind that Lonetree's heavy sentence was imposed solely because of the secret panic and hysteria in the CIA and Defense and State Departments induced by my compromises," was flashed on the screen. Even Dave Beck, the government prosecutor, filmed in his office in Knoxville, Tennessee, went on the record as saying, "Clayton Lonetree should be released from confinement."

It was also a remarkable piece of theater that cast Clayton and Violetta as characters in a Cold War version of *Romeo and Juliet*: the children of two families (countries) that did not get along, who engaged in a forbidden love and were guilty of little more than a crime of the heart.

Even the finale was a scene worthy of Shakespeare, who loved plot twists that resolved personal plight and ended with ultimate reconciliations. After the correspondent revealed that a recent letter from Clayton to Violetta contained a proposal of marriage, an American TV audience, along with Clayton Lonetree, who was watching from prison, read her handwritten response:

Yozhik,
I got your letter. It made me feel the happiest woman in the world.
I do want to marry you.
The answer is Y E S.
I love you.
I miss you terribly.
Your Violetta

ACKNOWLEDGMENTS

As tricky as it is to research and write about intelligence issues, acknowledging everyone "without whose help . . ." can be just as problematic. There are people who gave me their trust and time and who, for legitimate personal and professional reasons, spoke only on condition of anonymity. There are people who continue to be employed in sensitive positions whose careers would be jeopardized were I to credit their contribution publicly. And there are people in Russia who spoke openly to me only on the assurance their names would never be revealed, because a lesson of their country's history has been that what it is permissible to say today could be grounds for punishment tomorrow. So to all those who helped but do not find themselves mentioned—and you know who you are—you have my gratitude.

While I'm still in a covert state of mind, I'd like to thank the Central Intelligence Agency—for nothing. I share the frustrations expressed by virtually everyone in this story who had to deal with the CIA. Direct letters to the public affairs office, requests under the Freedom of Information Act, intervention by sympathetic congressmen, all elicited the same response: "We can neither confirm nor deny the existence of any information relating to your appeal."

The KGB was more cooperative with this endeavor than the CIA. It was Soviet intelligence agents, not American, who initially parted the veil for me on the Vienna intrigues involving Yuri Lysov and the CIA "hooded witness" at the court-martial.

The CIA, it turns out, had been aware of Clayton Lonetree's espionage activities before he turned himself in.

As I later learned, Yuri Lysov had been servicing other American personnel at the embassy, some in positions significantly higher than Lonetree's, and the CIA was allowing him to continue to operate in order to determine the full range of the people he was in contact with until it sprang its own recruitment trap on him. This was an operation it had been committed to before Lonetree came on the scene, which was why it took so long for the Agency to make up its mind how to handle Lonetree. It was considering whether or not there was a way to use Lonetree to get to George. Detailed questioning of John Doe at the court-martial could have jeopardized the CIA's plans, which were still in progress at that time.

Perhaps it will come as no surprise that information relating to CIA activities as they pertained to the Lonetree case comes, in part, from Aldrich Ames. Mr. Ames's efforts to shed light on whether or not and how the KGB might have used Lonetree to divert attention from his activities, as well as the way losses due to him factored into the CIA's perception of the seriousness of the Lonetree case, were helpful and he deserves to be thanked.

As long as I'm dipping the pen in gall, this appears to be the place for me to mention Ronald Kessler, author of *Moscow Station: How the KGB Penetrated the American Embassy,* which covered some of the same ground I have, although in dramatically different fashion. Published within two years of the Marine Spy Scandal, Mr. Kessler's book alleges that the NIS had criminally mishandled the investigation, the KGB had successfully penetrated the embassy code room, and the U.S. government was engaged in a massive cover-up. Mr. Kessler was kind enough to share with me the transcripts of many of the interviews he conducted, for which I am appreciative. But in all honesty, looking at his book now, I feel it is so full of erroneous presumptions that it is best viewed as a cautionary tale that illustrates the trap a writer of fact-based spy books falls into when he's in a hurry to publish provocative claims. *Time* magazine reached a similar conclusion when, just months after turning its cover and eight inside pages of extracts over to the book, it conducted its own investigation into Mr. Kessler's assertions: The printed results amounted to a remarkable retraction. Even Aldrich Ames, in a letter to me, described *Moscow Station* as a significant piece of disinformation that provided him with almost as much cover as the Lonetree case did. According to Mr. Ames, when Kessler resuscitated the fear that the embassy had been penetrated, the CIA took a second look at the case, which meant more wasted energy and diverted resources. "It was sensationalism and lies . . . but of course I was rooting for the Kessler thesis."

In the process of reconstructing the internal consciousness of Clayton Lonetree, I drew on a number of sources, including a personal conversation and letters from Lonetree to me; interviews with his mother, father, and sister; interviews with all his attorneys; notes taken by the defense team's investigator; interviews with psychologists who interviewed him; letters he wrote to a variety of people; published articles and books; and conversations with teachers, counselors, and friends of his. My ability to do the same with Violetta comes from personal conversations with her; questions submitted to her and answered through an intermediary; interviews with her mother, her sister, close friends, former instructors, and her coworkers in the KGB; and letters she wrote to Clayton Lonetree.

From the Marine Corps, both active and retired, I want to especially thank Lt. Col. Dave Beck, Maj. Dave Henderson, and Lt. Col. Mike Powell for the hours they gave me. As well, Col. Craig Mayer, Col. David Breme, Col. Jim Schwenk, Maj. Jay Drescher, Maj. Dwight Sullivan, Col. Tom Bowman, Mast. Gun. Sgt. Joey Wingate, Cap. Andy Strotman, and Brig. Gen. Mike Rich. And for allowing me to experience what it was like to be a Marine security guard in training for a day, my thanks to Major Milburn, Colonel Benson, Master Sergeant Roland, and Captain Whielden.

From the Navy, my appreciation to Lt. Comdr. Forrest Sherman, Commander Mounts, Capt. Phil Roberts, and Lt. Comdr. Jerome Cwiklinski.

From the Naval Investigative Service (now called the Naval

Criminal Investigative Service), which was understandably reluctant at first to participate in what might have been another round of NIS bashing but took a chance in order to have its side of the story told more fairly, I'd like to extend my appreciation to Lanny McCullah, Goethe "Bud" Aldridge, "John Skinner," and Angelic White. As well, Kent Walker, Dave Moyer, John Triplett, Robert Powers, Vic Palmucci, Ron Larsen, Diana Collins, Al Reese, Al Billington.

From Capitol Hill, I want to recognize Rep. Christopher Shays for his personal support of this project; Sen. Jeff Bingaman for his ongoing interest; Rep. Olympia Snowe and former congressman Dan Mica.

From the State Department, past and present, I am obliged to Ambassador Arthur Hartman, Robert Lamb, Mark Sanna, Jefery Chapman, Tom Macklin, Greg Guroff, Warren Zimmerman, and Effy Wingate.

From the intelligence arena, I am indebted to Donald "Jamie" Jameson, Joseph Evans, George Carver, Herb Romerstein, Angelo Codevilla, David Whipple, Robert Mayhew, and Stan Levchenko.

From the FBI, thanks to Mike Giglia and Dick Ault.

From Russia, I can't say enough good things about my interpreter, Natasha Lebedeva, and my three research assistants, Elena Vasina, Vasilli Gatoff, and Valentin Korolev. It goes almost without saying that I am also grateful to Genrietta Khokha, as well as Violetta Seina and Aleksei Yefimov. Additional thanks must go to Valery Tishkov, Maj. Gen. Oleg Kalugin, Natasha Gevorkyan, Raisa Drobyazko, Nikolay Khalip, Galya Moravyova, Yuri Zakharovich, Sergei Kondrashon, Rem Krasil'nikov, Vittoria German, Ludmilla Vronskaya, Galina Oleynick, Nikita Petrov, Andrei Semirot, and Mikhail Lyubimov.

Before listing the many civilians who contributed to the making of this book, I would like to single out Amy Knight, who began as a valuable resource and ended as a close friend; Mike Stuhff, who throughout this incident gave a lot and received very little; Diana Ingertson, an unexpected but rich source of information; William Geimer and Larry Uzell of the Jamestown Foundation, for their aid and advice; Tom Williams, for his confidence that I would handle the material he shared with me in an understanding manner; Eileen Stombaugh, for her excellent research assistance; Pete Earley, who introduced me to Aldrich Ames; and Lee Calligaro and Lou Saccoccio, for including me in their appellate efforts. Thanks too to Sally Tsosie, Spencer Lonetree, the late William Kunstler, Ronald Kuby, Rich McBride, Ken Peel, Boris Boguslavsky, Donna Hartman, Hank Holzer, Jay Peterzell, Stan Cloud, Don Oberdorfer, William McAllister, Robert Cullen, Peter Carey, John Peregoy, Reuben Snake, Johnny Whitecloud, Val Anisimow, Danny Devine, Tom Holm, Catherine Werner, Mary Ann Razim, Diane Saenz, Robert Slusser, Martin Cruz Smith, Dave Williams, Nancy Snyder, Valerie Manning, and Talia Carner.

Also deserving mention are Drs. Hugh Hill and Sandy Read, who kindly provided me with comfortable quarters while I was in Washington, D.C.; Donald Barliant and Janet Bailey, oh that everybody could have such friends; and my agent Anne Sibbald of Janklow and Nesbit Associates, who has been more than that.

Last but hardly least, I want to acknowledge the enthusiastic support and help and everything else I asked for and received from Rita Feinberg; the enlightened counsel of my editor, Michael Korda; and the patience and creative partnership of my wife, Star Liana York.

INDEX

PHOTO CREDITS

U.S. Marine Corps: 1, 2, 3

CBS, *Eye to Eye:* 4, 8

Benson / Tribune Media Services: 11

UPI / Bettman: 12

Courtesy of Lanny McCullah: 13

Courtesy of David Henderson: 14

1987 Star Tribune / Minneapolis-St. Paul; staff
photo by Ragene Radniecki: 15

Courtesy of David Beck: 16

AP / Wide World Photos: 17